LUTHER
HIS LIFE AND WORK

by

GERHARD RITTER

translated from the German
by John Riches

GREENWOOD PRESS, PUBLISHERS
WESTPORT, CONNECTICUT

Library of Congress Cataloging in Publication Data

Ritter, Gerhard, 1888-1967.
   Luther, his life and work.

   Translation of Luther, Gestalt und Tat.
   Reprint of the ed. published by Harper & Row, New
York.
    1. Luther, Martin, 1483-1546. 2. Reformation--
Biography. I. Title.
[BR325.R633 1978]   230'.4'10924 [B]   78-2717
ISBN 0-313-20347-4

Luther: His Life and Work. Copyright © 1959 by F. Bruckmann K. G. Verlag., München. Copyright © 1963 in the English translation by William Collins Sons & Co., Ltd., London and Harper & Row, Inc., New York.

All rights reserved. No part of this book may be used or reproduced in any manner whatsoever without written permission except in the case of brief quotations embodied in critical articles and reviews.

Reprinted with the permission of Harper & Row Publishers, Inc.

Reprinted in 1978 by Greenwood Press, Inc.
51 Riverside Avenue, Westport, CT. 06880

Printed in the United States of America

10 9 8 7 6 5 4 3 2 1

LUTHER

Preface to the English Edition

The author is aware that, for non-German readers, and in particular those of the English-speaking world, the path to an understanding of Luther is beset by considerable difficulties. The German idiom of his time is difficult to convey, and in translation its peculiar charm—the intense force of expression, the colourful image—is all too easily lost. Furthermore, the modern reader is not helped by the fact that Luther's work is dispersed over a countless number of writings which in the main are concerned with specialised and specific questions of a character which can be familiar only to the student of history; nor is a systematic analysis of Luther's religious concepts available, of the type provided by Calvin in his *Institutes of the Christian Religion*. Perhaps the greatest barrier of all to an impartial historical appreciation of the German Reformer lies in the centuries of ecclesiastical argument upon the subject; nineteenth-century liberalism, in dealing with these arguments, in its turn introduced new misconceptions concerning the character and significance of his achievement in the world.

From earliest times both the Anglican Church and the Roman Catholic have depicted Luther, not as a 'reformer,' but as a revolutionary, a destroyer of ancient and hallowed traditions; as a plebeian; as an enemy of all ecclesiastical hierarchy; as a barbarous and immoderate quarrel-seeker. They have accused him, because of his unrestrained accusations against the Old Church, of destroying not only the world dominance of the Roman Papacy but, simultaneously, of shaking the very foundations of that wonderful edifice, a unity of culture in

Europe, based upon Christianity. The resultant antipathy was further heightened by the extremely violent polemical treatise written by Luther against Henry VIII, the founder of the English national church.

Anglicans and Roman Catholics have viewed Luther as an extreme revolutionary. Nineteenth-century liberalism in Germany, and also on occasion in France, hailed him as a liberator, freeing the world from the domination of priesthood and dark medieval superstition; but this, too, as first France and later Germany discovered, was a misconception. To the forward-looking liberal, now estranged from Christian dogma, Luther's Reformation was soon to appear simply as a half-measure; it even preached the old dogma and was far removed from that view of the world, secular and freed from religious 'prejudices', which the enlightenment of the eighteenth century, as first conceived in England, was to project to the world. Of political freedom of speech, in the sense of liberalism, Luther had not the remotest conception. On the contrary: the greatest reproach which the liberals of Western Europe level against Luther is that, in his sermon 'Of the grace of God', he persuaded the Germans to maintain an attitude of pious obedience vis-à-vis the authorities, causing them to become servile lackeys of the princely class and quite devoid of any sense of freedom. It was, indeed, the very memory of Luther which, in the period of nationalism, served to sharpen yet further the contrasts between Germany and Western Europe.

Given these circumstances, does it not seem a hazardous undertaking, to offer to the English-speaking world a biography of Luther, written by a German historian of Lutheran persuasion?

The task would be, perhaps, a hopeless one, had not present-day research on Luther advanced beyond the level it occupied in the nineteenth century and had not the terrible first half of the twentieth brought about considerable change in the spiritual climate of Europe. An attempt has been made in the last chapter of this book to assess Luther's historical significance from the new viewpoint of our own day. It is sufficient here to indicate briefly just why and in what way the picture of Luther to-day differs from the former image.

In substance, of the writers on Luther before the First World War, by far the majority recognised him only as a campaigner against Rome and the founder of German state churches. Often, and particularly in the case of non-German writers, they were acquainted with only a very limited portion of Luther's writings. During the first decades of this century highly intensive research originated in Germany, and is to-day keenly pursued in nearly all Protestant countries; this study has been supported in its original premises by new and important manuscript discoveries and has succeeded in penetrating to the innermost structure of Luther's thought.

In spite of the many paradoxes and contradictions contained in his writings, and his own at times inconsistent behaviour, what emerges from this work is the final, magnificent unity of Luther's theology—and this, moreover, a unity rooted in religious experience of quite exceptional depth and power. Luther is a religious prophet: his public acts, his militancy, his efforts as organiser of church life—all stem from this. Only those who view Luther in this light can hope to arrive at any understanding of his essential character.

Such an understanding was only partially attainable in the age of religious liberalism. To-day, in a world which has become godless, Europe has had experience of devils so frightful as to render doubtful in her eyes any belief in the steady forward progress of humanity; on the other hand the religious concerns which exercised Luther, the agonising question of the 'secret' and invisible aspects of God, have all been brought sharply back into focus. Upon us Germans, at any rate, his spiritual world has dawned anew, and the author of this book has to acknowledge the fact that the basic attitude of his own work, which appeared in its original form shortly after the First World War, was considerably modified by the experience of the Hitler régime and the Second World War. It remains true that Luther reflected to a very high degree the German character and left his own imprint on it, but the fact has become less important. What emerges from our present-day view of him is above all an impression of enormous power of faith and in his dealings with men an astonishing fearlessness, all springing from his true reverence for God.

This impression has for some time no longer been confined merely to Lutheran circles. To-day it is to a far greater extent shared by Roman Catholic theologians; never in the past four hundred years of Catholic church history has the question of the Lutheran Reformation been considered with such absence of hatred and prejudice as to-day. This is true not only of Germany. The oecumenical movement of churches and religious communities, which has shown such a powerful upsurge since 1945, has paved the way in the Anglo-American world to an understanding of Luther. In the U.S.A. Lutheran studies are already intensive and widespread. An English edition of his collected works is being prepared (St. Louis), whilst the periodical *Archiv für Reformationsgeschichte*, which is under my supervision and which since 1951 has been directed by a mixed body of editors, appears in several languages and has served to link in the closest possible way the study of Luther in both lands. My friend and fellow-editor Roland H. Bainton (New Haven) has published a widely read, new biography of Luther which in many respects accords with my own. In England, too, James MacKinnon's older and comprehensive work on Luther (1925-30; four volumes) has now been joined and supplemented by the work, conducted with great zeal, of younger church historians, such as Gordon Rupp and Philip Watson. It seems, therefore, that an advance company of deeply experienced people, which has originated in the oecumenical movement and

PREFACE TO THE ENGLISH EDITION 9

whose members are drawn from all denominations, is labouring to bring back to the general awareness of a strongly secularised world the oecumenical significance of Luther as a major prophet.

In such a changed situation the translation of this book into English may claim to be justified. It is the work of a historian, not a theologian; it is not written in order to contribute new findings to the body of Lutheran theology. Its aim is rather to present to the reader in as vivid a manner as possible the humanity, the religious experience, the historical role and the tragic destiny of the Reformer. This approach, by fostering a sense of participation and eschewing false heroism, is intended to let the reader see Luther clearly, his greatness as well as his demoniacal characteristics and the limitations of his human condition and power.

The chronological list appended at the end of this book may prove useful to the reader unfamiliar with the highlights of Luther's career and the main historical events of the German Reformation.

January 1963

Author's Note to the Sixth Edition

The main section of this book, which records the actual story of Luther's life, has changed little since the earliest editions (1928-9), although careful note was taken of all criticisms offered by experts in this field, and of course attention has been paid to the advances made in the general sphere of research on Luther.

The introduction and conclusion (Chapter 9) have, however, been more extensively rewritten. The original plan of the book, made shortly after the end of the First World War, emphasised Luther's importance as a national hero, as the central figure of

German culture, with a vigour which I to-day feel to have been exaggerated. The catchword which was coined at that time—'the Eternal German'—has been cut from this edition, without, of course, neglecting the particular national importance of the greatest of German theologians. My own theological understanding of Luther was considerably deepened by my activity as editor and critic of the *Archiv für Reformationsgeschichte* (since 1938), by the preparatory studies for my history of the sixteenth century (first published in the *Propylaenweltgeschichte* 1941), and not least by my active participation in the struggle of the Church against the National Socialist régime in the thirties. In retrospect I feel that my book reached full maturity only in the third and extensively revised edition which appeared in 1943. The world catastrophe which we had already sensed then and which broke on us in 1945 brought Luther's ideas of the hidden God and the twilight of world history home to us Germans with a remarkable actuality. This led me to rewrite the introduction almost completely in the fourth edition (1947). The aim of the fifth and sixth editions has been to extend the revision begun in 1943, above all by re-examination of the conclusion, and to bring out more strongly the universal significance of the Lutheran prophecy.

Many of the ideas in this book have been developed since in two essays published in the journal *Zeitwende*—'Luthertum, katholisches und humanistisches Weltbild' and 'Luther und die politische Erziehung der Deutschen'—both appearing in 1946-7, while the former has been reprinted in the collection of essays *Die Weltwirkung der Reformation* (new edition, R. Oldenbourg, Munich 1959).

Freiburg i. Br., January 1959   GERHARD RITTER

Contents

	Introduction	*page* 15
1	The Early Years	23
2	The German Scene in 1517	55
3	The Break with Rome (1517-19)	68
4	The Reformer (1520)	93
5	Hero of the German Nation (1521)	114
6	First Signs of the Storm	129
7	The Storm (1522-5)	144
8	Founder of the Evangelical Churches	172
9	Luther's Historical Importance	210
	Chronology	249

To the memory of my son Berthold,
killed in Russia on
Christmas Eve 1941

Introduction

Everywhere Western civilisation stands bewildered at the sight of the ruins of its thousand-year-old culture. No corner of its territory has been left unscathed, no part of men's material possessions left undamaged, none of men's spiritual foundations left unshaken. Everything has been turned upside down by the great cataclysm of the last thirty years. Everything seems to have become meaningless. Everything which before was certain has been plunged into doubt, and again and again our faltering footsteps stumble into confusion. Stark fear stares out of the depths of the darkness which obscures our future. Will the wheel of a seemingly unrelenting fate roll on over us, and what will remain of everything which till now had made life seem fine and pleasant; or are there still springs of truly vital spiritual power, pouring forth from the very depths of life, which is pure and strong enough to restore our courage—courage not merely to carry on with life which for so many has become impoverished and uncertain, but courage to fight defiantly against the fate which threatens to overtake us.

One may approach the life of a great man such as Luther from many different angles. To a German, Luther's character has always borne an unmistakably national stamp and he has appeared as one of the most important architects and personalities of the national, intellectual tradition and way of life. In Germany he has always been hailed as a 'national hero'. All this has now changed. To-day the survey of his life affects us no longer simply as a portion of German or Western intellectual history: it now bears upon the whole question of our spiritual existence, with those basic questions on whose solution the formation of human culture is completely dependent. All the questioning of our age can be reduced to the single question: does God exist? If God is really dead, as we are assured now in despair, now in triumph, then we are faced with complete nothingness, and we can no longer entertain any idea of reconstructing a genuine culture. For true culture always draws on the very depths of being, and must wither away if its roots no longer reach down to the true springs of life. If God is dead, then only time remains, but time without eternity; only the foreground remains, yet without depth; our whole existence becomes meaningless, since now it is without future, without a fixed goal set infinitely high above the humiliation of our animal existence. Then we shall drift helpless on the endlessly tossing waves of time, without guide under a starless sky. We have already had a first foretaste of the uncanny cold and darkness which will then come over the earth. We have already seen the bestiality in man unleashed, which is always waiting its time, and we know the crippling fear which reigns over men in place of the confidence of belief, in a world which has become godless (and so heartless). What has collapsed in these last few years, finally and irrevocably, is the attempt of European humanity to build and maintain a society divorced from real belief in God, a world of the humanities, of civil order, of national cultures, of an international community of peoples. To-day we see that such a society dispenses with the vital life-giving forces, and is therefore doomed as soon as the bottomless pit is opened and the battle of the demons begins.[1]

What did Luther learn about the reality of God? This is the question which above all others opens up for us an approach to him to-day. It is just this approach which leads straight into the centre of his life. It is when we start from this point that every-

[1] cf. Book of Revelation, chapter 9. The reference is to the plague of locusts, which is the first of the woes to come on the earth. (Translator.)

thing else becomes important: the translation of his experience of God into a message, the founding of a new community centred round its proclamation, the building of his Church, the light shed on human problems by this central message, its expression in practical life and its effects on economic and cultural life, and on national characteristics and the State.

But of course, what also becomes apparent in all this is the figure of a great man of unforgettable originality, who has made an impression on the German character such as scarcely any other man has. Lastly we see a period of German social history without which his development and work would remain incomprehensible.

Whether all this is mere history, the simple record of the distant past, or whether in the end it contains an answer for us too, to our needs and questions (or at least a signpost for our further search), remains to be seen when we have completed our journey with him along the path of his life.

Before we move on to a closer examination of Luther's life, we must take a quick look at the spiritual world with which he was confronted, into which he was born—a look at the world of medieval Christianity. To ask whether there is any historical precedent for his preaching is much the same as to ask whether it is possible to distinguish anything of the peculiarity of German piety within the spiritual universalism of the Roman Catholic West.

This hardly permits of any single answer. For how is it possible to determine closely the spiritual character of Germany before the arrival of Luther? One may perhaps receive a general impression. In a thousand instances one can catch a glimpse of it —but who can hold it, who can distil its essence into words? What is the peculiar secret of the German character? All that we can grasp is the historical destiny of the German nation, as it is shown in the clear light of the records of its past: that as a people set in the centre of Europe, the Germans were to be more strongly opposed than others to the infiltration of foreign influences into their culture. A destiny which at all times has exerted an enormous pressure in the formation of the German character and at no time more than at the beginning of Germany's national history. For it is a most remarkable and important fact that the first beginnings of a higher culture were introduced to the Germanic tribes, who inhabited the Teutonic territories, in the ready-made forms of the late classical civilisation. Later, however, these forms were forced on them by the Church, whose mission it was to try to root out the pagan folk elements in their culture. So it is that only the most scanty fragments of the early pre-Christian German traditions have been preserved under a huge mound of Church traditions; yet we believe that in the earliest centuries of German Christianity we can perceive more of the native spirit of defiance of German folk-lore, even from within the Church, than in the following centuries when the uniform cloak of Roman Western civilisation was laid more closely over it. The advantage which Germans possessed over South and West European nations (especially over south-west Germany, which had been so much exposed to the late Roman civilisation) as a result of achieving political order in the tenth century was quickly reversed, as soon as the great struggles of the Empire began with the Papacy and the Vassals. We celebrate the Middle High German court epic as the first-fruit of Germany's national literature; we seek hopefully and not unsuccessfully for expressions of the German Spirit in the works of Roman and early Gothic architecture and painting. Yet everyone knows that the supremacy of French culture over the West was never more strongly assured than in the period of Court poetry. The elegance of its forms, the fantastic world of the poet's imagination, had such a deep influence on the hearts and minds of the Germans, that even in their noblest creative works the particularly German element is hidden deep under the luxuriance of the foreign forms—and is indeed often

INTRODUCTION

scarcely perceptible from the standpoint of a later age. The foreign element seemed to penetrate into the innermost recesses of German spiritual life. Even German poetry, above all in the monasteries, began to assume the dark ecstatic traits of Rome with its reverence for God and its renunciation of the world. After the victory of the Roman Popes over the Empire, scholasticism, too, begins to penetrate slowly into Germany with the help of the Mendicant Orders. In this we can perhaps see the clearest symbolic expression of the victory of Roman universalism.

It is interesting—and yet by no means a matter of pure chance—that it was precisely in the German Mendicant monasteries, those seats of lofty devotion and learned contemplation, that German sensibility and thought came into conflict with the spirit of Roman dogma and first broke through the hard shell of pious obedience to find its own means of expression. From Meister Eckhart, the Dominican, to Luther, the Augustinian Eremite, stretches a series of theologians in whose literary works we believe it is indeed possible to find for the first time certain clearly definable traits of German piety. Nor is their circle by any means limited to the mystics and men of similar temper: in the fifteenth century we find undertones of humanism in these voices, above all with Nicholas of Cusa, about whom now far too little is known, yet who was without doubt the foremost (even if not the most characteristic) figure of his century in Germany. And there were the 'silent figures', such as Wessel Gansfort, Johannes Popper of Goch, and other like-minded men. History has passed them all by and many of these men are now partly or wholly buried in obscurity beyond the reach of even academic research. We do not even know the name of the author of the Frankfurt 'Theologia Deutsch' which Luther later republished. Only recently has more light been thrown on the writings of Johann of Wesel with their similarities to work of Hus. At first sight the diversity of all these undertakings may seem to far outweigh the one element which they all have in common, and it would certainly be a mistake to see these men as in any sense early reformers—none of them really broke through the magic circle of the medieval, hierarchical world-order. But one can see quite clearly how in these isolated attempts at self-expression a strong spiritual need common to them all struggles to be heard. It is a need to see religion as personal knowledge of God, to gain a deeper spiritual understanding of the religious way of life, and, if not to dispense with the position of the priest as mediator between God and man's soul, at least to let it sink into unimportance by comparison with the one thing which really matters—the immediate experience of God in the heart of the believer. These are external symptoms of a hidden spiritual process, a study of which is more relevant to the history of the German spirit than to the history of Western theology. They begin to show themselves first at the height of the Middle Ages, with the beginnings of German theological speculation, and from the outset they give it—by contrast with Parisian scholasticism—a character which is more edifying than rationalistic. Then, in the later Middle Ages, the growing emphasis on the spiritual life began to upset the harmony between reason and revelation, and between the human and spiritual way of life which had been everywhere dominant in the Western Church in its best days. It was then that the hidden contradiction between the spiritual needs of the devout soul and the seemingly inflexible ordinances of the Church began to assume the character of a spiritual dilemma. It was at this point that religious life in Germany began to be subjected to an extreme tension which already gave signs of its presence in the strange conflict between the increased devotion to the Church and the simultaneously growing criticisms of her internal and external weaknesses. Only in Germany did this conflict become a decisive mark of ecclesiastical development. The Spanish Church drew new vigour through its spiritual roots which stretched back

INTRODUCTION 21

into the thirteenth century, and this produced a new flowering of the old ideals of Roman Catholic piety. On the other hand, in Italy, cultural life began to grow out of the bonds of ecclesiastical tradition as the world of Christian ideas began to lose its completely exclusive hold on the minds of men. It was only in Germany that the growing religious needs of men, that Christian piety in its most intense form, came into conflict with the traditions of the Church because of its own deep spiritual failings. There can be no other explanation: the distinction between the history of the German spirit and the general development of European culture first becomes clear at the point at which the religious needs of the German soul came into conflict with the spirit of the Roman Church; and if the fifteenth century has been called the most German century of our history, this can only be maintained, if indeed it can be, by pointing to the increasing fervour and sincerity with which the Germans of that period tried to make the spiritual treasures of the Christian inheritance their own. Whatever the art and literature of this century may have produced (including the so-called Folk-Books) outside this circle of ideas, in no way bears the unequivocal marks of the true German spirit.

Seen from this standpoint Luther's life-work might well appear as the final crowning point of a development which had started centuries before. He found the decisive word, for which others had searched in vain; he it was who helped their vague longing to its fulfilment. Indeed without these spiritual antecedents it would be quite impossible to explain the success of the great revolution which attacked the very foundations of the political and spiritual life of the West among a people separated by numerous geographical divisions and noted for its political inertia. Yet it is not possible to speak of a specific development of the reformation idea without completely distorting the course of events. When Luther set in motion the revolution which broke the spell of a tradition which had lasted for more than a thousand years, he was able to do this because he based this revolution in the very depths of his religious consciousness. This decisive element in his action is the element which is completely new, completely unprecedented, completely unexpected. This one startling fact brought the Germans, who till then had been regarded by the other nations more as enjoying, than helping to create, Western culture, for a few (admittedly short) decades to the forefront of the spiritual development of Europe.

Yet we must be careful, for it is not in this way that we shall find the true meaning of these events. Not as a German, but as a Christian, as a living witness to the reality of God, Martin Luther became the Reformer of the Western Church. There is no real precedent for his work, for his rediscovery of the mystery of primitive Christianity. It can only be understood when we see it relived in the spiritual life of the man himself.

1. The Early Years

It will soon become clear that the central task in any study of the life of Luther is to penetrate to the roots of his personality, into the innermost regions of his spirituality. It may be that biographers of other great spiritual leaders have found it easy to pass from the external to the internal, from the historical environment to the core of the personality as it gradually develops in response to external influences. Luther's spiritual development has its starting point in the depths of his soul, where no external influence could penetrate. Whoever wishes to understand him must seek him first in his solitude. Of course, the fact that, in contrast to so many other medieval movements which were quickly suppressed, Luther's efforts met with such great external success, was due amongst other things to a most remarkable and unique set of external circumstances which also claim their place in history; but the real secret of his power cannot be found here but in the period of his spiritual development, the foundations of which had been laid long before he stepped out into public life. It can only be found in a spiritual life of such force and depth that nothing comparable to it can be found in the Middle Ages, in spite of all the traces it betrays of its origins in that period. How many had already tried in vain to break the spell of the priestly domination of the medieval church! Some had failed because they could not really break away from the idea of the church as a sacramental institution; others because they gave expression, less to their religious experience than to the rationalistic criticisms of secular thought; a third group (among them forerunners like Wycliffe and Hus) because their opposition was at first inflamed by the external abuses of Church life and was thus from the start tainted with earthly and political demands before they penetrated to the fundamental spiritual issues; but the one thing which all these men had been unable to do was achieved by the monk from Wittenberg with his deeply spiritual and religious firmness of will. It was out of the innermost stirrings of this will that were to come the most far-reaching historical consequences, because it had to draw all its strength from a source which lay beyond the reach of all human and earthly endeavour. The spiritual struggles of this man have become history to an extent which is indeed rare. One is immediately reminded of the great mysterious figures who stand at the very beginning of the history of religion; but they are obscured in the half-light of semi-legendary traditions, while the picture of Martin Luther is already bathed in the full light of historical knowledge.

Now of course it is true that in the life of any man (even if he were as incapable of concealing the thoughts of his heart from others as was Luther) there remain secrets which no book can relate. Even the dedicated study of sources which has for centuries been part of research into Luther's life has not been able to dispel all the shadows which cluster round the figure of the lonely warrior in the monastery cell at Erfurt. Even the criticism of the last few generations had to break through a romantic garland of legend which, not without complicity on the part of the old reformer, whose memories of his early days had grown remarkably dim, had for a long time been twined round the story of his youth. Martin Luther was born on 10th November, 1483, in Eisleben, the son of parents whose circumstances were modest but by no means so far reduced as to have caused him any great suffering. From 1484 he grew up in Mansfeld. There seems to be no need to speak of any particularly severe hardship in his childhood and even less of any disturbance of his nerves and temperament as a result of brutal mishandling by his parents and teachers. But there are indisputably darker undertones in the impressions of these early years. His country parents bore the unbending sober uprightness of people who with tenacious endeavour and sharp business sense had worked themselves up quickly into a position of modest prosperity. This, coupled with the barbaric school discipline of those days, was here brought to bear on a personality in which the powers of genius were slumbering, and which therefore (in spite of his crude and primitive manners) must have been infinitely more susceptible to influence than one would have expected from a glance at his rough village environment. But is it not possible to distinguish positive elements which he inherited from his home environment? One thing above all appears to be determinative; that is his descent from peasant stock, and from the heart of the German country. His heritage is to an extraordinary degree German, and he was never for a moment able to put off the country boy, either outwardly or inwardly. For the rest, there appears to be nothing in what we know of his family home and his forebears which goes beyond the ordinary and everyday. Nor is there anything particularly remarkable in the very ordinary piety of his parents. Thus, to be more precise, the only spiritual inheritance which he brought with him from the miner's house in Mansfeld was an inexhaustible fund of popular wisdom and mother-wit, in speech and thought—but spiced with a strong dose of superstition in which was to be found not a little primitive folk-religion, with its dull fear of invisible, mysterious powers holding sway between heaven and earth. The devil in the mine, the witch in the next-door house, the goblins of all sorts in the woods and fields, against whom one had to invoke all the protective spirits and weather charms: these were the very real trials which even such sober and businesslike people as Hans and Margarete Luther had to put up with. It was only at fourteen, when he went to grammar-school at Magdeburg, that the Church with its mysterious power of attraction seems to have made an impression on the soul of the young boy, particularly in the religious instruction of the Lollards, who had set themselves the task of converting the exponents of wordly scholasticism. When, in 1498 he moved to a new school in Eisenach, his 'favourite town', he came into contact with a warmer church life than that to which he was accustomed at home, in the circle of his relations and friends, among them Frau Ursula Cotta, who with her family entourage played a legendary role in the earlier traditions. Yet Luther was hardly a beggar boy whom she took in off the streets, as they would have us believe. Some fortunate recent finds of letters give us a clear picture of the atmosphere of warm friendship, musical company and devotion to the church in which the boy grew up into a youth. Yet in all this, scarcely the outlines even of the man become visible. His biography only really begins in Erfurt, where he entered the university in 1501. But even here the reliable sources for this period, which come from the time of his entry into the monastery, remain extant only in scanty fragments. Little remains but the picture of a hard-working student, sincerely devoted to the Church, held up to others as an example, who quickly assimilated all that the Erfurt philosophers had to impart in his rapid rise through the academic degrees. As well as scholastic learning his interests included the reading of old Roman and Neo-Latin poets, but this hardly entitles one to speak of a circle of 'humanist friends'. At the same time he was 'an alert, gay character', who could play the lute, had many friends, and always carried a sword on his journeys through the countryside. Nothing in this mode of life would indicate that he was destined for any other future than that of the normal German scholar. Nowhere was there any trace of external disturbances which might have thrown the student off his expected course of action. All the same he was a gifted young man for whom his father, who had meanwhile become an alderman in his small town, had great hopes. Since taking his

THE EARLY YEARS

master's degree in philosophy he had been preparing for a lawyer's career, with the aim of a respectable post as counsellor to a prince or town. A suitable match was being considered for him—and then, suddenly, this model son threw over all these plans with the decision to disappear for ever behind monastery walls. The break with his father marked the beginning of the wanderings through the desert which led Martin Luther to the forefront of history. ' For I have come to set a man against his father, and a daughter against her mother; and whoever loves father and mother more than me is not worthy of me.'

Martin Luther himself was never in doubt that at this point in his life (which otherwise, in spite of great dramatic tensions, bore no sign of any other really remarkable occurrences of this kind) he felt directly the intervention of a higher power. A great deal of doubt surrounds all the reports of his spiritual trials and his fear of sin in that early period, which are supposed to have driven him into the monastery. Nevertheless it does seem that the shadows of deep spiritual unease and of a deep concern with matters of religion were appearing across the picture of the young student with his bright, laughing features. Throughout his life he was subject to a far greater degree than others to stormy changes of mood. Certain events, such as the supposed death of an unknown friend, a narrow escape in an accident in 1503, the raging of the plague in Erfurt in 1505, and others, may have given him cause for deep reflection and spiritual distress, but they hardly offer an explanation for the catastrophe of the summer of 1505, for the entry of the young Master into the monastery of the Augustinian Eremites at Erfurt. Only one thing is certain: the vow to enter the monastery, which he made during a storm in an open field near the village of Stotternheim, was made at a moment when the youth was overcome by terror. ' Encircled by the milling forces of the terror and fear of death, I made vows which were wrung and pressed from me.' When the lightning struck so close to him that he was thrown to the ground with such force that he 'nearly broke his foot', he let forth a cry, which did not come willingly from the heart but was like a cry of terror, and which was decisively to alter the course of his life. Visions, a main characteristic of the Romantic mystics, were always foreign to the temper of the melancholic German; but, at least afterwards, he seems to have thought of this experience as of a voice from heaven. Only much later did he begin to doubt, as did his father, whether it was God or the Devil who had spoken with him then.

For us to-day the whole occurrence seems to be nothing but the first rumblings of the storm which was to overtake Martin Luther in the monastery.

His 'conversion' in the monastery is one of the most disputed points in recent research on Luther. Nevertheless nothing has become clearer than that one cannot in any sense speak of a once-and-for-all conversion. What we see before us is a hard, wearisome struggle step by step over more than ten years in which there are indeed moments of joyful elation, occasioned by moments of sudden insight, but in no sense that flash of enlightenment which in a moment buries an old existence in darkness and opens up a new path clearly in front of one's eyes. 'His soul was the battleground of two ages.' Even this does not express an entirely accurate view. For this monk with his deep anxiety about the merciful nature of God is not consciously seeking a new answer to old problems. One cannot stress this point too firmly. No echo of the universal opposition to the secularised papal church and its assumption of wordly power can be found in the loneliness of the purely personal struggles in which Luther freed himself from the spiritual world of the Middle Ages and fought for the courage to live on the basis of a new and infinitely deeper understanding of the message of salvation.

The form which these struggles assumed is well enough known, at least in its outward pattern: his crippling feeling of

THE EARLY YEARS

sin; his terror of the wrath of God, which he tried in vain to placate by intense contrition, ascetic penances and an ordered sanctification of his way of life. ' If ever a monk got to heaven by monkery, I would have got there too; all my brothers will testify to that. For if it had gone on much longer, I would simply have martyred myself to death with vigils, prayers, reading and other work.' This was no exaggeration; during his whole life his body never recovered from the effects of these years. But where did this powerful need for the self-mortification of the earthly man stem from? It is in no sense a purely artificial product of the cloister, just as his fear of sin cannot simply be explained as a ' monkish disease '. It may indeed be that even before his entry into the monastery Luther had at times felt a burning desire to be reconciled with God through the ascetic life (although in fact we have little specific knowledge of this); and yet he would have been able to find ways and means of having the hurried vow at Stotternheim annulled. What then was the root of all these fears?

People have often tried to produce a psychological or rather medical explanation for his case, and it does suggest itself very readily for a young man of heated temperament. If one reads how Luther portrays the power of original sin, the evil desire which rages like a devouring fire in our veins and destroys all free will, then it is difficult, even if one is without prejudice on the subject, to avoid the impression that it is the sensual passions in a sexual sense which he is describing. But it is unlikely that temptations of this kind played a particularly important part in the life of the young monk. The testimony of all the sources, even when subjected to the most searching inquiry by bitter opponents, speaks against this. It is no mere chance that the vow of celibacy was the last of all the Catholic vows which the reformer renounced. The internal trials which tormented him most of all were set on a much higher plane. They disturbed him as profoundly in old age as in his youth; the only difference was that as he grew older the outward occasion of these trials changed and that above all he had meanwhile achieved an incomparably greater insight into the means of overcoming them. He was never seriously concerned with temptations of a worldly nature, with the struggle of the natural man with the strict monastic vows. All this lies far beneath him, and one can make no more radical misjudgment of him than if one sees his soul as the scene of a battle in which the natural desire for happiness of the earthly man struggled against the ascetic's longing for salvation. It was not that the asceticism of the monastery seemed to him too strict and too impossibly hard to fulfil, but that it seemed totally inadequate in face of the infinite demands of the divine commandment. Nor was it longing for heaven or fear of hell which rent his soul; his own personal wellbeing fades into total insignificance by comparison with the terrible force with which his spirit was torn by the question of an ethical religion as such.

A more accurate interpretation of his distress of soul may be found not in a 'natural' but in a theological explanation, which takes as its starting point the internal tensions of late medieval piety. These sprang from the difficulty of reconciling man's free will in his own actions with the ideas of predestination forged by men like William of Ockham, that is from the internal contradiction between the idea of the retributive justice of God and his irrational and arbitrary election of men. On the one side stood the ability and duty of man in his free will to make himself worthy to receive grace by preparatory works, the ability particularly to produce in himself by means of self-abasement a complete hatred of evil and an infinite love of God; on the other hand the dependence of all moral achievement, of all worth in the eyes of God, on the mysterious co-operation of the grace of God poured into the sacraments, which grace (unaccountably only present in the sacrament through the mediation of a priest) immediately disappears as soon as a mortal sin gains a foothold in a man's heart. Against both these there is God's arbitrary decision either to reject or to accept the works of the man which have been produced in this state of grace; to destine the sinner for eternal salvation or eternal damnation as an act of grace apparently without rhyme or reason. So many propositions, so many doubts and questions, so much cause for inner uncertainty and new fear. In this theology a lively active will meant everything and pious abandonment to God was of no real importance (quite in accordance with the English attitude to the world and life, as one would indeed expect from its ancestry). By its strong emphasis on the responsibility laid on man in his free will and at the same time on the unfettered arbitrariness of God's decisions, it forced the antinomies which are of necessity always to be found slumbering in any high religiosity, right out into the open. One can imagine the effect this must have had on the monk in Erfurt with his intense German sincerity and penetrating insight, as he attempted with trembling conscience to fulfil the moral demands of such a theology and to unravel its secrets with his restless, searching intellect. How could he approach with composure a God on whose grace he could not count with certainty, when his whole life was one long struggle to make himself worthy of this grace? In such circumstances does not justice come to be more a matter for fear than for hope? Did he not indeed have cause for despair as he contemplated a life full of uncertainty and unending yet fruitless striving for righteousness?

Our understanding of these things and of the religious ideas with which Luther was in daily contact in the monastery has undoubtedly been deepened by the extensive research which has been made into Late Scholastic theology in the last few decades. Even this does not bring us right to the heart of Luther's problem. Countless others had had to deal with the problem of this internal contradiction in their religious ideas. Why then was it that it was only in his case that it led to such violent explosions? Whence comes this new conscience which made him feel this dilemma so deeply and directly—to such an infinitely greater extent than the rest of the world around him and in fact than any other theologian since the days of Augustine? Only now do we arrive at the secret of his greatness: that he was infinitely more than a theologian, that in a strange way for a man in the sixteenth century after 1500 years of Christianity he was able in spite of his scholastic heritage and upbringing to remain ultimately independent of all doctrinal traditions; that he was able to grasp anew the eternal mysteries of the divine in an utterly original manner. It is only when one passes beyond all rational concepts and the questions of doubt which they raise, that the primary religious phenomenon becomes visible. It cannot be compassed in words, but at least an echo remains here and there struggling for expression.

Such things could only be related in the third person:

I knew a man, who told me that he had often borne these torments, although admittedly only for a short while. They were so great and hellish that no speech can tell of them, no pen write of them, indeed that no one can believe in them, who has not himself experienced them./ They were of such a kind that if they had grown any more in intensity, or even lasted another half an hour or even only the tenth part of an hour, then the man would have been completely overcome and all his bones would have turned to ash. In such moments God appears in his terrible wrath, and all creatures are at once before him. There can be no escape, no comfort, neither within nor without, nothing but accusation and damnation for all. Then the man cries out in his fear, as it is written: 'I have been cast forth from the sight of thine eyes.' He dare not even cry: 'Oh! Lord, deal not with me in thy wrath.' In such moments, strange as it seems, the soul cannot even believe that she could ever find salvation. She can only see one thing: that the punishment is still unfinished. For it is indeed an eternal punishment and impossible to think of as temporal. And so nothing is left to the man but the longing for help and the horrifying cry of fear; yet he does not even know to whom he should turn for help. Then the soul is stretched out on the cross with Christ, so that one could number all her bones. And there is no corner in her which is not filled with the most terrible bitterness, with terror, fear, anguish—but all this eternal, infinite.

What is this? What caverns of the human mind are here revealed? Here is nothing of the ecstatic contemplation of the heavenly glory which Roman mystics extol, nothing of the blessed solitude, the self-abandonment to the eternal being of God of Meister Eckhart and Tauler. Nor will we find anything of the God of the medieval church, meting out his laws and ordinances, with whom the individual can converse only through the mediation of the well-ordered official hierarchy of the church (as if through successive stages of appeal) and whose throne is approached by a thousand steps of devotion. God is the 'mysterium tremendum', the 'awesome secret', just as he appeared at the beginning of religion—as soon as, or perhaps even before, men recognised in him the source of all happiness. It is a terrible thing when God speaks to man—'a dreadful greeting as if we had seen lightning strike a tree or a man'.

Would you know the time, the place and the way in which God speaks to us? Then listen: 'As a lion he has broken all my bones.' In his majesty he does not speak with us so directly that we can see him, for 'no man shall see me and live.' Our nature could not even endure the smallest spark of his speech. And so he speaks with us through men because we could not bear to hear him himself. And what more? If indeed it were possible for God's majesty to speak kindly to natural man, would this not have killed man and caused him to shrivel away, so that his evil stench might no longer infest the air? For he is a devouring fire.

'He swallows us up and takes such delight in it because he is driven to it by his zeal and wrath to destroy evil.' 'For he is more horrifying and terrible than the Devil. For he deals violently with us, and tortures and torments us, and has no care for our persons.' 'For no man can avoid this; that when he thinks of God, his heart in his body takes fright and would take refuge in the world. Indeed as soon as he hears God mentioned, he becomes fearful and timid.' Now these are indeed religious images and sentiments which to the modern man with his rationalised and conventional feelings and conceptions, which he calls his religion, may seem completely foreign, like a piece of primeval rock. But it is precisely this which is the mark of great men of history: that they do not comply with our standards and ideals but bring their own standards and ideals into the world. Whoever wishes to understand the fullness of the historical achievement of Luther, the warrior of God, must become fully acquainted with this dark mysterious force underlying his piety. Only then does the boldness of his decision of faith become really clear, the unheard-of strength of this soul which struggled constantly in extreme despair, even against God himself, to achieve a childlike trust in this Old Testament God of terror, to see him as 'our dear Father', and to make this trust the central core of his life. For it is by no means true to say that these struggles belong only to the period of his monastic life or to the early years of his life there, and that they then died away thanks to a new knowledge of the salvation of the Gospel. The reformer admitted that he had been pursued by such trials from his early youth. His experience

THE EARLY YEARS

in the storm before he went to Erfurt was certainly nothing more than a particularly violent attack of that religious fear, whose close relationship to primitive folk-religion, to the irrational fear of the 'uncanny', has only recently been fully explained by research into the psychology of religion. He was always a man of deeply religious temper, who could at times be frightened by 'every falling leaf', because he thought he could sense the breath of God in its movement. Right up to the last years of his life these disturbances recurred again and again, sometimes as temptations from God, sometimes as from the Devil, his dreaded companion, with whom he 'ate so many bushels of salt'. Indeed it seems that they only reached their full intensity at a time when he had already gained the basic insights of his reformation theology; they oppressed at their worst in the years when he publicly broke with Rome. His life was always a fearful walk with God where every moment could bring new storms in his soul. The real secret of his prophecy is the highly paradoxical fact (perhaps because it is a religious fact) that it was precisely this domination of the natural man by fear which became for him a never-failing source of strength, of that freely-flowing strength which overwhelms the world because there is nothing left in the world which can terrify it. It was precisely at the times when the storms in his soul were at their fiercest that the confidence of the prophet in his mission was at its greatest. For it was then that he was most confident in the holy purifying flame which burnt in his soul.

Now of course, only when this primitive religious experience had penetrated his whole being could he reach such a peak of certainty, and this was the particular historical contribution of his years in the monastery. For it is only because, and indeed only in so far as we are dealing with spiritual processes of a very high order, that these very personal experiences have become historically important. Nevertheless it is possible that their psychological roots, like those of so many spiritual phenomena of first importance, reach down into those dark regions of the life of the soul in which the psychological and the physiological become indistinguishably entangled. At least after his stay at the Wartburg in 1521 we hear a great deal about his severe physical illness (stones, chronic digestive disturbances, sometimes combined with palpitations), which he explained by his excessive asceticism in the monastery, which had destroyed the strong physique of the peasant boy long before its time; yet nothing of this is mentioned during his stay there. Nevertheless it is possible that even at that time he showed the strong nervous susceptibility which is common to all great enthusiasts. Those brothers at Erfurt who did not wish him well were very ready to complain of his vehemence. If one wished one could find in this a certain connection between his physical characteristics and his psychological depressions. In a historical appreciation, it is clearly of no importance. Spiritual inadequacy may perhaps be satisfactorily explained by physical causes. It is part of the greatness of a genius that even physical limitations only act as an external pressure bringing him wider and deeper experience of the torments of the human condition and making him realise the possibility of overcoming them, forcing the slumbering spirit to ever greater efforts against the flesh, and striking new and bright sparks from the dead stone. The historical importance of his work is therefore in the last instance independent of the history of his psychological development; it is a work not of the psyche but of the spirit, freed from its human frame and forcing its will on history.

The historical importance of Martin Luther's religious temptations lies in the fact that they acted as a spur to an intellectual undertaking of enormous range and depth—to such an extent that it is not possible in detail to distinguish his religious struggle for reconciliation with God from his theological struggle for a proper understanding of the Bible. And it is remarkable that this spiritual illumination, this many-sided development of a theological doctrine, was never able to quench the original fire and passion of his religious experience—indeed it seemed at first to have been heightened by the struggle against spiritual and temporal opposition. It is this which gives his life such dramatic force and which lends it its heroic character.

The spiritual content of Luther's life's work is predetermined by the ethical rather than by the mystical element in his religious experience. What distinguished his temptations from the dull fear of the primitive levels of religion was not his overcoming of a sense of despair by a concept of the absolute which embraces God and man in a perfect unity, but their ethical character. For him the infinite distance between God and man found expression in his consciousness of sin. All the concepts of late medieval Christianity are inextricably bound up with this idea. The peculiarly personal element in Luther's piety is first seen in the strange sensitivity of his conscience, in the scrupulous excess of the moral and religious impositions which he laid on himself. Only one must be careful not to imagine that one has exhausted the significance of the matter by emphasising the ethical element in his piety, its origin in his feeling of guilt, and his constant concern with the central problems of sin, grace and salvation. Beneath this ethical element there is an even more radical, purely religious element, behind the fear of the damned lies the completely primitive fear of the creature confronted by the sight of the Eternal and Almighty. It will of course be difficult to find a single utterance of Luther's, particularly in the later years of his life, from which the ethical interpretation of this relationship is completely absent. He is never content with the purely natural experience of religion. Everywhere he presses forward to a clear ethical spirituality. But the source of the uncanny power of his religious experience, which compels him to take the demands which God makes of men so seriously, is none other than this feeling of the creature separated from the source of all life, this destructive consciousness of his own insufficiency, which is always present, even if he has not committed any particular sin. 'If God abandons our hearts, so that we lose all sense of confidence, then we are faced by blank despair; for *whether or not we know sin in our hearts*, we flounder on the one thought: who can say if God wants me.' Luther had already been clear in his own mind for a long time about the solution which could release him from his fear of sin, when he suddenly experienced the most remarkable but perhaps most characteristic of his temptations, a sudden fear of death at the sight of the blessed sacrament in the great procession at Eisleben in 1515, which came on him with such force that he felt he would die. This all points to a level of existence which has nothing to do with moral experience; only of course as a monk and a Christian his first reaction in such circumstances was to resort to the traditional practice of penance and to torture his conscience in a search for sins of one sort or another—to resort to an excess of confessions, which even in the company of professional ascetics was quite unheard of and which must indeed have seemed quite unintelligible and even grotesque to the normal conscientious, morally-minded man.

Even Johann Staupitz, Luther's much respected and loved Vicar General, with his well-meaning and ordered humanity, could not understand it; he thought he could help the terrified and despairing brother by brightly scolding him for his pangs of conscience, terming them 'bunglings and toy-sins'. The whole of the life-work of this man, who was important enough in his own way, was directed towards helping his pupils and hearers out of the anxieties of late gothic piety, occasioned particularly by the doctrine of predestination, by pointing them to the fatherly goodness of God and to the saving act of the Crucified. In this way he did in a certain sense anticipate the later teaching of the reformer, and it was largely as a result of this that the reformed congregation of the German Augustinian monastery became under his direction the rallying point for a new spiritual life, for a deepened and intensified piety. Nevertheless even he did not penetrate into the very depths of Luther's experience. And it is even less likely that the other members of the monastery will have understood what it really was that tormented their remarkable brother, even if their well-meaning comfort could temporarily ease his burden. And although Staupitz's warning that excessive and self-tormenting exercise of the sacrament of penance was against the will of God could sometimes snatch him out of the depths of despair, just as he threatened to go under completely, no one could bring him real, lasting help. For what he himself felt as the original and inherited sin of his humanity could in no way be grasped by the moral sensitivity of the average man—it was basically nothing other than the purely spiritual self-affirmation of the creature in the face of the Almighty, it was the despairing self-defence of the natural man in his terror of being enveloped in the infinite will of God. He carried this struggle through with that uncompromising honesty against himself which characterises only the strong in spirit; he carried it through to the complete self-destruction of his own will.

Meister Eckhart and Tauler had believed that the greatest of all human delights was the extinction of the self in the union with the infinite being. It was reached when the will was completely stilled as the soul sank in contemplation into the infinite depths of the Godhead. For Luther with his masculine, self-willed religiosity, it seemed the hardest of tasks, beyond the reach of human ability. Admittedly he saw the task in an entirely different way. They had found the essential source of all happiness in the contemplation of God, before whose majesty Luther felt his bones crumble away, the God who made relentless demands on his moral will, which in truth he could never fulfil, who arbitrarily called some to salvation and damned others. And yet the love which was demanded was to spring from a joyful will, breaking forth under the deepest compunction, freed from all impurity and selfishness. It was the impossibility of this task which drove him to despair, and not as many have mistakenly supposed, the 'natural' and 'egoistic' fear of 'hell', that is to say of arbitrary damnation by the Almighty. He knew this fear too, but rejected it as a temptation of the flesh and the Devil. What terrified him most deeply was the impossibility of fulfilling the divine commandment in its fullest sense. The Church indeed offered numerous aids for coming to terms with this impossible task, toning down the full severity of the demands by admitting the possibility of offering at least a 'natural' love in which egoistic motives were mingled, accepting 'attrition' instead of a full contrition. It made the sinner whole by the miraculous infusion of the substance of grace through the mediation of a priest in the sacrament of penance or in the Eucharist. The Church could offer participation in the store of grace and merits of others which it controlled; it offered a means of increasing one's own holiness by the ascetic life in the special vocation of the monastery: all this and much else besides. Luther exhausted the possibilities of all these methods. The spiritual results which he expected from them, the melting away of everything earthly in the joyful enthusiasm of the love of God, still escaped him. Only for a short time, particularly in his first year in the monastery, do they seem to have had any deeper results. All means proved inadequate before the unconditionality of the moral demand. There were moments, which recurred ever more frequently, when an overpowering hatred of the God who seemed to desire to bring all men to despair outweighed all other feelings in his heart.

Until the moment came when the solution, at first only faintly perceived, became clearer and clearer. Whoever tries to define his solution is soon taken in the nets of theological formulae, which never really exhaust its spiritual content. For what is really expressed in the Lutheran doctrine of justification is in essence no theory, no dogma, but something of the realm of pure experience achieved and maintained only by constant, bitter struggle. It means that in the struggle with God one takes the enormous risk (and it is always felt to be such) of laying down one's arms, exposing oneself to the danger of eternal damnation and doing what would seem impossible in such a situation: trusting oneself wholeheartedly and in complete faith to the wrath of the angry God, because he commands it and because it would be blasphemy to show the least mistrust for his love; in other words to perceive, in the moments of greatest spiritual torment, the loving God behind the angry God; to perceive behind the terror of the infinite wrath of God the mystery of the infinite, inconceivable love which is shown to the Christian in the saving work of the Son of God; in Luther's own words, ' to hear above and below the " No ", God's deep mysterious " Yes ".' 'For the true master-stroke is to force oneself to take the leap from our sins to Christ's righteousness.' Just as Christ, in his moment of complete abandonment by God in his agony on the cross, nevertheless experienced the merciful will of God, as he commended himself into his Father's hands, so must we; only the sight of the Crucified can give us courage for this; only his victory makes possible our victory over hell and death—a victory which we receive purely as a gift from God. Only when man's natural desire for happiness, only when the very last remnant of man's *claim* on certainty of salvation has disappeared from his soul, when nothing remains but the readiness to surrender to God's almighty will ' even if the soul thereby were to remain in the grip of fear for eternity '—only then is the point reached to which God wishes to bring men, only then does 'justification' become possible. 'If you do not want to die, then die; if you do not want to go to prison, then give yourself up; if you do not want to go to hell, then go there.' The irreducible antinomy of his religious presuppositions is here experienced and affirmed in a single intense experience, as the will reaches at once a climax in its striving and in its total self-abandonment. If this succeeds, if union with God is established on this basis, then the belief in God's mercy assumes heroic proportions; all the petty fear of sin falls away from man, and its place is taken by a truly regal consciousness of the self, far surpassing any casuistry of the moral commandment, because the believer now knows that he is secure in the heart of his personality. It is true that he has not become 'one' with the Godhead, like the mystics (with the consequent disappearance of the willing self), but has been united with God, the Lord and Father, through Christ, who comes alive within us; in this he is filled with supra-terrestial, immeasurable powers, which spring from the depths of life. In the place of the pious man of the Middle Ages, whose confidence stems from the confessional and is always restricted by the thousand barriers of ecclesiastical law, by 'evangelical counsels' and priestly judgments, there appears the 'freedom of the Christian man', which excels all other freedom, as heaven excels the earth, and which gives the right 'to boast of God, to be bold in him, and to be happy'. The highest degree of attachment, attachment to God, is at the same time the highest degree of freedom—freedom from oneself and thus from the whole world. Man can in the last resort only become free from himself when he has been confronted with the absolute, with God, and has come to realise the total insignificance of all the efforts of his own will and has borne all this until he can at last abandon himself completely to God. Only out of such experience is born the true inner freedom which is much more than the precarious security of the 'demonic' man whom Goethe admired so much,[1] is born the disposition of a man who needs no signposts or encouragement from outside to guide him on his way, because he is not creating himself but experiences himself as the creature of a higher power which works through

[1] cf. Goethe's characterisation of, for example, Egmont and Faust. (Tr.)

him. Such a man knows that his actions are directed from the highest court of appeal and need fear no human command or judgment. For him it is the inner disposition which is all-important, while the external act counts for little or nothing, because 'God tries the hearts alone.' In his actions he has no further desire than to fulfil God's commandments, simply for God's sake and not for the sake of his own salvation, and is for this reason free from the wills and ordinances of men.

In these experiences and in their interpretation (which for him was only the rediscovery of divine truths which had been revealed long before) lies hidden the true genius of Martin Luther. They are the experiences of a spirit which had stood firm as he struggled alone against the great spiritual torments which rose up out of the mysterious depths of primeval humanity. As he slowly pressed forward along untrodden paths he eventually reached a depth of religious understanding of the primitive Christian mystery which far surpassed both the shallow outlook of ordinary churchmanship and also the many-sided attempts at reform which had been made by the medieval heretics and saints. Again and again men had tried to reform the Church without the necessary means; by imitating the external forms of early Christian community life or by putting indiscriminate emphasis on the literal meaning of isolated early Christian doctrines. Only Luther penetrated to the heart of the matter; his mission was not to re-establish the forms of early Christian life and doctrine, but to reveal the religious strength of the Christian tradition in a way which was closely related to the spirit of the earliest beginnings. In so doing he in fact discovered what was at the same time the oldest heritage in the Christian tradition. It was the all-dominating central idea of God's holiness and majesty, casting aside all men's claims to self-sufficiency, unconditional and unlimited in its moral demands, and yet at the same time God who is the Father who has pity on the fallen son, on the sinful creature in all his inadequacy as much as on the man made pure and raised again to a new dignity by moral effort and sanctification in worship. The inconceivable paradox of Christian teaching, which is intolerable to all those who are sensitive about man's natural dignity, and which pours scorn on all the humanist ideas of morality, was again lived out and preached by Luther with rugged determination: that even the noblest efforts of man as such are vanity before God; that all human virtue, even in its noblest form, is as far from the goal of divine holiness as are the highest mountains of the earth from the infinite distance of the heavens; that all our striving towards God will never bring us to him; that there is no possibility of invoking God's mercy, not even of influencing it, even through the highest moral achievements; but that nevertheless the majesty of the Eternal and Holy One can make a covenant with the transitory and guilt-laden creature, because he comes to us with merciful love. A paradox which is not softened but taken to the point of mystery by the Pauline 'Theology of the Cross', the doctrine of the incarnate God, whose sacrificial death on the cross should, in Luther's mind, act as a revelation and mediation of God's merciful will to us, and not as a trial forced upon us; this incarnate God was the most certain, indeed the only certain, revelation of his fatherly love. Truly a highly paradoxical doctrine, which, as Luther characteristically expresses it, 'allows God to have the victory over God'. If this, as has been said, shows the true mark of the Christian religion as against all other salvation religions—the unheard-of teaching that God has mercy on the sinner and not on the just man—then Martin Luther did in fact achieve nothing less than the re-establishment of the religious mysteries of Christianity with its strange primitive power, and in doing so he consciously flouted the attempts of scholastic philosophy to make it more accessible to human reason. 'At once sinner and justified'—this summary of Luther's central idea shows most clearly the contrast between the religious themes which are here brought into mysterious union; the enormous tension and feverish activity which this produced in his religious life is, in essence, the same which in the very beginnings of Christianity provided the driving force for a world historical development on an incomparable scale. There is something terrifying in the bold way in which Luther dares to speak of these tensions. 'No one is nearer to God than those in despair, who (in their trials) hate and curse God, and none of God's sons would be more dear and welcome to him. For they make more recompense for their sins in a single moment than if you did penance on bread and water for many years.'

This is the spiritual temper of the man who, tested and strengthened in his spiritual struggle for life and death, would one day step out of his monastery cell on to the stage of the world. Meanwhile in order to achieve this incomparably steady disposition, he needed a spiritual armament which was more suited to defence and attack than mere religious moods, mannerisms and attitudes. He would certainly not have become the prophet of his age, but one of the 'silent figures' buried and hidden from the world, if he had not carried his struggle relentlessly and logically into the sphere of the religious traditions of his time, into the sphere of late medieval theology. Only so did his personal experience gain the external force and abundance of ideas which enabled him to reshape the whole course of the century. He was driven to take this further step by external and internal motives, by the deep-felt need for an objective confirmation of his personal conviction of salvation in the earliest traditions of the Christian revelation, and also by the duty of academic teaching which was imposed on him as a curative measure by his superiors.

Luther had already undergone a thorough training in the arts of scholastic science. It was therefore to be expected that the Cloister at Erfurt would destine so pious and talented a brother for theological studies. They were proud of this 'second Paul' who had fled from his respected position as 'Master of the Free Arts' and prospective lawyer, to take refuge behind cloister walls, and whose spiritual zeal now seemed to know no bounds. They hoped that he would become a learned and illustrious member of the Order. Immediately after his priesting (in May 1507) he embarked on the normal theological course at the school of the Order at Erfurt and at the university. A year later when Staupitz, the Vicar General, needed capable young teachers for developing the new University of Wittenberg and the small Augustinian Convent there, Brother Martinus was lent to them as a teacher of philosophy. Yet in the autumn of 1509 he was called back to Erfurt, probably because he was needed already as a lecturer in theology. He rapidly took one degree after another at the university in a way possible only under the special statutes applying to the religious clergy. If he eventually applied for a chair in Wittenberg rather than in Erfurt it was probably because of personal feuds within the order which divided the reformed monastery at Erfurt and the Vicar General Staupitz. For a time even Brother Martin lent his support to the opposition to Staupitz, but only so long as he felt he must fear that Staupitz's efforts to unite the German Augustinian Convents would lead to a serious relaxation of ascetic zeal. He even made a pilgrimage to Rome in the winter of 1510—all on behalf of the opposition party—although without any practical result and without receiving any deep impressions from his visit to the Holy City. Shortly after this he realised that his fears had been exaggerated; the two parties came to an agreement, although the majority of the Erfurt party still remained intransigent. As a result, Staupitz's and Luther's trust and confidence in each other grew even more. Luther now left Erfurt for ever; at the end of 1511 or the beginning of 1512 he moved again to the 'Black Monastery' in Wittenberg, soon became sub-prior, with charge over the studies in the monastery, and eventually, not without the friendly pressure of

THE EARLY YEARS

the Vicar General, became public preacher, Doctor of Theology (October 18th, 1512) and Staupitz's successor in his 'biblical' chair at the university.

For practically every stage of his rapid rise to academic honours there are fortunate new finds of manuscripts which cast most interesting light on the subject: an abundance of lecture notebooks, memoranda, and jottings of various types, whose study, interpretation and evaluation is still to-day awaiting completion. They show us Luther as a scholar, as the connoisseur and exponent of a centuries-old literary tradition, as a systematic thinker working out step by step his theological terms from the most penetrating study of the Bible, but with constant reference to the great Church Fathers, and above all to Augustine. He appears in a light which earlier generations who had only known his popular and polemical writings had never suspected. In this way it will one day become possible to establish more clearly the role which different elements played in his theology. But we already know clearly the important part which the Ockhamite theology of the late Middle Ages played in his thinking. Its strong emphasis on the part of the divine will was something which he himself felt most deeply and he was to take its biblicism to an even higher level. At the same time there is the strong influence of Augustine, certain contacts with late German mystics and also with Bernard of Clairvaux; but the most important element is still the ever more intensive study of the Bible and its earlier commentators in which he gradually tried to introduce the new aids of humanistic philology—all in all, the very worthy scientific achievement of a man who never allowed himself to accept an easy answer, but who moved increasingly from traditional problems to new-found ones which he then investigated with complete thoroughness.

To be sure, Luther was in no sense a scholar by nature; if he had been he would, as Erasmus's example shows, never have been able to answer the historic demands which were made on his will; he would never have been able to take issue with the whole world on those supreme questions of faith which allow of no answer on academic lines. One could hardly make a more radical misjudgment than if one were to see (as did his immediate successors) the chief importance of his work in his new formulation of the faith, in the deepening of the scientific understanding of the Bible, and so on. Indeed the sweeping, basically unscientific partiality with which he used even the earliest traditions of Christianity to support his own basic assumptions in matters of faith is an accompaniment to his prophecy. Nevertheless it is decisive in an understanding of Luther's life-work to know that he never based his right to proclaim a new teaching on a special gift of the spirit, on an extraordinary vocation by any sort of divine suggestion or miraculous revelation, as do most religious leaders of mankind, but exclusively—quite simply and naïvely—on pure study, on his profession (not even of his own choosing) as 'Doctor of the Holy Scriptures'. He never even thought or intended to say anything really new with his understanding of Christian truth —indeed he would have despaired if he had had to force himself to this judgment of his work. Even the formulations of scholastic theology, in which he interpreted his religious experience for himself and for others, were for him in no way a mere expedient which he accepted for want of any better; they were indispensable to him because they ensured the unbroken continuity of the Christian tradition, of which he saw himself as the reformer and not the destroyer or overthrower. Just as he would never rely on pure meditation, on the intuitions of the 'inner light', but only on the firm and clear word of the Bible—in this sense a true son of late medieval biblical theology with admittedly a particularly radical inclination against traditional post-biblical doctrine—similarly his religious experience would never allow him to rest until he had fitted it (sometimes not without ambiguities) into the firm system of the traditional early Christian doctrine of Christ's all-sufficient saving act. This rooting of highly personal experience into a world of ideas which traditionally were held to be universally valid was certainly not without danger. But on the other hand one can see clearly how this very thing, the anchoring of his own corpus of belief in the traditional world of ideas of the Church, enabled him to be the first to achieve that highly original compromise between revolution and restoration, which is the essence of the Reformation: and this in the founding of a new Church, which, in spite of all, set out with the sole aim of reviving and continuing the old. Luther never wanted to make the way clear for religious individualism, but only for God to work in the hearts of men.

Yet there have been many vain attempts to date the various stages through which Luther struggled to his new position of faith and tore himself free from the scholastic doctrinal system. But what happened here was a piece of pure 'revelation' of a deeply spiritual nature; who could ever hope to draw back the veil from processes which by their nature could only partly have been played out in the regions of pure consciousness? Equally, anyone who asks when Luther eventually overcame his spiritual trials will never receive an answer. For Luther never managed to rid himself of them. On the other hand, one must not imagine (as it might well seem from the later accounts of the reformer) that there were years in the monastery which were unrelieved night and despair. Fragmentary records from the early years show that precisely during the period of his much discussed attacks of depression, which at times are reputed to have seriously endangered his physical health (although we have no clear evidence for this), there were also brighter times when he praised the cloister life to others as a 'fine, satisfying life'. His stormy soul was never without its ups and downs. If we may trust his earliest lecture notes

(1509-10) then it seems that as a young theological don he had hardly begun to take even the first steps which would lead him out of the magic circle of the scholastic system. We do however know with some certainty that already individual points of his later theology were fermenting in his mind; but as yet nothing of all this could be stated positively in the lecture room. Only in the years which followed, during the quarrels in the Augustinian orders, the journey to Rome and his second stay at Wittenberg, did the core of his own piety begin to take its place in the centre of his theological thinking, and this in his discovery of a 'new conscience', of the duty of the unbounded surrender of the heart to God as the unconditional prerequisite of all true religion; what up till now he had felt rather than known, began now to change his whole thought. At about the time he received his doctorate, he had already forged the basic concepts of his new understanding of justification; they appear more or less clearly in his first great course of lectures on the Psalms (1513 to 1515). But it is deeply characteristic of Luther, the biblicist, that he could never be content until he had made sure that it agreed with all the more important biblical witnesses. Above all, one passage in Paul (Romans 1. 17) was for him a source of endless fear and worry, because it proclaimed not the mercy, but the justice, of God as the true content of the Gospel. The solution of this doubt is the only part of his theological development which one might be tempted to call dramatic. One day as he was preparing one of his lectures on the Psalms in the study in the tower of the Black Monastery, he was suddenly overcome by a sense of deep happiness at the discovery of the solution of his worries ; for it suddenly became clear to him that Paul in this passage meant not the punitive but the 'justifying' justice of God, which gives, pardons and awakes new life—'justitia justificans'. He himself always considered this realisation as a turning-point in his spiritual development. Later commentators have even seen it as the 'hour of the birth of the Reformation'. This, as the lecture notebooks show, is a big exaggeration: in them the new element in his thought grows gradually so that it is impossible anywhere to discern a sudden leap forward or to fix a precise date for the 'experience in the tower'. Nevertheless, from 1513 onwards, a new stage is reached in his work with the lectures on the Psalms. As Doctor of Theology, he now began to devote himself more and more to the criticisms of the scholastic tradition. It was still a long and wearisome way, but yet every step brought him further out into the open. The decisive turning-point had been reached.

By 1515 we find notes in the margin of the standard theological textbook by G. Biel, which was then used in his school at Erfurt, which dub the latter's scholastic arts with such terms as 'utter nonsense' and 'enormity of the human mind'. One can see clearly in the biblical lectures for that year, on the epistles to the Romans, Galatians and Hebrews, the completion of this truly liberating process of simplification which replaces a mass of theological niceties by a few simple basic concepts. Naturally the lectures retain the scholastic form for a long while; but it is highly interesting to see how this form is imperceptibly filled with a new content. Again and again outmoded elements of thought are reworked to fit in with a completely changed spiritual outlook. Once the antithesis has become really evident, it is no longer possible to think (as many have often tried since then) of synthesising the two elements. The contrast is not so clearly seen in individual theological formulations; indeed in the transitional years it is sometimes difficult to point out the precise difference. But essentially it lies in the strong change of emphasis from the man, from the world, from the Church, to God; in the unexpected and radical way in which he stresses God's exclusive power in his dealings with all living creatures. Clearly Luther's religious sense spoke so strongly on this point that it would hardly brook contradiction from traditional Church doctrine for long. Because his immediate experience was so strongly theocentric, his theology began to develop more and more along these lines. This marked the return to a theological discussion which was pursued with a relentless seriousness of purpose, with a passionate religious force which since the days of Augustine had been gradually losing ground in Scholasticism. If medieval theology's main purpose had been directed towards constructing a well-ordered cosmos with the aid of Greek philosophy, descending by degrees from the divine Trinity to the human creature and his earthly surroundings, in which the Church, the great institution of grace, assumed a decisive position as mediator, then this artistic creation was now gradually to fade away like a castle in the sky before Luther's penetrating gaze. Neither the biblical metaphysic of dogma into which Christianity had been distorted by Greek thought, nor the essentially Roman legalistic concept of the Church, could stand before his exclusive and unconditional interest in the question of the ethical nature of religion. Just as the all-important concept of divine grace had developed from the idea of a spiritual substance into a pure process of the will, so it was with the dogma of the Church and finally with the Church itself—the whole religious tradition was, in the strict sense of the word, now to be spiritualised and stripped of all its magical and miraculous elements. It is not the sacrament, so we read in the lectures on the Epistle to the Hebrews, but faith which justifies. A new, purer, personal belief was to take the place of unthinking devotion to the Church. In this sense Luther's theology may well appear to us as the highest realisation of that tendency which lay deep in the German character, whose first stirrings we have already seen in late medieval piety, of the desire to express the religious way of life in personal terms, to set the direct personal relationship of the individual to God in the place of the mediation of salvation through the priests and the sacraments.

The fulfiller and destroyer of the Middle Ages: in the period of his lectureship we can gradually see Luther assuming this unusual position. There was nothing new in religious opposition and in criticism of the spiritual roots of the hierarchical system of the Church. But Luther was the first to get to the very heart of the matter by, in a remarkable way, both developing and countering these older tendencies. The earlier critics had for the most part refrained from active opposition, burying themselves in the silence of pious contemplation. If Luther's message was to have a wider audience, then one day he would have to be drawn out of the confines of his monastery and be forced to speak freely in front of the whole country. There on the stage of public life in Germany and elsewhere the wild and unruly cries of the most varied factions had long rung out against Rome and the Romish priests: there was no slogan which provoked the masses to louder cheers than the call to fight against papal usurpation and the lust for power and the hypocrisy of the priests. But all this would die away again so long as the Church held the keys in its hands which were to decide between bliss and damnation. With these it could always in the last resort compel even the most defiant spirits to submit to its will. The criticism remained vague and aimless, clinging to externals, attacking political institutions, here and there trying to achieve more by political means, but all without lasting effect. Did it not seem as if time was just waiting for the man who would unite all who were discontented and ready to fight, the pious and the impious, the ' silent figures ' and the politicians, and with his spiritual aims give to their zeal the necessary impetus and direct it with deadly aim right at the heart of the Church's key position,—a man who was at once a prophet and a nationalist, a religious thinker and a popular agitator in the grand manner?

So much depended on Luther's deeply penetrating mind becoming more and more independent of the restrictions and prejudices of monastic introspection. The lectureship at Wittenberg provided the external impetus, the solution of his theological doubts in the tower gave him the inner strength and freedom. It is worth noting that since that time even his external bearing changed, the steps of the fearful monk became firm and sure as he approached his real life's work. After his lectures on the Epistle to the Romans, the monk and professor began to look out eagerly into the world beyond the cloister cell and the schoolroom. Everywhere he was met by sounds of opposition against worldly and spiritual government. As a theologian, he was not afraid to mingle a strong note of criticism into his scientific and edifying observations. He rapidly became the most celebrated teacher in the young university, which owed not least to him its reputation as the most progressive university in Germany in theological as well as in philosophical and humanistic studies; as a preacher and pastor, as the busy District Visitor of his order, and finally as an academic, he daily accomplished an amount of work which everywhere aroused amazement—he could employ two secretaries for himself, he sighed in 1516. His strength grew in measure with his duties, as he realised to his joy. The reform of theological studies seemed to him to be his particular vocation. Then he directed ninety-seven theses against scholasticism to the academic world and all at once was plunged into the battle against Indulgences. Without even suspecting it, he was called before the people in a role for which he alone had the strength. He walked on to the stage of great history. He appeared before the eyes of the whole nation.

2. *The German Scene in 1517*

What a scene of unrest and disturbance met him—a world filled with dangerous tensions. He came into an atmosphere heavy like the air before a downpour, with the first thunderclaps rumbling in the distance, announcing the approaching storm. The German nation, full of defiance, lay helpless like a captured giant, bound by the unwieldiness of its own limbs (in Machiavelli's mocking words), only waiting for the liberator who would unleash the eruptive forces imprisoned there.

The great dream of the universal hierarchy of the papal dominion over the states of the West had long since been shattered. Long since, the great nation states of the European West had raised themselves to their full stature and, conscious of their independent secular power, had shaken off the yoke of Peter's seat. It was Francis I, the Renaissance prince who stands at the beginning of the history of Royal Absolutism in France, who made a treaty with the Pope in which the Curia and the State divided the control of the Church, but in such a way that the State had the lion's share. Similarly the English Church had to accept the position of a national church under the supremacy of the monarchy. Even the bigoted Spanish monarchy, the most faithful, if also the most embarrassing, friend of the Papacy, used the Church of Spain as the sharpest weapon of its secular power. Italy, on the other hand, with its colourful collection of states, was basking in the glory of a new, highly secular culture which threatened to drive away the secretive shadows and candle-light of the medieval Church. Only the 'dumb, fat' Germans, as Hutten complained, still acted (as they themselves thought) as the footstool of the Papacy's power. And indeed they had come off by far the worst in the great new definition of boundaries of spiritual and secular power in the period of the great councils. Since then the huge mass of 'the German nation's grievances' against Roman irregularities had flowed from decade to decade to the steps of the papal throne, in a thick dirty stream: thousands of justified and unjustified complaints about foreign tricks and exploitation; cases where the clergy had overstepped the bounds of their jurisdictive powers, or where German benefices had been distributed to favourites and 'courtisanes' of the Roman Curia, to the detriment of the German nobility; where lawsuits in the papal courts over benefices had been prolonged and the costs raised; complaints about the exploitation of the right of the German clergy to raise taxes by tithes, annates, expectancies and other impositions; about the simonistic misuse of the papal office of the Keys; about the increases in the charges and taxes for dispensations, privileges, provisions and absolutions of all kinds; about the undermining of the rightful authority of the bishops and the destruction of the diocese by direct intervention of the Curia, by the liberal distribution of papal privileges; by the arbitrary distribution of clerical benefices to privileged monasteries—about all these and a hundred other abuses. Every session of the German Imperial Diet was filled with this endless cry of anguish (often with the German nobles, for whom Hutten later spoke most eloquently, joining in with their spiritual cousins); yet no one could find a way out of the situation, because for the Germans the first and most important prerequisite for self-defence was missing: the national state.

It has been noted, as a characteristic peculiar to German development, that for several centuries the German nation had remained more or less at the point which it had reached at the end of the Staufic period. This is certainly an exaggeration; only by contrast with the rapid cultural development of Italy may that of the Germans be said to have remained at a standstill. But it is remarkable how long the old ecclesiastical and feudal culture of the height of the Middle Ages retained its appeal in Germany, even in the eyes of the new middle classes. Even more remarkable was the lapse of time before permanent new political forms, adequate to the needs of the future, emerged from the political chaos which had gradually developed in Germany since the fall of the Staufic Empire. The form which was eventually to become a kind of substitute for the crumbling Empire (which now, with particular affection, was called 'holy' since it was but a ghost of its former self), the princely state was, in 1500, still only gradually beginning to develop. Nevertheless, one can see clearly how by the middle of the fifteenth century the traditional continuance of general anarchy was beginning slowly to resolve itself, as some of the greatest princely houses began methodically to pursue the end, not only of rounding off their possessions externally, but also of securing them internally by developing the forms of State government. In this respect, the great reform councils, whose effect was felt on German soil for decades, were not without far-reaching consequences for political life in Germany. From their close contact with the representatives of foreign states, above all from Western Europe with its more developed administrative institutions, and also from the exponents of Italian Renaissance politics, the cleverest of the German princes learnt the importance in the development of princely power of a systematically ordered administration, of legally trained officialdom, of a centrally constructed judicature and of a comprehensive legislation. Above all, these ideas of reform were transferred from the realm of ecclesiastical politics to that of temporal politics. Nor did this only happen in the Empire, whose weaknesses had been painfully exposed by the prolonged catastrophes of the war with the Hussites, and whose reform was now inseparably bound up with the plans of the Church

Reformers. But much more now the rulers of the princely states and civic authorities were beginning zealously and successfully to undertake practical improvement in the Church in their own smaller spheres—well aware of the increase in power which would indirectly stem from such efforts. After they had succeeded in excluding the influence of the Monarchy almost entirely from their own political territories, their efforts were directed with even greater determination, either by means of bitterly fought law-suits or by means of pure force, towards similarly excluding the influence of the central ecclesiastical authority, the Papacy, from their own lands, towards reducing the legal privileges of the clergy, and towards bringing the episcopal sees under their own control. Yet we must be careful not to fall into the error of thinking that the primary motive of the princely and civic authorities was always provided by the desire for secular power. At least the better men among them took very seriously their Christian duty as 'God's officials' of caring for the spiritual salvation of their subjects and the well-being of the Church. In their active spiritual zeal they were not afraid of delving deep into the heart of ecclesiastical affairs. In a constant struggle with dissolute monks, with bishops and spiritual corporations who had become negligent of their duty, they tried to improve degenerate monasteries, to stem concubinage among secular priests, to ensure the conscientious administration of Church property, to control sellers of indulgences, to institute strict legislation about Sabbath Day observance and about prayers and processions and to hinder the misuse of spiritual sanctions and of the rights of spiritual superiors to levy taxes. Since papal absolutism with its 'exemptions' had done extensive damage to the old authority and supervisory powers of the bishops, and had abolished diocesan boundaries and everywhere interfered indiscriminately in spiritual government, the serious advocates of reform had for the most part little choice but to appeal to the secular authorities.

THE GERMAN SCENE IN 1517

Rome was far away, the State government with its officialdom and courts near to hand. It seemed pointless to seek justice from the Papal Curia, or to expect any correction of moral misdemeanours from that quarter. Long before Luther's appearance in public life, the Germans had become accustomed to calling on the 'emergency powers' of the princely or civic authorities as soon as the question arose of getting any Church reform under way. This of course did not in any way prevent the hope of a great and overall reform of the nature of the Church in the interests of the Empire from flaring up again and again.

And so the beginnings of a political reformation of German life had indeed been made. But everything still remained on a revolutionary footing; when nothing further could be achieved by inheritance, purchase and law-suits, then people had few scruples about resorting to force in order (in the majority of cases still without any higher political aims in view) to assert their rights as rulers over some tiny scrap of land. The decrees for preserving the public peace, which had been instituted by the Empire at the great Reform Diets at the turn of the fifteenth century, were able to make their effect felt, and could begin to abolish feuds and to win a certain respect for the highest imperial courts, at least among the lower estates of the Empire. Yet the bitter family wars of the great dynasties still continued, as did the smaller feuds between towns, princes and the imperial nobles; while here and there robber-bands of the impoverished lesser nobility hid out in deserted spots or in their nests in the mountains and endangered the lives of travellers. The emissaries of the Imperial Diet, travelling clergy, and even the princes themselves, were not safe on the country roads. Had it not been for the help of the 'Swabian' league, even the imperial house would not have been able to muster a substantial enough force of troops to ensure the peace of the land in north Germany. It is true that the chaos of feudal anarchy was hardly less serious in the West European states in the fifteenth century, and in England was certainly more marked and oppressive. But in these countries the legal and political bases of the national monarchy had for centuries been too firmly established for them ever to have been so completely shattered, as they were in Germany. It only needed a few strong rulers to root the new political order (which, particularly in England, was so successfully and firmly established) in a central authority. Yet in Germany the construction of a new, more modern State organisation was carried out—in so far as it was undertaken at all—in small scattered districts, without consistent or connected planning, on the meanest scale, depending on a thousand chance circumstances, on the fluctuating whims of countless petty lords, narrow-minded, rough boorish fellows, on the changing fates of many dynastic houses and of tiny civic communities. It was no wonder, then, that like the constantly repeated attempts at Church reform, this effort, too, never achieved more than a small, chance measure of success. From the historical standpoint of a later age, one may indeed recognise a new permanent element in all this, under the cover of external events. A contemporary saw only a wild, confused and multifarious activity before his eyes, a seemingly pointless brawl for petty changing ends.

Even before this development in the princely territories, the idea of the State had been fostered in the legal training in the cities. Here above all was the source of Germany's economic power; here was established the far-reaching wealth of the bourgeois, with his well-tried skills and his bold business acumen. More and more the bourgeoisie became the real vehicle of secular culture after the half-French *Courtoisie* of the Staufic knights had faded away. A middle-class literature was gaining in popularity, which although relying for the most part on the Romantic echoes of the Middle High German epic nevertheless contained many elements of unsophisticated folk-lore. There was already a wide readership among the middle classes for the products of the new printing press, and a stream of pamphlets were published which dealt in a common-sense way with every possible question of practical life and contained a considerable measure of reasoned criticism of the age. Finally, too, the universities, which had all been founded at the end of the Middle Ages, were gathering around them in the towns a small group of academics, interested both in the theological questions of the age, and in the flow of humanistic ideas from Italy with their sharp criticisms of Scholasticism, the officially accepted science of the Church. Of course, the time was by no means ripe in Germany for the new secular ideals of culture of the Italian humanists. This is most clearly shown in the bourgeois art. It is precisely now, at the height of its late Gothic glory, that it brings home to us most clearly just how deeply and firmly the ideas and outlook of the Church were rooted in men's minds; never before or again was art so deeply pious and at the same time so much a part of the folk tradition. It was in these cities that later the preaching of the Reformation met with the most immediate understanding and most quickly bore fruit. Behind their thick walls and towers, in the shadow of their cathedrals, there was a spirit of defiance among the citizens which would resist even the Emperor and the Empire if it came to attacks on the new doctrine. Yet, of course, politically they were dwarf-like institutions, with all the weaknesses of the small state, unable to carry through large-scale measures, and besides this hard-pressed from within and without—on the one hand by the bloody struggles of clan and class, against which even the most elaborate constitution was often powerless to help, on the other hand by the eternal feuds with princes and nobles, of which Köln alone was accused of seven hundred within a space of thirty years! These tiny republics were beset by the hate of the haughty Junkers, who would have rather seen the despised 'pepper sacks' dead than alive, and who took every opportunity of 'cutting their throats'. There was a never-ending series of Customs disputes and bickering with the lords, both great and small. At the Diets the bourgeois appeared mistrustful and sullen, embittered by a thousand small local grievances; he knew full well that the nobles were only interested in his money bags. Petulant and cautious, he guarded the secret of his finances, refused to pay taxes, and jeopardised any comprehensive measures with a thousand objections and evasions.

If the cities sought to protect their own skins against the rising power of the princely states, then the politically under-privileged lesser nobility (and in particular, the knights, who enjoyed the freedom of the Empire) were no less zealous to protect theirs. Since the end of the imperial politics in the grand manner and of the great imperial armies, they had been forced to seek advancement in the service of the princes, as cavalry officers and commanders of mercenary troops, or (and this held out the best prospects) as lawyers, for it was no longer always the case that noble birth would be an adequate qualification for the post of councillor or chancellor to a prince. But all were not willing to bow under this yoke; there were whole groups of political malcontents, above all in Franconia in the Central Rhineland, who insisted defiantly on their inherited imperial freedom and even leagued together for protection against the desire of the princes for universal control, and formed a strong element of political opposition, constantly ready to embark on any new feud.

Hate, mistrust, fighting and violence on every side! Only in one thing were all these classes united—in their desire for a share in the possessions of the Church, in its enormous capital, its fat benefices, monasteries, privileges and incomes of one sort or another. Everyone was ready and eager to devour these. Nothing is more typical of folk-art than the lampoon against the useless rich clergy. This is not to say that the Church in

THE GERMAN SCENE IN 1517

Germany had really become as black as she was painted! For a long time the work of the great councils had been to set in motion internal reforms of the spiritual life of the orders and the secular clergy. The number is great of faithful vicars of souls and important popular preachers, whose work has been recorded. Alongside the many characteristics of the clergy, so well known to us from protestant criticisms—the external lip-service, repellent superstitions, vulgar avarice, deep depravity and moral decadence—there was no lack of witnesses to a more sincere and passionate piety, a deep inner fusion of the poetic traits so characteristic of the German people, with the revered body of German legend and the deeply inspired liturgical forms of the old Church, particularly in the Mary cult, which was never achieved again in later Protestantism. But respect for the Church was shattered once and for all— among the ranks of the scholars chiefly by the ethical and rationalistic criticisms levelled by humanism at the education of her clergy, at the effectiveness of her sacramental institutions, and at her many miracles; at the level of the commercial middle classes by their disgust at the privileged separation of the clerical life from secular bourgeois society, which with their practical outlook and democratic ideas, they resented so strongly. Finally, in the lower classes, the way had for generations been made open by the preaching of the mendicant orders, above all by the radical wing of the Franciscans, of the ideal of the ' poor Church ', of the unconditional discipleship of Christ: a revolutionary teaching which was taken to the point of a fanciful communism by the numerous sects and secret societies whose underground activities could not be stifled, no matter how much heretic blood was shed. The less so as the sparks flew out again and again over the Bohemian forest from the furnace of Central Europe, from the heretic state of the Hussites.

Thus for a long time the earth had trembled under the blows of the coming social revolution. Here and there the great mass of the underprivileged, the peasants, was beginning to rise. What drove them again and again to revolt was not so much economic misery—they had long grown accustomed to these old burdens—as sudden defiant outbursts against social and political oppression, above all against the introduction of new rights for the ruling classes and against the extension of old ones. For everywhere in the largest and smallest states, even down to the smallest local authorities, the lords and their councillors were constantly striving to exploit the refined methods of legal government to increase the subservience of their subjects, to raise the level of public taxes and to levy them more rigorously, and to extend their own rights in many spheres, over forests, hunting, water, grazing, and to limit the rights of their subjects. If the ownership of the land and the strings of government happened to be in the same hands, then the task of the lords became particularly easy. And yet the peasant of those days was no longer the dumb, helpless blockhead still portrayed with such arrogance and condescension by the courtly and bourgeois singers; especially in south-west Germany in the great farmhouses of the Black Forest or among the rebellious people in the area round Lake Constance, there was a defiant aggressive spirit abroad among the peasants, who were prompt to counter the demands of their petty secular and spiritual masters whenever they attempted to use coercion. Had not their Swiss neighbours, who were of their very own stock, been the first to resist the proud Hapsburgs and the lords of the Swabian League ? Here as everywhere else in the villages of Upper and Central Germany one could meet returned mercenaries, aggressive peasant lads who had fought for money on the battlefields of Italy, Burgundy or Hungary and who now paraded in the fantastic splendour of their uniforms, thirsty for action and hungry for booty; it was the natural centre for a country uprising. The German country folk who had been systematically disarmed in the Middle Ages were now again partially rearmed, because their superiors needed the support of their arms. And as they were rearmed, so their resistance grew to serfdom, and to any further restrictions of the old rights of those who had formerly been joint-proprietors of the Mark. Resistance was greatest in those areas where the authorities could least justify their use of force by actual achievements in state administration, where it seemed to be based on nothing more than private avarice and hard-heartedness; in the smallest territories, the most unbalanced political forms of the German Middle Ages. The smaller the means of power at the disposal of the rulers, the more bitter was the opposition of the peasants, the more defiant their insistence on old rights and traditions and the greater their intention to reinstate them at all costs. Nowhere, however, was the confusion of these dwarf-like political forms, both spiritual and temporal, greater than in the south-west of Germany, in the Frankish and Swabian territories on the Upper Rhine, Neckar and Main. Here both subjects and rulers felt most directly the loss of the strong central authority of the Empire, and so it was here that the call was loudest for the Reform of the Empire and the restoration of the old, long-since-legendary glories of the Emperor. Here the peasants suffered most severely from the plundering of a nobility who had no more effective way of carrying on their feuds than by setting fire to the villages on the lands of their opponents. Here lay, huddled close on top of each other, the spiritual princedoms of the imperial abbeys: monasteries and sees with their fat benefices for the nobility and their miserably paid, grumbling clergy, their superfluity of spiritual possessions and badly supervised, dissolute cloisters, their administration weak and disorderly, their rulers even more powerless than their secular counterparts, and yet doubly hated by the common man (for was not the contradiction between Jesus' commandment of love and the harsh government of these spiritual tyrants, and between their ascetic duty and their shameless worldly activities, clear for everyone to see ?). Popular leaflets demanded the complete reorganisation of the Empire and the Church. Every popular preacher screamed loud accusations in the ears of the people against the morally depraved and sated rich clergy. Religious epidemics played their part in rousing the opposition of the masses yet further. Thousands flocked to see the Saint of the Taubergrund, Hans Boehm, the 'tub-thumper' of Niklashausen, with his miraculous picture of Mary, and to hear him preach deep threats against the feudal oppressors, and the wickedness of the Emperor, and above all against the priests: the time would soon come 'when the priest will feel like covering up his pate with his hand and when he'll be happy if people don't recognise him'. Here and there arose new peasant leaders to whom the masses listened, among them honourable and respectable men, driven by a genuine popular desire for justice; yet there were, too, the irresponsible figures, seducing the people with their fanciful ideas of communism; lapsed clergy, mercenaries out of a job, peasant have-nots, publicans, village musicians, rabble-raisers and agitators, among them such notable men as Jost Fritz, the famous conspirator from Breisgau, Gugelbastian from Buehl and the Swabian Gaispeter of Beutelsbach. Stories were circulated about Friedrich, the Emperor of the Second Coming, who would shortly appear under the protection of the yellow cross to make the poor people free and the clergy poor; stories, too, about the overthrow of the Anti-Christ in the Papal See. Words became actions. On the Upper Rhine, on Lake Constance, in Swabia, later in Carinthia, Carniola and Styria, and on the Bavarian banks of the Lech—everywhere, risings flared up. Hardly had one been put down with bloody reprisals than another would start up somewhere else. Again and again the Emperor and the Imperial Estates proposed new ways of dealing with the affair, but in vain. Everyone sensed where the root of the evil lay: in the unhappy political state of the Empire, in the lack

THE GERMAN SCENE IN 1517

of a strong unified State authority, in the insecurity of public law. The complaints of the Estates were for ever growing that one could find no justice in the Empire; for the struggle of all against all appeared endless, ever since the great attempts at imperial reform had faltered in mid-course. Yet no one knew what to advise as long as the chief cause of the failure still appertained—the particular egoism of the Imperial Estates and the incompatibility of their interests with the high-handed, fantastical European politics of Maximilian with his plans for world domination by the house of Hapsburg. The general confusion was never more clearly demonstrated than at the Imperial Diet at Mainz in 1517 just a few weeks before Martin Luther nailed up his theses against indulgences on the Castle Church at Wittenberg. They no longer dared to grant military aid to the Emperor 'for the common peasant might become even more incensed in his present raging temper'. The Estates pleaded desperately with the Emperor that for the sake of God and Jesus Christ, he should gain some insight into the grievances which were disturbing the peasant and that he should help to right such enormous injustices. But no one could suggest what should be done.

This was the moment when Martin Luther stepped out of his monastery cell. This was the nation to whom he had fitted himself to preach the deep doctrine, born of the struggles of his sensitive and heroic soul, of justification by faith alone, of the inadequacy of all external action, which does not spring spontaneously from the depths of a pure heart, reconciled with God. Could it be expected, was it in any sense conceivable, that he would succeed in preserving the pure flame of divine truth through all the storms which his appearance would unleash, unclouded by the smoke of purely earthly passions? Until now all attempts to improve the Church had ended when the fire from heaven had finally been extinguished in the steamy mists of earthly desires, human greed, political ambition, the impure misinterpretation of the will of the All-Holy. What would be the fate of the new community of the saints, which Martin Luther preached to his Germans in the context of a world so full of hatred, so steeped in sin?

3. The Break with Rome (1517-19)

Luther himself stepped on to the scene with the happy and naïve confidence without which no truly great work of man has yet been ventured: that is, in the belief that one need only put the light of truth on its stand for it to light up the whole world of its own accord. In 1518 he was already protesting to Staupitz that he would rather have stayed 'in his corner', if it were not that others had dragged him out of it. And it was certainly not the mere desire for a fight which drove him to the forefront. Academic brawls and tourneys never came naturally to him as they did to his opponent Eck. Whoever inquires into his motives must always go much deeper than that. For him the strongest impulse for external action was always the trials of conscience of the pastor. So here, too, right at the beginning. His attention was drawn by penitents in his congregation at Wittenberg to the scandalous trade in 'letters of indulgence' (which released the penitent from ecclesiastical punishments on payment of a sum of money as penance) which was being plied with charlatanistic methods by the Dominican monk, John Tetzel, under a papal commission for the sale of a so-called Jubilee indulgence. Behind his sermons lay a most unsavoury transaction of the great princes of the Church. The Curia, impoverished as ever, had demanded large sums of money

THE BREAK WITH ROME (1517-19)

from Archbishop Albrecht of Mainz and Magdeburg for the privilege of uniting the benefices of two archbishoprics in his person at the same time, which was contrary to canon law. Albrecht had had to incur large debts with the banking house of Fugger in order to raise this sum of money, and to help him pay back the money, the house of Fugger received a certain portion of the indulgence money which Tetzel collected from his penitent audience, and for this reason he was accompanied by agents from the bank on his journeyings. Luther himself had at first no suspicion of these underhand monetary transactions, a full-scale contrivance of cunning Roman courtiers and aristocratic German prelates and skinflints. What brought him to announce a public disputation on the true nature of penance and indulgence was, in the last resort, the clearly unchristian and unscrupulous exploitation of the sacrament of penance by the travelling sellers of indulgences and preachers of repentance. The methods used by a man like Tetzel to stimulate the fast-waning interest of Church people in indulgences were nothing short of mass deception. It was impossible (in Luther's opinion) that this could be the real intention of the Pope and the Church. He only wanted to warn, not to destroy. He was only concerned with the sanctity of the sacrament, to whose practice he wanted to lend a new spirituality. He knew enough of the centuries-long history of indulgences to give crushing grounds for exposing the late medieval forms as crude distortions of their earlier counterparts. However, unlike all earlier critics he was not content merely to appeal to earlier Church laws, but unearthed the deepest roots of the sacrament of penance in the early Christian revelation; this particular question could now be seen in the light of his new religious understanding. In any case why should he worry about the financial difficulties of the Papal Curia and of the Archbishop of Mainz (for whose benefit the latest sale of indulgences had been instigated) or of other great lords! In the same Castle Church on whose door he nailed up the famous ninety-five theses on October 31st, 1517, there were 217,443 holy bones and similar objects on view— the favourite (and highly lucrative) possessions of the pious Elector Frederick; anyone who managed to get through all the rows on his knees, and donated something for the building of the Castle Church, earned himself each time 127,799 years and 116 days indulgence from the fires of Purgatory as Spalatin, Luther's friend at court, reckoned it up in 1520, not without a mischievous grin. In the next few years the ceaseless and costly activity of the agents of the Elector of Saxony brought about a large increase in the number of these 'cures'. In 1520 they attracted many thousands to Wittenberg for the great exhibition of relics, for which the year before Pope Leo X had granted an increase of indulgences of nearly two million years (one hundred years for every relic) in order to gain the Elector's support in the Imperial Election. So Luther could have inflicted no greater injury on his own ruler than by taking this public stand on indulgences and the idolatry of relics. Yet he was unable to understand considerations of this sort, just as no one outside in the world could understand his deeply spiritual motives. Already right at the beginning of his journey it becomes clear how lonely his way must be. Those who fêted him still thought only of the most superficial implications of his theses: the unmasking of this profiteering, the bold protest against the extortion of the indulgence vendors, He felt it himself; at first this unexpected response worried him more than it encouraged him. The others, however, diligent servants of the existing authorities, saw nothing but the petty ambition or the devilish defiance of the zealot, casting the tables of the money-changers out of the temple.

It was precisely this which roused him and drove him on further; this contemptuous way in which his warning was treated. At that time the theory of indulgences had still to be formulated in a precise dogma; the discussion about it still

THE BREAK WITH ROME (1517-19)

seemed open. Despite this, the miserable charlatan Tetzel could dare to threaten him straightway with the stake. And then from the beginning the dispute about relics became involved in the shameful bickerings of the monks, in the Dominicans' jealousy of the Augustinians. For a considerable time Luther remained silent, obedient to the warning of his ecclesiastical superiors. Instead of bursting forth in a series of pamphlets, he first established an unassailable scientific position for himself, by working out the thoroughly scholarly 'resolutions' (appendices to his ninety-five theses). Even then he waited obediently for his bishop's decision before he published them. But he could never give in over these issues. At the very moment when Rome was trying unobtrusively to quench the fire, to warn him off through his superiors of his Order, he stepped forward once again. His Heidelberg theses on sin and grace, delivered in 1518 to a chapter of the Augustinian congregation as a conscious challenge to the teaching of the Ockhamites, were received by the audience of this professor who had so rapidly risen to fame, as an academic sensation. Moreover the sermons and writings of the summer of 1518 struck a new note which made the world listen in astonishment. All at once men saw what demonic forces of anger, irony, of supercilious humour, of the most arrogant self-assurance, were released in this man as soon as one touched on that most vital, sensitive point: his conscience. In these writings we find a feeling of personal, practical and scientific superiority, anchored directly in the depths of his religious experience. This gave his self-assertiveness its incomparable, masculine ring. 'Here I am at Wittenberg, Doctor Martin Luther, Augustinian, and if there is any grand inquisitor who feels like scoffing iron and tearing down rocks, I'm telling him, there'll be safe conduct and an open gate and free lodging for him here.' He graciously suggested to Tetzel that he might do better roasting geese at his stake: for he knew more about that than theology. It was already clear that this monk with his faltering conscience and meek heart was called to pour iron into his nation's blood. People had been complaining for long enough. Now it was time for action. 'Ho! ho! he'll do it,' was the cry like a sigh of relief on the lips of many. How sorrowfully had all the worldly-wise, even at Wittenberg, shaken their heads at the beginning. 'What you say is true, brother, but you will achieve nothing by it. Go to your cell and say " God have mercy on me."' Now he bore them all away with him: the majority of his order, against the specific orders of their Roman superiors and in the face of the hatred of all their enemies; the university, particularly the young students, the Saxon court, and many theological circles elsewhere in the land.

Things seemed to be coming rapidly to a head. We will not pursue here the pattern of intrigue set in motion against him in Rome, the different denunciations brought against him, particularly by the Dominicans, the most reliable champions of papal dominion and its trusty police-force. Luther at first heard of it only from rumours. Any of his supporters with political understanding must have wished that he would prove himself to be a loyal moderate son of the Church and would show his orthodoxy in matters of dogma by skilful reticence. Yet the increasing danger only served to raise his confidence; for him it was nothing other than the surest pledge of the 'truth, which is contradicted of man', as he wrote in truly exultant tones. He believed he possessed the truth, even if all the centuries of Scholasticism had taught otherwise. It was just at this point that he first really burnt all the bridges behind him, publicly challenging the unconditionally binding power of the ban and frankly opposing the misuse of this for political and financial ends—one of the greatest evils of late medieval Church practice. On August 7th he received the formal summons to Rome. If he obeyed he knew it meant death or life-imprisonment. The following day he was already at work on a polemical treatise which from start to finish, with a sort of mocking respect, tore to shreds the official judgment of the papal palace theologian, Prierias, as a pure contrivance of Italian superficiality. He even reprinted passages from it word for word in order to expose it to the mockery of German theologians. To the horror of the Saxon court this was followed in August by the publication of the sermon on excommunication, whose basic themes had already been spread abroad in a grossly distorted form by his opponents in an attempt to blacken him. 'Pray for me,' he wrote to Staupitz on September 1st, 'lest I should become too jubilant and over-confident in this struggle.'

It was precisely this overwhelming conviction of the rightness of his conscience which made it impossible for him to submit to men's judgments without first being allowed the possibility of free discussion, which made it impossible for him to run straight into the clutches of the Roman dragon, which would have devoured him without doubt. Had he obeyed, it would have meant giving himself up and at the same time abandoning his cause. And he clearly never for a moment entertained such an idea. He was still a long way from condemning the Papacy as such; but he was much too firmly convinced of the evil intentions of his Roman judges to waver for a moment. In him they wanted to suppress the pure Word of God. He never considered the idea of pressing forward pathetically to a martyr's death, if the matter did not require it. Just as it never occurred to him to stimulate his 'trials' artificially as had so many mystics and pietists (indeed he anticipated them with terror), he equally never pressed forward for the cross which God wished to lay on him. His way was the heroism of suffering rather than of the desire to suffer, which by contrast characterised the ascetic nobility of so many medieval saints.

But how was he to persevere with the power of words alone, now that Rome had spoken? Now all ways were barred to the truth, if secular power would not come to her aid. The

German Reformation would have been lost right at the beginning if it had not found political support in the political power of the landed princes. Without hesitation, and yet reluctantly, Luther appealed to the Elector to intervene. It embarrassed him not a little that his cause should now become the affair of the princes and the great lords; how far this pact would one day lead him, he could clearly not have suspected at that time. For the rest he did not refuse outright to come before the judges; he was not minded to creep into a corner, without giving reasons and answers, for this would only have harmed his cause. So it was in accordance with his wishes and proposals that the Elector agreed with Cajetan, the Papal Legate, to hold first an inquiry on German soil. Of the details of the agreement with the legate, Luther could learn nothing more precise. When at the end of September he set out for Augsburg, he knew little more than that the decisive turning-point of his life was now before him.

It was without doubt the hardest journey of his life; incomparably harder than later the triumphal procession to Worms. In Wittenberg he had hardly had time to worry. Melanchthon had just moved there and Luther had been concerned along with everything else with the reform of the college. Now, however, on the journey he was assailed by uneasy thoughts. Now that the affair was becoming serious, he met with nothing but dark pessimism on all sides. 'My dear Doctor, the Italians are learned people in God. I am worried that you will not be able to maintain your cause before them. They will tax you sorely,' Staupitz wrote darkly of the cross which had now become inevitable. The brothers in his order from all the houses advised him to turn back. Lonely and depressed, he went on his way, tortured by physical illness and depression. 'All the time I was thinking, now you will have to die. I was so frightened by the flesh.' Or in a childlike way typical of him: 'Oh what a disgrace I shall be to my parents.' Moods of Gethsemane. But it was not the fear of the flesh alone which overwhelmed him. We can only suspect what was taking place in the depths of his soul. At the beginning of September he had written to Staupitz hinting at the incomparably more terrible thing which he had to suffer and which compelled him to think of all temporal terror as insignificant. The summons to Rome worried him little, ' only that I genuinely want to honour the power of the Church'. Now, it seems, the old religious terrors assailed him, more terrifying than ever. But now they clearly sprang from another source. 'How often,' he wrote later from the Wartburg, 'my heart wavered and punished me and reproached me with its strongest argument; are you the only one who's clever? Can you really say that all the others are wrong and have been wrong for such a long time?' Now his thoughts may have begun to run along these lines. Up till now he had always hoped that truth would conquer by virtue of its own pure power if only one could give it space and time to have its effect—it must transform from within the old Church, on which, as a good Catholic, he hung with all his heart. Now for the first time he was faced with the real and immediate danger of a complete break with Rome. His own destiny reared itself up like a terrible monster before him. He arrived at Augsburg in a state of extreme spiritual distress, deep depression and physical exhaustion.

Yet his will remained as firm as iron. 'Even in Augsburg, even in the midst of his enemies, Christ reigns. May Christ live and may Martin and every sinner die, as it is written,' he wrote on his way in answer to the voices which warned him against his course of action. But as soon as he came into contact with the urbane Italian diplomats who surrounded the papal envoys, he was overcome by a proud sense of his own German nature which he felt to be so far superior. With what contempt he rejected the 'typically Italian' suggestion of one of these lords, that he should go through the form of recanting merely to avoid condemnation as a heretic—after all, others had done it before! Indeed two worlds confronted each other here, the politicians par excellence and the man who in the Italian sense was certainly the person the least qualified for politics in the whole of Germany at that time.

Was it possible that there could be a compromise between them, that the already gaping crack in the building of the Church could be patched over? This was, at bottom, the object of the discussions. Cajetan was not the judge Luther took him for. For some weeks now the wind had again been blowing in a different direction. A happy chance in higher politics, the estrangement of the Saxons and the Hapsburgs, had given the Curia cause to hope that they could rapidly overcome the Saxon heresy with the power of the Empire. And so it went quickly ahead with condemnation and warrants for arrest; all this in a great hurry, without giving the accused a hearing or a regular trial. And yet the wind changed again just as quickly. Even before the thunderbolt had arrived in Augsburg from Rome, it had become clear that it would have been best not to have sent it in the first place. The election of a new Emperor was due. All hope of defeating the Spanish candidate the Hapsburg Charles, hated by the Curia because he was the greatest threat to the Papal State and to the House of Medici in Florence, rested on the Saxon vote. It was impossible that they should drive the reluctant, procrastinating, pious Saxon into opposition just at this time—just at the very moment when, to the joy of the Curia, he had refused to sign an agreement which would have committed him in the Imperial Election to casting his vote in favour of the Emperor's grandson, Charles (August 27th). Over and above all this, Cajetan was left in no doubt about the present hostility of the Imperial Diet towards Rome. The tithe which was so urgent for the Crusade against the Turks could not be carried through in any circumstances.

THE BREAK WITH ROME (1517-19)

Never before had so much dust been raised in the Imperial Diet against Italian arrogance and the deception of the priests whose only purpose was to exploit the Germans. Also, at this time the danger from the Turks was more pressing than ever. If papal diplomacy did not proceed with extreme caution in the matter of indulgences, everything would be lost. Cajetan himself, one of the most honourable figures in the Curia of Leo X and the only theologian in the Renaissance court who was capable of making a judgment of his own accord on the dogmatic aspect of the dispute, recognised perfectly well that Luther's teaching about indulgences was by no means to be condemned out of hand as, in the strict sense, heretical. He had himself only just finished a treatise on indulgences which equally condemned certain abuses in recent practice. And so he had agreed to the wish of the Saxon, even though it meant going against his own instructions, to summon his professor with safe-conduct and without any danger of arrest, to justify himself, in the hope that he might gently persuade him to make the recantation which was so urgently needed. If this did not succeed, then perhaps threats might help. But for the moment there could be no real force behind them.

This was the state of affairs which Martin Luther found in Augsburg, even if he did not see it quite so clearly. No sooner had he arrived than he found himself entangled in the confused net of higher politics. What enormous consequences for world history were to result from the fact that during the development of this crisis, which shook the Western Church, its leaders were more deeply involved than ever in political action which distracted their attention from their universal spiritual task; that precisely at this moment Peter's seat was occupied by a very average man, living only for pleasure, who was basically, and indeed wished for nothing better than to be, an Italian patron and 'tyrant' in the style of his Florentine house, with all its calculating subtlety, all the delight in underhand diplomatic techniques, but also all the impoverishment in higher aims, which was now natural in the politics of these small states. What did this bright, corpulent, elegant Medici with his puffy, blasé features, who spent the majority of his days in his hunting lodge at Magliana in diversions which were not always of the most tasteful kind, what did he understand of the religious ideas of this remarkable, pious German, or what at all of the spiritual torments of the rebellious Saxon Mendicant! True the politicians of the Curia with their traditional political instinct needed no theological understanding to sense that the man was a firebrand of the most dangerous kind who must be quickly stamped out. But to be able to appreciate the spiritual depths from which this time the outburst had sprung forth was a task for which they had no scale of values. They knew of no other way of controlling it than by the blind affirmation of papal authority, and yet, because of the political troubles of the day, possessed no means of enforcing its recognition—least of all by a man like Luther! Even in conversation he made an uncanny impression on Cajetan—if later reports are not legendary. From the deep flashing eyes, and the lean, bony features of this face, which still bore clearly the marks of countless sleepless nights and days full of activity and fierce spiritual struggles, there spoke a fiery spirit whose demonic glint would not easily escape even less skilful judges of character. However that may be, the small, slender Eminence—himself a professor under his Cardinal's robes—condescended to give in to Luther's demands, which only the day before had been dismissed as laughable by the Italians—an action which he later tried to have deleted from the reports, as it had been expressly forbidden in his instructions: and he embarked on a theological disputation with the notorious heretic over the most important of his theses. In all seriousness he had hoped to be able to convince the rebel by his Thomistic arguments and to win him by the impression of paternal mildness. Indeed if Luther had been at all susceptible to the pressure of earthly might or to the fear of men, he had scarcely found a better opportunity of beating a retreat and making his peace with the Church, as many had done before him. For now the representative of the Roman see was himself attempting to bring him back on to the right way. The Italian cleverly omitted the fearful demands of his instructions—abjuration and church penance (which at the least would have to be made in strict imprisonment) even if he recanted of his own free will—avoided any discussion of the practice of indulgence and instead posed Luther two essential but purely dogmatic questions for debate. But the stubborn German was unable to realise how much these concessions from the highest quarters really meant. He had only heard in all this the one word: 'Recant!' It is dramatically clear from the accounts in his letters with what defiance and self-assurance he met this suggestion: the consciousness of the unconditional superiority—both religious and scientific—of his own hard-won conviction in comparison with the 'crass Italian idiocy' of the Thomist, which was to him like 'children's jibes': and then his demand following naturally from this, not to be admonished like a lost sheep, but to be recognised as an equally privileged opponent of the might of the Church and to be allowed a thorough discussion of all points at issue on neutral ground. Cajetan soon saw what sort of 'beast' he had allowed himself to get involved with; his Italians sniggered at the angry Fratello who dared to spite the Legate to his face. Losing his temper, Cajetan shouted him down. But this completely spoilt everything. Even Luther became violent: 'Your Excellency must not think that we Germans do not know our grammar either!' The discussion had been in vain. 'Get out!' shouted Cajetan, 'and don't let me see you again unless you come to recant!' If this was an attempt to scare him into submission, it was unsuccessful. Luther went and did not return.

Later, the Curia, when it was vainly courting the favour of

the Saxon court, reproached Cajetan with having mismanaged the whole affair with his high-handed threats and with having driven the heretic to obduracy, and later Luther also passed similar judgment. But in this he misjudged himself and his position at that time. The Roman did all that he could within the limits of his instructions and of the state of affairs; persuasion, threats, and even, when all was in vain, pleading through Staupitz's agency. All to no avail. What Luther for his part demanded, the Curia could never offer without abandoning her whole tradition. It is most noteworthy to see how he held his ground without wavering in the midst of all political attempts to force him to a compromise. The Saxon councillors and Staupitz had long been uneasy about these strange proceedings. They were looking for a way out, for a way of removing their protégé from the verdict of the papal judges and of yet avoiding a formal break with Rome. Luther, who had no knowledge of the ways of canon law and politics, complied with their advice, expressed in a skilfully-phrased document his obedience to the Church, appealed to the judgment of learned, non-Roman judges, and in an almost pleading letter asked for gentle treatment; a letter in form subservient, in the strict sense of the Middle Ages, but as far as the matter itself was concerned, unprecedentedly bold and firm of purpose. After all his protestations of obedience, he eventually came to the conclusion that he could recognise only his own conscience, bound as it was to Biblical revelation, as judge in this decisive question: that he must place the Word of God as he understood it from the clear words of scripture over against all papal decrees. Practically speaking it meant that he was prepared to accept 'human' authority, as he called it, only in so far as he was inwardly able to agree with it. By any standards of the Middle Ages, this was in effect nothing but a declaration of revolution.

Staupitz sensed this immediately. He felt uneasy now in the

THE BREAK WITH ROME (1517-19)   81

company of his favourite and much-admired pupil and friend. He released him formally from his vow of obedience to the Order and hurriedly left the city. There followed a gradual estrangement which for years he vainly tried to arrest. It was for Luther by far the most painful loss which he had to suffer on his journey. For now in fact the break with Rome had become inevitable and it was only a question of time before it was declared openly. This is the meaning of the days at Augsburg. Luther himself would not recognise this immediately. In vain he awaited further action from the Legate, and again in writing protested his formal subjection. Then when no answer came, it suddenly became clear to him that the already threatened ban could fall on him like a thunderbolt at any minute. At dead of night he fled the city, without suspecting at all how firmly the Legate's hands were tied. In Nürnberg he received a copy of the earlier papal brief, later to be withdrawn, which declared him, the Son of Evil, to be a notorious heretic, demanded his imprisonment without further trial, and threatened all his supporters with excommunication and interdiction. In vain he tried to persuade himself that the document (Spalatin had managed to lay hands on it only by bribery) must have been forged. But he could no longer hide from the fact that he had been cast out into the wilderness.

His answer again shows us the whole man. It was to publish an account of his hearing at Augsburg together with the brief which had come into the hands of the Saxons by such devious means, accompanied by an utterly scornful and passionate attack on the Papacy, the 'Behemoth' who devours the witnesses of truth. For a long time he had been 'itching to have a little game' with these Papists and to let them feel more clearly how little effect their decrees could have against the divine Word. It is strange that as soon as he felt the presence of danger close upon him, he became suddenly more certain of his own ground and all the more doubtful of the legitimacy of the authority which threatened him. How was it possible that there should be this gaping contradiction between the commands of God, the clearly felt rightness of his own moral conviction and the action of him who called himself God's representative on earth? He worked himself up into a violent state of spiritual ferment. 'My pen is eager to give birth to something far greater. I do not know where these thoughts come from. But this business, I suspect, has as yet not even begun. There is still a lot to be done before it can be allowed to rest, as the great clowns in Rome are hoping.' Demonic powers inside him were bearing him off to an unknown destination. For the first time in his life there flitted like a shadow over his soul that dark medieval idea of the approaching end of the world, with which the heretical radical Franciscans, the Eremites of the Italian mountains, had once tried to interpret the appearance of the great Babel of sin in Rome, and which since then had occurred again and again, wherever this dull, powerless feeling of resentment was straining in its bonds. 'Just see if I'm not right in my suspicion that the real Anti-Christ in Paul's sense is now reigning at the Roman court; I'm certain I can prove that he's worse than the Turk.'

When Martin Luther wrote this, scarcely more than a year had passed since he had first taken his stand against the sale of indulgences. How impetuously had he, who had matured so slowly, rushed since then to the attack! In the heart of the battle he had hardly noticed how his opponents had lured him from position to position out into the open—a little further now and he would stand there alone at the most dangerous outpost leaving all his flanks exposed and abandoning all the restraints of human authority way behind him, with his only weapon, the Bible, in his hand. This did not scare him for a moment. He knew he was at one with his God, so what need had he of man? For a long time he had sensed that with his unpredictable outbursts he was becoming more and more of an embarrassment to the Saxon court in spite of all their

THE BREAK WITH ROME (1517-19)

good-will, and that they would be glad to be rid of him if he went. Yet he neither intended to take this into consideration nor to drag his rulers into the abyss with him. As soon as the bull of excommunication appeared, which he expected any day, he would go—'anywhere under heaven', perhaps to Paris to seek protection from the powerful university corporation. He looked forward to shaking off all his worries. 'Then I will pour out my heart and present my life to Christ.' He had already taken leave of his friends and congregation in case he had to leave. He was ready and girded like Abraham, he wrote, to go out from his Fatherland and his friends, for God was everywere.

But still the bull of excommunication did not come. First came a warning, indeed a threatening note from Cajetan to the Elector urging him not to besmirch the ancient honour of his house with the reproach of having harboured a heretic, advising him to deliver up the little brother into the arms of justice. A year later there appeared at the court in Attenberg the Junker Miltitz, announcing the gift of the golden rose. Instead of trumpets blowing for war, there came the peaceful music of the shawms.

We cannot here trace more closely the remarkable mixture of personal and political intrigue, of weakness and folly on the part of the Roman lieutenants, and of over-subtle calculations of the part of the central authority in Rome, which led to this reversal of policy—a train of circumstance which for a long while seemed insoluble and which has only recently been explained in detail. Ever since the great event in Europe of the election of the Emperor in 1519 had been imminent, and the rivalries of the new great powers of the West, France and the Hapsburgs, had been thrown into the game, all other worries had for many months been forced into the background. Rome had only one aim in view, to prevent the formation of an overwhelming Spanish power-bloc in Italy by the unification of the Spanish possessions in Southern Italy with the means of power of the German Empire. To this end they sacrificed first the trial against Luther; all decisions taken against the heretic up till the autumn of 1518 were quietly dropped when the Saxon proved himself obstinate on this point. For a long time the Holy See wooed the leader of the opposition in the German Diet with concessions of all sorts: by granting a substantial number of indulgences for his Wittenberg 'relics' and so on. Now they needed him even more to support the French candidature for the German imperial throne which was so unpopular in Germany, and, later, even as their own candidate against the 'Hapsburg Charles'. Once this course had been decided on, the Church was forced, step by step, to take measures which its lieutenant Cajetan, probably their only diplomat who realised the terrible seriousness of the situation in Germany, seems to have carried out with increasing concern and reluctance. The Pope's friendly offer in the spring of 1519 to his beloved son (who had only just been denounced as a heretic and a 'Son of Evil') to pay the costs of his journey to Rome, where he could make the recantation which he was supposed to have offered of his own free will, came as a result of the misleading reports of the idle gossip, Charles of Miltitz, who was trying to curry papal favour with his more than amateurish attempts at reconciliation. But more was to come. In the height of the political tension of the last weeks before the imperial election it was even possible for one of the papal agents to offer to the Elector (admittedly in very ambiguous terms) the cardinal's hat 'for a friend', if the Elector was ready to accept the German imperial throne against the Hapsburgs—an offer which the artful old Saxon could on occasion interpret to others (and perhaps not entirely without reason) as if the Pope had been thinking of Luther, so little were the people in Rome seriously disposed to consider the Lutheran heresy as 'damnable'. Whether this was a conscious misinterpretation or not, taken on the whole the papal diplomacy of these months is remarkable for its frivolous misunderstanding of the danger which threatened Rome from Wittenberg, much to the advantage of Saxon politics. One can see without more ado why Luther (who for the rest learnt little of the details of these transactions) poured out the scorn of the self-assured theologian on the transactions of these diplomats of the Roman Renaissance court, who were as fitted to deal with these spiritual affairs ' as an ass to play on a harp '. As for the Papacy, its policy (which moreover failed to achieve its aims) can only be seen as the most fateful omission of duty in its whole history; for Luther's person and work it meant salvation.

But already, just before the decisive turn in affairs which was brought about by the death of Maximilian II (January 1519), he had received the assurance that the Elector would take responsibility for his protection; with increasing determination the court pressed him to stay in Wittenberg and at the same time rejected respectfully, though carefully, the Legate's demands for his surrender. Luther's affair must first be discussed and clarified before learned and impartial judges, before judgment could be made. Above all, the policy of the Saxon Elector in these years was to delay the solution of ecclesiastical disputes for as long as possible in the interests of his university and its most famous teacher, by all manner of evasive and destructive tactics. The successful execution of this policy was made much easier for him by the great crisis in the distribution of power in Europe. To what extent this attitude was determined more by secular political motives than by the Elector's personal inclination towards the personality and teaching of Luther is disputable, and difficult to establish from the ambiguously cautious utterances of the ponderous and sly old ruler. It is typical of him that he never spoke to Luther in person; for he was always uneasy about his fiery spirit. On the other hand his behaviour cannot be explained by purely political motives; it was without doubt determined by his religious conscientiousness. Elector Frederick was the first in a long series of princes sternly devoted to the Church and surrounded by theological advisers and confessors who gave the characteristic stamp to the policy of the Saxon Electorate in the age of the Reformation. Perhaps nowhere else in Germany was the political atmosphere so suited to Luther's needs at this moment; for he had to be free to develop his ideas quietly without the all-too-frequent disturbance of external and political pressures. And this is precisely what this Saxon state with its modest secular ambitions could offer him, even if for a time it had by a fortunate chance been able to tip the balance in the struggle between the great powers. Yet its size was small enough to allow the personality of this un-politically-minded adviser to have a decisive influence and large enough to play a leading role (as the most powerful champion of the 'liberty' of the princes) in the German Imperial Estates. To leave this land without compulsion, and with its university which had just begun to flourish so unexpectedly, would now have been pointless and foolish.

Luther used the many years of protection (though not of course of absolute security) from Rome, which he owed to his Elector, as a period of intense study in which to embrace increasingly wider spheres of Church life and also of secular culture within his system of thought. It was in these years that he assumed the full status of a reformer. Yet not quite in the way in which he later felt it to have happened: as if the enmity and malice of others had driven him step by step from the path of the old Church. Much more the fire of the central blessed knowledge of divine truth had once and for all been kindled in him. One can see it flaming up irresistibly inside him, again and again devouring the ruins of dead traditions. All the storms which blew on the flames from outside, in a vain attempt to put it out, served only to kindle new coals; indeed they could do nothing but drive the heat of his religious passions now this way, now that. He himself—and this sheds great light on his character—was still as incapable as ever of gauging the force of his own passion. He still had no means of taking sight of the distance between his new-found position and his own past. In truth, his own attempts, which he had still not abandoned, at clinging onto his connections with the past and at portraying himself as the obedient servant of the Papacy, in which, at the same time, he thought he recognised the Devil in person, are nothing but misinterpretations of his own being, birth pangs of an unconsciously creative soul; torments which always remained strange and unintelligible to the clear understanding of the humanist Zwingli. But in all this there is no faltering, no inner uncertainty, as soon as the core of his own conviction, his new understanding of religion, is itself challenged. We look on with astonishment to see how all the weight of learned arguments, of accumulated authorities from the thousand years of the Church's history which are urged against him, not only by petty bitter opponents but by sincere and serious men, rebound without any effect whatsoever, how he dismisses everything with sweeping authority as the 'idle works of men', as soon as it is directed against the foundations of his hard-won faith. Warnings, too, from true and pious men of such great moral sincerity and spiritual authority as, for example, Ulrich Zasius, to moderate his polemics and to consider into what whirlpool of confusion he is dragging the Church, ring in the ears of the warrior without causing him for a moment to falter. Whoever wishes to achieve truly great aims must be able to shut his ears even to the well-reasoned considerations of wise but cautious men. Martin Luther possessed this rare gift of the historical hero to an extent which has been known only once since in German history—in the iron will of Otto von Bismarck. Whoever reads the countless polemical treatises of Luther in these years cannot help being reminded of the picture of the heroes of the old

German sagas; not only in the fierce joy with which these men did battle and which comes out quite naïvely in the first few years of Luther's struggle, happy and confident in all his wrath, still without the addition of his melancholy contempt of men, and the choleric irritation which embittered his last treatises; still more characteristic is the wild burlesque humour of this warrior, who not only hurls endless abuse at his enemies but pillories them mercilessly in front of the whole world. This side of his character, most noticeable perhaps in the grotesque dual between 'the raging bull of Wittenberg' and 'the ram of Leipzig' (the court careerist and intriguer, Emser), won him more than anything the attention and applause of the Germans; barbaric and foul-mouthed in his denunciations of his opponents—to an unusual degree even for that uncouth age, but for all that, speaking in the popular idiom with a degree of power which had not been heard since Berthold's sermons; full of vivid imagery in his speech and, lastly and above all, inspired by a deep conviction of his divine mission and therefore ultimately triumphant and ascendant, in spite of all his swearing and thumping like a peasant. Certainly, if it is one of the German's hereditary faults to tend to extremes in dispute and in anger, then Luther had his fair share of it. Who could deny or dispute that thereby the trials of German fate and its Church have been made more severe? He himself never denied that he was 'hot-blooded' and uninhibited in his attacks; but even if he lamented this as a sin, he was always conscious that he was not pursuing his own advantage, but his Lord's. For himself, he would much rather have remained in retirement: 'I don't mind whether it goes through or not. I don't stand to gain or to lose by it. But God is always dragging me off. So many frightful blasphemies are being spoken *against me and God's Word*, that even if I'm not immediately swept away by passion and violence as is my manner, nevertheless anger about the whole business would drive even a man with a heart of stone to take up arms.' Remarks in which the natural and complete identification of his person with his mission remind one almost word for word of sayings of Bismarck: only that the Reformer knew nothing of the personal desire for revenge and the cunning of the great politician (as his dealings with Tetzel, the unfortunate first victim of the papal policy of reconciliation, clearly show). In any case his Christianity was virile and active in all its aspects, the exact opposite of the purely passive teaching of obedience which was later ascribed to Lutheranism. 'I implore you,' he once wrote to the constantly faltering Spalatin, ' if you uphold the rightness of the Gospel, don't think that its cause can be furthered without worse bitterness and revolt. You won't turn the sword into a pen, or war into peace. The Word of God is sword, is war, is destruction, is offence, is ruin, is poison, and like the bear on the way and the lioness in the wood, it meets the sons of Ephraim.' 'I have not come to preach peace, but the sword,' was one of the sayings of Jesus which he was most fond of quoting.

How hopeless from the start was any attempt by papal or Saxon politicians to enforce silence on this man, or even to procure an extended truce in the matter. In February 1519, he began on the preparation for the great disputation which was planned in Leipzig, and to which he had been challenged by Professor Eck, the conservative theologian from Ingolstadt, who had gained such fame for his abilities in debate. The theme was to be the origins, age and limits of the authority of the Roman Papacy. To this end Luther was obliged to embark on a more thorough study of canon law and the collected decrees of the Popes. He was horrified to find such a mass of ungodliness and of devilry in one place. He immediately decided to write a book which would for the first time take up the issue seriously with the ' dragon of Rome '. Everything else up till now had been merely ' playing '. He contemplated with glee the prospect of completely destroying this whole deception, the work of centuries; for a long time he had wanted to do it, but had not till now had the courage to start. 'Now the Lord is drawing me on and I will not follow unwillingly.' In terror, Spalatin wrung his hands over the new unheard-of indiscretions which Luther was about to commit in Leipzig. But he was imperturbable. 'This affair will not end (if it is of God) until just as once the disciples left Christ, so do all my friends leave me, and only truth remains to protect me with her right arm, not with mine, nor with yours nor with anyone else's. For this hour I have been waiting from the beginning.' There was no going back; on the contrary, he felt compelled to say a great deal more which until now he had held back out of consideration for the court and the university. Indeed, in Leipzig he cast doubt not only on the spiritual authority of the Pope but also on the infallibility of the great councils, even on the famous reform council of Constance and its damning of the heretic Hus.

These were the finest years in Luther's life. Daily he grew closer to the heart of his nation; his writings circulated in countless copies, were devoured all the world over, even far outside Germany's borders. Even the German humanists, under Erasmus's leadership, who had long been interested in ecclesiastical and theological problems, but who were still embittered by the dispute at Reuchlin with the monkish champions of the old Church, began to recognise in the Wittenberg monk their fellow soldier in the fight for the reform of the outward Church life and study, and for the simplification of sacramental practice, the abolition of countless abuses and the restraint of Roman greed. It was thanks to their recommendation and widely enthusiastic agreement that Luther's Latin writings received such an unbelievably rapid and wide distribution. After the great disputation in Leipzig (summer of 1519) they listened even more intently. Admittedly, Luther himself was deeply disappointed by the course of affairs in these week-long discussions. He had hoped to clarify the questions which affected him, to convince his opponents, by the weight of his arguments from Scripture, of the justice of his cause; in the happy confidence of victory, almost arrogantly, with a bunch of carnations in his hand, he had taken his seat at the disputation. But all such hopes were destined to come to grief. The others had never wanted to make any real progress, as he thought, but only to gain superficial rhetorical and dialectical triumphs in the style of all scholastic disputations. He felt he had wasted his time unnecessarily; in any case it had now become clear to all the world that he was not prepared to accept unconditionally even the authority of the councils, to which some months before he had appealed to decide his affair. This caused a new sensation. The letter of his childhood friend, Crotus Rubeanus, written to him from Bologna, mirrors beautifully, with its almost stormy tenderness, the admiration of wide humanist circles for the bold theologian, who was able to restate and reapply so many of their catch-words in a completely novel way. Obviously their common interests lay more in their outward front than in their inner conviction. The humanistic mixture of heathen and Christian ideals, the cool *bon sens* of Erasmus and the moralistic shallowness of his theology was always basically foreign to Luther. But for the while this stepped into the background. Persuaded by his friends, he himself courted the favour of the great scholar and took delight in carefully considered, patronising recommendations which the latter sent to him through the Archbishop of Mainz—much to the satisfaction of Melanchthon and the Saxon court. Even a group of German prelates, led by the Archbishop of Mainz himself, did not look unfavourably on the proceedings of this man from Wittenberg against Rome. How long they had groaned under the financial oppression of the Curia, which dealt more harshly with them than with anyone! But all this approbation from men began to worry Luther. Instinctively he may have felt how much material greed, how much criticism completely foreign to his nature, and how much purely anti-ecclesiastical feeling was beginning to cling to his heels. Nothing worried him more, he said once (at the beginning of 1520) than when he wrote to men's satisfaction. In the midst of all his feverishly busy pamphleteering and teaching he again and again withdrew into the quiet haven of his devotional life. But above all he loved to work on his edifying and educational writings, his commentaries on Galatians and the Psalms, his book of sermons, his beautiful message of comfort for the sick Elector, his exposition of the Lord's Prayer, and others—in particular the great sermons, on good works and on the sacraments, in which already is contained the whole ' Summa of the Christian life ', as presented by Reformation teaching, and which are among the most permanently valuable of the products of his pen. When he was doing this he felt he was really doing the work he was called to: to lay a foundation for the inner spiritual life of the community of the believers, to help to renew the life of the Church from within. It was only here that his soul could always find firm ground into which to cast an anchor in all the storms of time. All external work, however much it excited him and drove him along, could never completely capture him; and now, above all, the attacks of religious depression returned, from which he always derived the greatest strength.

4. *The Reformer (1520)*

However much he might wish the quiet existence of the spiritual counsellor for himself, it was now that he was to be drawn out even further onto the battlefield. The year 1520 saw the composition of a whole series of important polemical treatises in which his activity as a reformer really reached its peak: the great sermons on the Mass, the Papacy at Rome, and on good works, the Latin tract on the Babylonian captivity of the Church, and the great address to the 'Christian nobility of the German nation for an improvement of the Christian estate'. Along with these goes the pamphlet (famous more for its title than for its content): 'Of the Freedom of the Christian Man' —essentially only a repetition of the basic ideas of the sermon published shortly before on good works. By far the most remarkable of these publications was the great political and social reform programme 'Of the Improvement of the Christian Estate'. Again it was as in 1517. What had been slowly maturing in the great depths of his soul suddenly revealed itself for all eyes to see. The theologian earnest for his faith seemed suddenly to have turned into a reformer, who drew together in his person all the ideas of the time which urged a remodelling of the present political and social state of affairs, who welded them together into a new unity through the innermost powers of his spirit, and now allowed all the great ideas which had been reverberating within him to flow out in mighty harmony into the world. Indeed this was a new turning-point in the life of Martin Luther. For it was at this moment that he was obliged to measure up to the external events of this earthly existence, which as we have seen was the hardest problem which the reformation idea had to face.

The enormous tensions of both his own life and of the life of the German nation forced the great reform programme out of him. In spite of all European counter-intrigue, 1519 had nevertheless seen the election of Charles I of Spain as Emperor, partly because none of the German princes had had the courage to set himself up against the pressure of the united power of Spain, Burgundy and Austria, and partly, too, because of the enormously strong national prejudice against the French claimant. Only in this way can we explain the misguided and wild enthusiasm with which the Germans awaited the arrival of the Burgundian Spanish prince. That which had in fact been brought about by the compelling force of a European constellation of fateful significance for the powerless Germany was now transfigured in a typically German way by all sorts of strange illusions. In Charles, 'of German blood' (about whom in fact they knew little more than that he could not understand a word of German), enthusiasts of all stations of life awaited the onset of a new age which would reprieve Germany from her political misery. All the countless grievances which had been stored up in Maximilian's last years till they had become almost unbearable would now all be resolved and Germany would tear herself free from the tyranny of Rome. A wealth of humanistic and popular pamphlets and poems conveyed such unbounded hopes to the new ruler. Above all, in the forefront was the valiant spokesman of the German nobility, Ulrich of Hutten, who kept the mood of opposition in the Augsburg Diet constantly on the alert and championed it further in his writings. In the spring of 1520 his fieriest and most effective pamphlets appeared, harsh cries of war against the Babel at Rome, whose sins, censured a thousand times before, had never yet been depicted with such animosity and with the adroitness of so great an agitator. There is no trace to be found here of Luther's deep religious sense, or of Erasmus's theological ideas of reform; but as if to make up for this there is more national pathos, as if with him the nation first became really aware of its slumbering powers—and more of the arrogant self-confidence of his estate which considered itself the supreme guardian of the national virtues. All this was not without its deep effect on Luther. Of course he had no need to go to the humanists to learn his nationalist feelings. It is clearly expressed in the German theologian's feeling of superiority over Prierias, and the moods of the Augsburg Diet found a sympathetic response in him, nourished as he was on his own experiences and the reports of men of affairs and by the study of earlier written complaints against Rome. But how could he help being fired by the national agitation of such wide circles? Deeply shocked, he read Hutten's edition of the Italian Valla, who revealed that the so-called Constantinian donation, on which rested the claims of the Papacy to secular power, was nothing but a forgery. Then from Bohemia he received the writings of John Hus. 'We are all Hussites,' he wrote, 'without knowing it. In my astonishment, I do not know what to think when I see such terrible judgments of God on man: the purest evangelical truth eradicated by fire for more than a hundred years, and even held to be damned!' Now he could hardly doubt that the Pope was really the Anti-Christ who had been foretold. Immediately the 'Roman hydra' stirred again after its long period of waiting and sought his life.

Ever since the failure of papal policy in the imperial election and since the outcome of the Disputation at Leipzig, no one could have doubted that Rome would again renew its persecution of the heretic. Yet all the same it was well into January 1520 before the Curia opened a new formal trial. Until then they had been vainly trying to threaten the Saxon into surrendering his protégé of his own free will. Again and again, Eck, Luther's personal enemy, had to urge the Holy College to take rapid and energetic action in this matter. Apart from him, only

Cajetan realised the true dimensions of the danger which threatened the Church here. It was only with the greatest difficulty, amidst secular and political business and diversions of all kinds, that the frequently changing committees of papal court jurists managed with the help of a few theologians who were co-opted for the purpose to secure a judgment on the basis of which the College of Cardinals then drew up, on June 1st, 1520, the Bull of Excommunication. It was a document drawn up in the most worthy and unctious tones, but clearly (to Cajetan's grief) highly inadequate theologically, which called down the mockery of those against whom it was directed, and made not the slightest attempt at a preamble, nor any distinction between heresy and mere errors and deviations. They knew practically nothing in Rome of Luther's writings, except a few individual sentences selected by the Dominicans, and indeed had no further interest in them. At first Luther only learnt of this activity by rumour. From all sides he was warned of Eck's machinations in Rome; hired assassins were supposed to be on the way to Wittenberg from Rome in the true Italian style. At the end of April the Elector sought advice from Wittenberg jurists as to what he should do if excommunication and interdict were proclaimed on himself and the town. How much longer, Luther must have asked himself, could he count on the protection of the Elector? Some months before, the imperial knight Sickingen had sent him an invitation through Hutten to seek shelter in his castle, Ebernburg. Now he repeated his suggestion. In June, the Franconian knight Silvester of Schaumburg offered him the protection of a hundred nobles who were ready to take up his cause. Luther listened with joy: with surprise he saw how deep an effect his words had already had on the nation. What a joyful picture he had once painted for himself after his return from Augsburg, of how freely and uninhibitedly he would be able to write against Rome once the hour had come to leave Saxony! He soon showed how little disposed he was to pay any heed. At the beginning of July the Elector sent, for his opinion, a sort of ultimatum which had come to him from Rome and which threatened the most severe spiritual punishments for himself and his country. Luther read it 'in silence', deeply serious; but as always, danger drove him into making stormy attacks rather than frightened him off. He wrote in reply:

> As far as I'm concerned the die is cast; to me the hate or favour of Rome is contemptible; I will not reconcile myself with them, I will have nothing more to do with them in eternity. If they condemn and burn my writings, then I'll do the same for theirs. If I can't have a fire then I'll condemn them publicly. Indeed I'll burn the whole of papal law, that monster of heresies. Now I'm finished with the meek face that I've put on up till now. I refuse to bow to the enemies of the Gospel any more.

The Elector ought to threaten that crowd in Rome; if they wanted to use force, then the whole of Germany would soon become a second Bohemia. For the Germans had a defiant spirit, particularly now that the laity had begun to think for themselves. There are clear echoes of Hutten's manner in such words, only these are infinitely more genuine and deep than in the mouth of the wandering knight whose blind desire for action eventually led him to sorry adventures on the highways. Even now cautious friends urged Luther more strongly than ever before to ward off the disaster which hung over him, by skilful moderation and offers of conciliation. But for him there was still only one way, which for him meant both his salvation and his duty: to step out now in front of the whole nation, to anticipate the threatened flash of lightning from Rome, by raising such a storm that the thunderclaps of the papal ban would roll away unheard. 'The time to be silent is past and the time to speak has come.' Almost arrogantly, as once at Leipzig he had taken his seat, he now stepped on to the platform of the People's Tribunal; with a joke about his own role as Court jester to the great lords and wise men of state of this world, he began to read out his programme.

Indeed it seemed, for a moment, as if the warlike theologian was to become a sword-rattling warrior like Hutten; but just at this moment, as he was expecting the papal ban which was intended to destroy his life's work, a new tract by the papal house prelate came into his hands in which the Papal Omnipotence and Infallibility were praised in an unbelievably exaggerated manner. 'I think,' wrote Luther, suddenly breaking into German in the middle of a Latin letter, 'that in Rome they must all have become mad, stupid, raving, senseless fools, stick and stone, hell and the devil.' The force of this agitation leaves an almost uncanny impression. It was indeed the angriest hour of his stormy life, when he wrote his much censured comments to Prierias. If the madness of the Papists went on like this then there would perhaps be nothing for it, but that the Emperor, kings and princes should attack 'this plague of the globe with force of arms, and make an end of the affair not with words any more, but with iron. If we punish thieves with the gallows, robbers with the sword and heretics with fire, why don't we even more readily, and with all the weapons at our disposal, attack these teachers of corruption, these Cardinals, these Popes and this whole seething mass of Roman Sodom, which unceasingly corrupts the Church of God, and then wash our hands in their blood?' It was through and through the late medieval anticipation of the end of the world which glowed so darkly in these words with its hope for the prompt appearance of the last Emperor who would put an end to the Kingdom of the Anti-Christ. Yet the last evening rays of a sinking day—and this really shows Luther's historical significance—were to be followed immediately by the morning sun of a new rising era. Almost at the same time as that tract against Prierias, there

THE REFORMER (1520)

appeared Luther's greatest and most lasting reformatory writings, the presages of a new epoch in Western history.

Seen in the context of Luther's life-work, they marked a first great climax. Yet at the same time, they assumed a special position of their own. To a far greater extent than elsewhere the theologian reached out here, particularly in the ' Address to the Christian Nobility ', beyond the narrow spheres of religious and ecclesiastical questions, and cast light on the world of politics, economics, social order and national interests. But of course, only with the searchlight of the religious prophet: everything was developed strictly logically from the central idea of the Reformation.

The point of departure was given in the new understanding of Christian Ethics, which the sermon on good works presented so impressively. For Luther there was no particular Christian morality, no Christian moral commandment, no catalogue of virtues and good works, which could in any way be distinguished from those of a pious heathen. The voice of natural conscience which told everyone who was not completely corrupted, what was good and evil, found in the ten commandments of the Old Testament, and in the commandments of love and equality of the Sermon on the Mount, only its assertion, confirmation, and, of course, also its justification, clarification and completion. An action became Christian only when it was born of faith: born of that disposition, itself brought about by God, of pure, unbounded love of God and men, which, as an overpowering, rapturous feeling of new life, drove away the shadows of self-love in the man who had been released from the fear of sin. He no longer needed any particular table of commandments of good works, pleasing to God: he would attempt to fulfil God's will in everything he did, by virtue of the overflowing love within him, and would always act in the consciousness of his ultimate responsibility before God. He was led on by an overwhelming inner impulse of such force that the leading strings of the priest and the casuistic moral precepts were no longer necessary. Just as it is with a man who does everything for the love of a woman, both great things and small, without needing any guidance, everything 'with a happy, peaceful, sure heart', 'so a Christian who lives unto God in this confidence, knows all things, desires all things, is ready for all things which are to be done, and does everything joyfully and freely, not in order to store up good works and rewards, but simply because it is a pleasure for him to please God, to serve God simply for the sake of serving him, content in the knowledge that it is pleasing to him. Whereas whoever is not at one with God, or who is not sure about it, strives and seeks and worries as if he wants to please and move God with many works. He runs to Saint Joseph, Rome, Jerusalem, here and there, says prayers to Saint Bridgit, this and that, fasts this and that day, confesses here, confesses there, asks this and that, and finds no rest, and does it all with great effort, despair and unwillingness in his heart.'

The Lutheran Ethic is therefore pure deontological ethics in the strongest contrast to the casuistic confessional practice of the Roman Catholic Church. The 'freedom' of the Lutheran Christian is certainly no capricious freedom: the conscience of the Christian remains strictly bound to the revealed law of God —indeed through Jesus' Sermon on the Mount it is brought for the first time to a right understanding of this law; it recognises in this way for the first time the real depth of the moral claims which God makes on us. But at the same time, it is freed from the fear of legalism, in the very moment in which it becomes conscious of the infinite character and practical impossibility of fulfilling the divine demand, the impossibility of moral perfection. The 'freedom of the Christian man' is salvation from the night of despair, despair in man's powerlessness, in the total failure of man's moral efforts seen in the light of the holiness of God. It is therefore also salvation from the

THE REFORMER (1520)

restriction of endless moral precepts, which forestall the free decision of the conscience, and which would regulate all moral life from the outset, and confine it within strictly defined limits. God did not create this beautiful world for us to withdraw from its pleasures into a life of self-torment. There is an infinite number of beautiful things which man should enjoy with a happy heart. God does not want us to shut ourselves away from them in a monastery, to avoid the married life and to mortify our bodies. Luther's view of Nature is full of uninhibited sensual joy and of acute observation of reality. He sensed God's active presence in every shooting grain of corn, in every flowering branch. To recognise and to praise the Creator in the splendour of his Creation was for him a purely instinctive need and duty. And so the gateway to a full life was opened wide—but it was never to be forgotten that, in the last instance, all creatures stand under the judgment of God. Against the danger of moral capriciousness, self-exaltation and self-righteousness is set the deep emphasis which is laid on repentance in the Lutheran faith; for at every moment the Christian knows that he is called on to answer to the Eternal and Almighty. He knows that he remains a sinner in God's eyes and will never have done exactly what he ought to have done. For Luther there were no saints, that is to say no men who had ever escaped temptation, or had been completely removed from the danger of moral error and relapse. The life of even the most pious and zealous is a continued struggle with sin and unbelief. Therefore there are no saintly works which as such are especially pleasing to God. Indeed, in the valorous deeds of conscious piety, there is normally to be found the greatest religious self-interest, striving to win itself rewards in heaven—whereas God is only interested in the free, purely selfless act of freely given love. For this proves itself to be of far greater worth in the faithful, selfless submission to everyday duties, in the things 'which are given to man to do', that is in his daily work, as well as in works of ecclesiastical sanctity.

Luther refuses to allow the old distinction between holy and profane actions, rooted as it was in antiquity, to have any further validity, because in his deepened understanding of religion there is no longer any possibility of invoking God by cultic acts. Everything is holy which is born of the right attitude to God, even walking, standing, sleeping, eating and whatever else is done for the nourishment of the body for the common good.

With this, the whole colossal construction of medieval sanctity of works collapses at a blow; fasting, saying the rosary, pilgrimages, donations of candles, altars, churches and cloisters, the whole ecclesiastical asceticism of monasticism—all these suddenly appear as pointless actions. There are indeed different levels of moral development, but no grades of saintliness and no difference between the moral demand which is made on the professional ascetics of the monastery, on the clergy, or on the lay-Christians. Only for the weak, immature, and criminal is the compulsion of the law indispensable, and only for them does the moral guidance of the Church become useful as a means of education. The Church's position of power as an institution of universal law and grace, which gathers together religious rewards and administers them, which rules over and supervises the life of the believer by legal judgments and laws which are canonically binding, submits him to its own strict corrective legislation, for the enforcement of which the power of the State is at her command—all this was now threatened at its very foundations.

The second blow was dealt, again from the same spiritual depth, by the scholarly treatise on the Babylonian captivity of the Church. Thanks to its being written in Latin, it was read in all the countries of Europe and everywhere received as a revolutionary deed of unforeseeable consequences. The humanistic circles in particular became acquainted for the first time with the true face of the bold Reformer, whom till now they had so zealously applauded. For many the treatise caused great scandal; conservative and conciliatory elements like Erasmus or Ulrich Zasius now shied away, declared themselves openly against the revolutionary, or retired to the neutral position of observers. The greatest offence was given by the radical denials of the magical character of the sacraments of the Church: Luther only wanted to consider them as the outward sign of a purely inward, purely spiritual process, the assurance of salvation of faith. They are a gift of God to men, but in no way a sacrifice of men to God and so in no way a means of appealing to the Will of God by sacred formulae. This completely destroyed the sense and the lawfulness of the central act of the Catholic cultus, the sacrificial mass with its miraculous transformation, however much Luther may have tried, by laying the foundation of a purely spiritual concept of sacrifice, to make possible at least the continuation of a part of these sacred and ancient rites. Later on, nothing was to cause more inward and outward torment than the task of maintaining the mystery of the real presence of Christ in its full form, without the miracle of the transformation of the bread and wine. The other sacraments, too, he treated with pious consideration for their traditional ideas and usages; he made no laws either about the lay chalice or about the abolition of private masses, of confirmation, the confessional or the supreme unction. Nevertheless the destructive effect of his attack was decisive: that he now only recognised baptism and communion (together with penance) as valid sacraments, declared the sacrifice of the mass to be pure idolatry, and the public constraint of the monastic vows and the priestly celibacy to be immoral tyranny, denounced the claim of the Church to regulate marriage as pure presumption, and declared the forms of adoration of God to be (against all Roman, and indeed medieval, sentiment—even of the heretics!) ultimately of no significance, since God was only interested in the hearts of men, and not in their outward actions, and because he would on no account allow his will to be bound by man-made legal forms. In this, the whole of men's religious thinking was changed: their converse with God now appeared as a completely free, purely personal, relationship of adoration, submission and trust, without any strict ties to outward forms. The Church, however, lost the majority of her income and capital, as the countless benefices for masses disappeared and as the canonical offices and the monasteries founded to say them were considered superfluous, as monastic vows and cloisters were abolished, and as the countless lay societies for the provision of masses for the dead disbanded (or as Luther suggested) turned into associations for the voluntary care of the poor and the sick.

But even this was not enough. With the difference between profane and holy actions there disappeared also the distinction between the spiritual and lay estates; as the Church changed from a ruling society into a free fellowship, from a legal institution with public power to coerce and punish, into a spiritual community, in which only the love-commandment of Christ was of supreme importance, the clerical orders lost their claim to a privileged legal position in the world. This was the most important message of the letter to the Christian nobility: the doctrine of the universal priesthood of believers. 'All Christians,' we read there, 'belong to a truly spiritual order, and there is no distinction between them merely because of their office. We are all of us consecrated as priests in our baptism—are all one body of the head Jesus Christ. Christ has neither two bodies nor two sorts of body, one worldly and the other spiritual. One body he is and one body he has.' This *corpus mysticum Christi* is the true Church: an invisible community of the spirit, scattered over the whole world—invisible because God alone who searches the hearts of man, can distinguish the believers from the unbelievers. How could such a purely spiritual community have any other head but Christ himself? From where could any sinful man derive the authority to play the worldly monarch as Christ's representative, that is, to rule over believers and unbelievers? There is no word in the Bible (as he had already explained in his treatise on the Papacy) which can in any way justify the secular power of the priests. He must no longer be the mediator between God and men, but only the servant of the Word, which God himself speaks to his children.

But when everything which has 'crept out of baptism' has been brought together in the unified body of Christendom, there is nothing which can prevent the secular authorities from undertaking the necessary great reforms on their own initiative. For they have 'an office which is useful and which has its place in the Christian community'. They have become 'a member of the Christian body, and although they have a physical function, they are still of spiritual rank'; therefore 'one must let them go about their business unhindered by the whole body of Christendom, no matter whom it may be—Pope, bishops, priests, monks, nuns or whatever else.' The secular sword (and he was thinking in the first instance of the Emperor and the Imperial Estates) must first summon, as in the fifteenth century, a great, general reform council. But if this were to founder on the resistance of the Pope and the prelates, then 'the masses (the Church people) and the secular sword' should continue independently in all places. For 'if anything is against God and endangers the body and soul of men, then it is the duty of every community, councillor, or superior, to abolish it or resist it by force; without the knowledge or sanction of the Pope or bishop, indeed he owes it to the blessedness of his soul to resist it, even if both the bishop and the Pope should try to stop him.' One can call this a restatement of the late medieval doctrine of the right and duty of the secular powers to give assistance in cases of emergency in the Church (when for example the Church cannot help itself as a result of schism); and Luther did indeed have in mind the 'reformation' of countless individual abuses of the Church by the civic and princely authorities. But at the same time, he far outpasses all such models; it is because he does not trust the Pope or the bishops that he wants to apply the reformation tenet of the power of the laity even against the will of the spiritual superiors and even without their knowledge!

After the proclamation of such revolutionary principles one expects a truly radical, perhaps Utopian, programme of reform. For example if one hears how he envisaged the installation of the clergy (any suitable member of the community can be called to this office in the same way as in the election of civil officials, but can also be deposed again and become a farmer or citizen as before), one is immediately reminded of the congregational methods of groups of extreme protestant enthusiasts. But the way in which Luther developed this shows that he only gave expression to such radical lines of thought in order to make his position in the struggle against the supposedly 'indelible character' and the particular holiness of the Catholic order of priests perfectly clear and evident to all. Although radical in the formulation of his principles, he proved to be remarkably conservative when it came to applying them, filled as he was with the very deepest distrust for the untutored masses, the 'Messrs Omnes'. In no circumstances does he want to produce a state of chaos, but an ordered reform. It is for this reason that he turned also to the Christian nobles of the German nation, by which he clearly meant, in the first place, the ruling princes, the greater estates of the Empire, and only in the second place unruly knights like Hutten.

When it came to individual criticisms, he presented an overwhelming mass of concrete grievances; the letter to the nobles marks at once the peak and the conclusion of a long series of ecclesiastical and political reform tracts, which had now been circulating for more than a hundred years. None of the complaints so often voiced against the greed of Rome, the internal corruption of the Church, and the suppression of the German nation by the Popes, is missing. But it was for just this reason that the letter had such a powerful effect, and became

THE REFORMER (1520)

known so much more quickly then Luther's other tracts. For all the discontent of the age felt that it was represented here. Yet everything had again been re-stated in a completely new form; it was not only that the Reformer exposed all sorts of other abuses, which his forerunners had not yet seen. Above all everything was approached from a much more radical standpoint, and everywhere the roots of the situation were uncovered in Rome's false understanding of religion. In this the force of his attack was mightily strengthened. One other thing made a deep impression: that his suggestions for reform in no way came from the mouth of a spiritual enthusiast living withdrawn from the world, but seemed to come from a well-informed, reasonable man who would take advice from men who really understood the subject and who abandoned the old traditional forms with more reluctance than relish. Not once did he talk of the complete abolition of the priestly Church and the Papacy, but only of the ending of papal abuses, the discontinuance of the secular power of the Church, the creation of a German national Church under the Archbishop of Mainz, the strict limitation of spiritual jurisdiction, of the monastic orders and of monasteries and cloisters, the admission of clerical marriage, the curbing of superstitious pilgrimages and miracles, the reform of Church punishments, and a great deal more in this vein. And he showed himself a true son of the Middle Ages by extending this activity as Church Reformer into the world of secular affairs; for at heart he still felt that spiritual and secular crime were one and the same thing. And so he demanded the reform of the schools and universities, the restriction of luxury, the prohibition of rates of interest (income from capital), and the abolition of usury, the restriction of the large import trade, of monopolies and guilds. Above all he advocated the struggle against large holdings of capital in favour of the honest agriculturists; police intervention against intemperance, prostitution and begging; the education of the people for work, for an industrious, undemanding, moderate, honourable and godly life. The ideals of the Christian Welfare and police state, which were finally realised in the late Reformation Period, can already be seen here.

We can see in all this the final conquest of the Middle Ages, and its equally radical development and supercession. We see the rejection of the assumption of worldly power by the priests, of the separation of the spiritual estate and of its position of authority over the secular powers, of the division of spiritual and secular law, of the underestimation of secular professions as against the clerical calling. Furthermore, since every profession, in so far as it is practised in a true Christian way, that is, as a responsibility before God, is itself a service to God, the earthly life of men receives a new value. The work of the secular professions ceases to be purely a necessary evil; it is done at God's command and the temporal prince acts under his command just as much as the Pope. But while this sweeps away the religious difference of values between the spiritual and secular estates, it does not overthrow the basic idea of the medieval society as a spiritual and secular whole; rather, for the first time, it is taken to its ultimate conclusion. Nothing could be farther from the truth than to say that Luther wanted to free secular culture and, in particular, the State, from its bondage of religious obligations. He freed them from the dominating power of the ecclesiastical hierarchy and the secular priesthood, but not from the Christian way of life. On the contrary, he was bold enough to call even the secular authorities and the whole laity spiritual estates. He was certainly not interested in making the world in any way more secular; he wanted to fan Christian piety into such a flame that it would have even more influence than before; but this by virtue of pure belief, pure love of God and fear of God, and not out of motives of pious selfishness, ecclesiastical habit and fear of Church punishments! He did indeed destroy the spiritual climate of the Middle Ages, but only to replace it with a Christian one. Nothing would have been more foreign to him than the idea of the moral autonomy of secular culture and, in particular, of political power. It is true that he wanted nothing to do with any sort of ecclesiastical religious consecration of secular power as known in the Middle Ages and, in particular, he would not hear of the consecration and ratification of the Emperor by the Pope. The exercise of authority is a profession like any other—like that of the shoemaker, tailor or farmer, with the sword and rule as its tools of trade. Nothing could be more simple, earthly or commonplace. Not the office itself but the personal disposition of the bearer of the office makes the actions of authority Christian in the first instance. In spite of all this, the prince remains, for Luther, God's officer and jailer, he remains of 'spiritual estate', because Luther could imagine no other situation than that in which the prince acts as a member of 'Christendom', of 'Christian estate', in the surroundings of a thoroughly Christian world. How else could he have laid the fate of the Church in the hands of the Christian nobles with such a carefree spirit? Even in his tract 'Of the Improvement of the Christian Estate', his trust in the Christian disposition of the secular authorities seems almost boundless; only later, when pressed by all the trials of the political storms which surrounded him, did he realise that a really pious prince, imbued with the Gospel, was indeed 'a rare bird'. It is then that he asserts that Church and Faith must 'indeed have some other protector than emperors and kings'. But even then he did not cease to speak powerfully to their conscience and to keep them constantly reminded of their Christian duties.

But how far could he be sure that this call to men's consciences would always and everywhere meet with any response?—particularly outside the narrow circle of the patriarchal princely houses of the small German states, who had now long been accustomed to think of Church reform as their most important task. Had not the great powers of the world now for a long time been on the road to a completely new world, which would be quite different from the Middle Ages ? Had not they for a long time now been in the process of emancipating themselves, not only from the spiritual authorities, but also, more or less consciously, from the principles of Christianity themselves ? Had not the Church itself in the great West-European states already become a means of power of the State ? Had not the great inspiring unity of the medieval cultural ideals of the Christian West long since been undermined by the advent of the Renaissance ? In this development of history the Lutheran Reformation assumes a unique and equivocal position. On the one side it threw itself with all its weight against the secularisation of all forms of life and not without resounding success: the intensity of religious life again rose to an unexpected degree in both Churches, in the new, as well as by reaction in the old; Christianity again appeared in the centre of all life, even though it had seemed to be in great danger of fading away, or, thanks to the unworthiness of its old servants, at least of losing its old glory and even its credibility. Politics, art and spiritual life were dominated by ecclesiastical and religious questions at the time of the confessional struggle, to an extent which was equalled only at the height of the Middle Ages and perhaps not even then. On the other hand, however, Luther—of course unintentionally and unsuspectingly—contributed more than anyone to the decay of the unity of the great medieval Christian culture by destroying the very roots of the enormously powerful organisation of the Western secular Church. In order to preserve the purity and authenticity of his religious message, he staked everything to make the Church again that outwardly invisible community of the heart and spirit which it had been in its early beginnings: how could it now possibly think of conquering the world as it progressed along its new path towards purity of conscience ?

THE REFORMER (1520)

It was the inevitable disadvantage of his Reformation, which he himself had not even suspected in his letter to the nobles, that as soon as the Christian community was no longer protected by the special privileges of the spiritual estates, it would run the danger of becoming dependent on secular powers and of losing its own independent existence; for who would guarantee that 'the secular communes, councils and authorities' would always use their power in the service of pure evangelical doctrine, in the spirit of pure Christian love? The chaos of a purely secular desire for power now threatened to take the place of the well-ordered cosmos of the medieval world order with its delicate graduation of secular and spiritual spheres. Very soon Luther was to feel himself forced, in the face of political intervention against his teaching, to make a sharp distinction between the spiritual and secular communities and to isolate a sphere of activity for the religious conscience, which no secular ruler might penetrate. But for the moment he saw the danger from the other side only; the secular estates seemed all to be submitting to the new Gospel—only the spiritual estate, the bishops and the Papacy, were showing resistance. Like everyone else, he hoped that the storm wind of the reformation would in a few years sweep Germany clean of all the clutter and rubbish of papal regulations and unevangelical superstition.

Indeed it was a historical moment of unforgettable importance —a spring day seemed to have arrived for the German people in which it was a 'pleasure to live', as Hutten wrote in his enthusiasm. For as Germany prepared to cast off its Roman fetters, it became aware for the first time of its own true national character. The powerful national movement which now rushed through the land, the blissful hope that now at last, even in secular life, everything could become different, new and better, if only the spell of old errors was once broken, was not (as we have just mentioned) without its effect on the Reformer. No one was more passionately concerned than he with the fate of the German nation, 'which nation with its noble nature is praised for its constancy and faithfulness in all history', but which had constantly let itself be ensnared by Italian wiles and cunning, and allowed the political freedom of its kingdom to be stolen by the Popes. An extensive addition to the second edition of the Address to the Nobility deals expressly with the sly machinations of the Popes, who used the pretext of the 'transference' of the Roman imperial office to the German princes, merely for the purpose of making the Emperor the 'vassal' of the Roman see, as was now again to be feared. Even the spiritual dignity of the Western Empire, its claim to ensure the obedience of Christendom to the Pope in its capacity as the secular arm of the Church, is disputed by Luther, although he does not entertain the idea of rejecting the leading position of the Emperor among the potentates of Europe, and of contenting himself with a purely German kingdom. In every case he always returns to the religious issue—to the rejection of papal intervention. But it is precisely here, in his determination to hold on to the German claims to universal power, that the warmth and genuineness of his quite naïve, involuntary and popular patriotism becomes really clear. Without the national arrogance and presumption of the humanist spokesmen of the time, but always ready to criticise ruthlessly the failings in the German character, he is still proud, as a German, to serve his dear Germans and to defend German freedom in the struggle against the Papacy. This side of his struggle was not the least of the factors contributing to the popularity of his writings, which now ran through the land like a forest fire. As the prophet of the Germans, Luther was greeted on all sides with shouts of triumph. For could not his Gospel seem even to the most pious like the fulfilment of an ancient longing in the German soul, like a last crowning glory of the German piety of the Middle Ages?

There was never a more fruitful moment in German history.

THE REFORMER (1520)

Its genius seemed to step forward into the limelight of world events, and to remould the spirit of the times. All the most talented men of our nation seemed to be drawn together to one point. They were to make the most original and important contribution to world history which has ever come out of Germany. Would it be possible to keep all the impulses which were here drawn together, working together in the same direction for any length of time ? In their first encounter with any resistance they proved themselves irresistible; the colossal structure of the medieval church tottered under the force of their impact. Rome's cries of 'Excommunication!' died away in Germany almost unheard. The heretic was triumphantly acclaimed as the hero of his nation. What would be the result if it should prove possible to preserve the enthusiasm and greatness of those days, when all Germany was fêting its saviour, and to transfer it into their everyday work—to translate the plans of the architect into reality without alteration—and to draw the whole nation with him along his chosen way, under the powerful leadership of an imperial authority, as had already been proposed at the beginning of his reformation programme ? Would any power on earth dare to resist such a united nation ? The fate of a large part of the earth, and above all the fate of the German people, hung on the answer to these questions.

5. *Hero of the German Nation (1521)*

He did not have to wait long for his first disappointment. A papal bull arrived in Wittenberg from Rome (dated 25th June, 1520) which declared forty-one theses of Luther to be heretical, which banned his books and condemned them to be ceremonially burned. In it Luther was summoned to repent within sixty days and threatened with excommunication should he refuse. In this case he was to be handed over to Rome for judgment and then to be given into the hands of the secular authorities for execution. At the same time as this bull arrived in Wittenberg, a note from Erasmus from the court of the young Emperor, who had meanwhile arrived in his inherited territory in the Netherlands, announced that it would be unwise to set any hope on him, for his court was dominated by the Papist mendicant monks. Immediately the first fires in the Netherlands were lit in execution of the papal judgment on the books of the heretic. Shortly afterwards came Spalatin's sombre report of the first impression of the bull on the electors just before their first meeting with the Spaniard on the Rhine. Luther received this news with a lack of concern which at first sight is more than a little surprising. 'It is no great wonder,' he wrote. 'Put no faith in princes; they are children of men, and can be of no help.' And shortly afterwards, almost joyfully, to Spalatin, 'I am glad that you have at last seen how vain are the hopes of the Germans and that you have learnt not to put your trust in princes and have ceased to care for the judgment of men. Were

HERO OF THE GERMAN NATION (1521)

the Gospel of the kind that it could be spread or preserved by the mighty men of the world, God would not have entrusted it to fishermen.' Was this still the same man from whose pen had come the rousing appeal to 'the Christian nobles of the German nation for the improvement of the Christian Estate', and who had set all Germany astir? But one can see from the first few sentences of this letter the deep religious concern which moved him in this matter: 'The first thing which we have to do in this affair is, in all seriousness, to put ourselves on our guard lest we should undertake anything merely out of faith in power or reason. For God cannot and will not tolerate it if a good work is begun out of confidence in one's own ability. He will cast it to the ground and that will be the end of it.' The particular character of the pure religious genius, and in particular the character of Lutheran piety, is nowhere more clearly seen than in this remarkably rapid retreat from the sphere of the world into the inassailable fortress of his own inner life. 'Never,' says a recent Luther scholar, 'was Luther at such a low ebb as in his letter to the nobles.' But it was as if he only delved for a moment into these shadowy spheres and then rapidly withdrew to calmer and purer regions. And indeed it was only under the pressure of external forces that this remarkable man became a reformer at all. 'If you did not drive me to it,' he wrote to Spalatin, 'I would leave the whole matter to God and do no more than I have done up till now; for I know well that it can only be carried on by his guidance and activity.' But in the last instance it was not the exhortations of his friends which kept him in the struggle; far more, rather, his decision was determined by opinions contrary to his own! In the end it was his constantly burning moral anger, which had already driven him out of his monastery cell and forced him to speak before the people, which now, again and again, overwhelmed him, however much his soul longed to find its rest in God. It is here that we can see that the prophetic element in his piety was ultimately stronger than the mystical element—that his warring spirit was stronger than that of the 'passive' contemplator of God's splendour, his will stronger than pious sentiment and speculation: to put it in his own terms, that in the end faith was of no worth without the good works in which it proved itself. But one can only fully understand the enormous tensions of his life, the stormy existence of his soul, which was far too deeply rent by its own internal conflicts ever to be able to settle into a comfortable and peaceful, ordered pattern of life; one can only understand this if one first realises what an enormous upsurge of moral indignation was first necessary before he could even set forth on his public career. It is no exaggeration to say that anger is the father of all his political writings: he 'cooled his blood' by writing them in the first flush of anger, and even today they bear witness to this. His biographers have often attempted to justify his 'uninhibited polemics', which gave offence even to his contemporaries. But can purely natural processes be excused? The unlimited passion of his anger was nothing more than the counterpart to the infinitely delicate sensitivity of his conscience. In both, he was completely unrestrained, because his moral consciousness far outstripped that of normal men. Just as he had to fight with the fleshly devil in himself, so he really saw his struggle with the world as a struggle with the princes of Hell. And naturally one did not go about such business with a feather duster, there was nothing for it but to go to it with both fists.

He had to hate and despise the opinion of his opponent, lest, in naïve and childlike confidence in God's help, he should leave himself and his work without any defence against his opponent. But in his faith he found a source of strength which astounded and terrified his advisers and friends no less than his refusal to set any store by human advice. He thought he was acting wisely and in the accepted manner of the Saxon court, when he publicly cast doubt on the genuineness of the bull of excommunication; but what good was that if, at the same time, he stated that, in case the Roman see really was responsible for this bull, he wished publicly and formally to curse that see, by appealing to his rights as a Christian, conferred on him in baptism, to curse it as a seat of Satan, of the arch-enemy of Christ, and to abandon it, with the bull and all papal laws, to the destruction of the flesh: 'In the name of the Lord Jesus Christ whom ye persecute. Amen!' Urged by the Saxon councillors, he allowed himself to be persuaded in the middle of October by Miltitz, that incorrigible schemer, to take part in yet another act of mediation, although any prospects of conciliation had long been vain. He promised to cease his polemics, to write a submissive letter to Pope Leo X, which was to lay all the blame on Eck's contentiousness and to dedicate a treatise to the Pope himself. And Luther kept his promise; but the treatise which he dedicated to the Holy Father was the essay on 'the Freedom of the Christian Man' and the letter of dedication which was printed at the same time, commiserated with almost fatherly sympathy with the 'most unhappy Leo, who sits in the most dangerous seat of all like a sheep among wolves and like Daniel among the lions and like Ezekiel among the scorpions. It is all up with the see of Rome, God's anger has fallen upon it without cease.' At the same time appeared the treatise on the Babylonian captivity of the Church, with its radical rejection of the medieval concept of the sacraments, that is to say, the most grievous of his heresies. It soon became perfectly clear that Karl Miltitz's promises had been without substance. Luther was seriously anticipating martyrdom. But this prospect, instead of crippling him as it had done in 1518, now produced in him a fever of activity such as he had never known before; for since then he had unmasked his opponent, and was quite sure that he was now confronted by nothing less than the demonic power of the pit. So he renewed his public appeal to a future council, and in a solemn proclamation, issued simultaneously on placards, called on the German authorities to support this step for the salvation of the honour of God and the Christian Church (November 17th). Three weeks later in a solemn and symbolic action he burnt not only the bull of excommunication, but also—and this made a far deeper impression on the world—the books of canon law, on the carrion-pit in front of the Elster gate in Wittenberg: a prompt reprisal for the burning of his writings by the papal commissaries—an act which made such an impression on people that even the moral success of that court of inquisition was completely undermined. This time, at least, he informed his electors first. But one can understand the concern which this incorrigible protégé caused the Saxon Electors and it is the most convincing proof of the devotion to the Gospel of the Elector's advisers, that they too in these critical months eventually found the courage to put all the skill of their ponderously careful but nevertheless successful diplomacy at his disposal in an attempt to save him from disaster.

We cannot here follow the intricate war of intrigue which was waged by both sides with great tenacity during the next months and preceded Luther's summons to the Diet of Worms.

To be sure, the Saxon was helped by the timely appearance of a favourable star over Europe: as long as the Medici in Rome held on stubbornly to their alliance with France, the Spanish Burgundian politicians found it advisable to worry him with talk of sanctioning the Lutheran heresy. But from the beginning it was clear that Germany with all her interests was only considered as a province or satellite of a world power at this truly international court. They thought to play with the heretical monk as with a piece on a chess-board which in itself is of no importance; and it was obvious that they would abandon this tactic as soon as it had achieved its object of driving the Pope into the arms of the Hapsburgs. Yet over and above this the Spaniards hated and despised this heretic with all the religious pride of a nation whose national conscience had been formed in the long centuries of the struggle against heresy. What a monstrous, almost unbelievable trick of fate for the Germans, that the two nations in Europe whose religious climate was as far opposed as possible should now be joined together politically. For of the two, one was in the process of rekindling the flame of medieval piety, while the other was already well on the way to a new form of belief! It is one of the most grievous misfortunes of our whole history that just at the moment when a great common purpose seemed to unite all the German houses and estates and bind them tightly together, our nation was governed by a foreigner who understood nothing, and could understand nothing, of its interests.

If it proved possible to gain a hearing for the heretic before the Diet, instead of following the traditional course of adding the imperial ban to the papal ban without further ado—in itself an unheard of innovation in canon and imperial law—then this was due to the general anger in the imperial estates against 'Rome's mismanagement' and also to the concern of the nobility at the 'burning rage' of the common peasant, who was not again to be cheated of his hope of a general reform. And it was then that the teaching of the new freedom of the Gospel began to penetrate even the lower levels of society, where the people, fired with a spirit of revolution, had long been awaiting their saviour. Now alongside and behind the threat of the knight with his sword and spear loomed the threat of the peasant with his scythe and flail, 'who now also understands the Holy Scriptures.' 'Nine tenths of Germany,' wrote the papal nuncio Aleander, 'are crying "Luther" and the other tenth are at least crying "Death to the Roman court" and everyone is demanding and crying out for a council.' And this was exactly how it was; the diplomats of the Renaissance court were amazed and disconcerted to learn that their normal methods of petty bribery seemed to have no effect with these 'beasts' who had simply gone wild; indeed they were even greeted on the streets with threatening fists. But, in the traditional manner, the cries of the people were wild and unintelligible, and in many ways without aim or purpose. For the rest only the Saxon court was ready to identify itself with Luther's cause—and even this kept up a pretence of being uncommitted. All the rest were only interested in their own particular grievances, which for the most part were purely materialistic, and saw in Luther a means to their own ends. This first Diet of the new Emperor was at last to put into force the reforms of the Empire and the Church, which had for decades been vainly urged and which in the end it had been impossible to discuss seriously with Maximilian. The imperial capitulation of Charles was to serve as a pretext to dispose His Majesty favourably towards the wishes of the imperial estates. Imperial reform, in the sense of government by the estates, the renewed weakening of the imperial power and reform of the Church in the sense of the renewed assertion of the sovereign of the princes over the Churches in the different territories, renewed limitation of the special legal privileges of the clergy, in taxation and other similar matters, and above all the rejection of papal interference in German Church affairs—this was the programme of the imperial estates (now presented for by no means the first time)—for whose promotion even the Lutheran opposition against Rome might prove, within certain limits, to be politically useful, although clearly dogmatic differences would interfere most unwelcomely in those purely political aims. And so the will of the majority prevailed, despite all the warnings, threats and entreaties of the papal envoys, and it was decided that they would at least first see and hear the heretic—although, of course, only for a short hearing, to see whether he was ready to recant from his public heresies, and not, as Luther had imagined, to a formal debate with disputation and ' arbitration by neutral experts '. Even here they could reach no agreement with the imperial government about what would happen if he should prove ready to renounce his erroneous teachings and doctrines; yet, in spite of this, the Estates were intending ' to hear him further on other points and issues ', that is to say they wanted to exploit his opposition against Rome to the full. Thus, when the imperial confessor Glapion secretly pleaded with the Saxon Elector (whom the imperial minister was certainly using for his own political ends) that he should persuade his professor to renounce the latest and most grievous heresies, which dealt directly with purely dogmatic questions, while leaving other matters open to discussion, he was also acting very much in the interests of most of the imperial estates. All was in vain; yet even Hutten, Sickingen and Bucer were persuaded to urge such suggestions on Luther, even as they were approaching the gates of Worms. Scarcely had the new Gospel seen the light of day than it had already become a factor in political bargaining.

And yet the man who had first proclaimed it was in no way worried by all this. Anyone who wants to see a historical hero, at every moment conscious of the sublimity of his mission, has only to read his letters in these months. Our literature has little that one would dare to set alongside them. Only a short while before, his little book 'Freedom of the Christian Man' had given the world an insight into his heart, into his own deep, personal secret. When he left for Worms, he had to break off his work on an evangelical exposition of the Magnificat. For this was the sphere in which his soul again and again found refreshment and strength, while his pen hurriedly sent out pamphlet after pamphlet against the Anti-Christ in Rome and his ' godless bulls and lies '. What use could he possibly have for the advice of friends, who would have had him write a letter commending himself to the German princes, or for the warnings of his own princely protector against the attacks of the ' little red hat ', the Papist at Worms ? He would neither trust the princes nor the warlike attacks of a man like Hutten on the priests; it was not the sword which would open the way for the Gospel (even if he had himself in moments of extreme excitement considered such a possibility), but the Word which must and would work through its own power. He could not possibly consider his appearance in Worms as a matter of high politics, but solely as a confession of faith: 'It is not our business to determine whether the Gospel and the public good are threatened more by my life or my death. We are only concerned that once we have begun to preach the Gospel we should not leave it to fend for itself, a prey to the mocking of the ungodly, and that we should not give our opponents any ground for self-congratulation because we did not dare to confess to what we taught or to pour out our blood for it.' 'You can expect everything from me except flight and recantation.' But even now he did not seek a martyr's death. He knew that God was still alive, who had saved the three youths in the fiery furnace in Babylon, and if he would not save him—then what would he have to bear, seeing that even Christ himself had suffered death. 'And even if they made a fire which stretched from Wittenberg to Worms and right up to heaven, because it is demanded of me I would still appear in the Name of the Lord and walk into Behemoth's mouth between his great teeth and confess Christianity and then let him do what he please.'

And so he embarked on his journey to Worms, without knowledge of the political machinations to which he had been exposed, but also without the slightest respect for them—only with the sure instinct of the religious genius that one thing above all was to be done: that he must preserve the message to whose service he was called, against all the trials which confronted him, and keep it pure and unstained by any concessions to the political needs of this world. The story of his progress to Worms, which practically assumed the character of a triumphal procession, needs hardly to be told again. None of the threats or enticements of his opponents could shake his firm resolve: neither the stern mandate against his writings, about which he learnt on the way, nor the statement of the Elector that if he wanted to come, then he did so at his risk, for he could no longer afford him protection, nor even the tempting invitation to Sickingen's castle at Ebernburg to a consultation with the imperial confessor—nothing could stop him going to Worms, ' even if there were as many devils there as tiles on the roofs'. He appeared, and thereby put to confusion the calculations of all those who had been counting on his staying away and had hoped thereby to expose him publicly and to forestall above all the heated discussion of the German grievances against Rome at the Diet, the range of which seemed almost unlimited.

No event in German history has been retold more often than the appearance of Luther before the Emperor and the Empire. The Imperial Diet of Worms in 1521 is of great importance for the history of the German constitution; all this has long since been forgotten, and only the proceedings with Luther have remained alive in the mind of the German people. In front of the full assembly he was challenged to recant his heresies. But he recanted nothing, and instead delivered a courageous confession of his own conviction and belief. The last sentence of his speech, ' Here I stand, I cannot do otherwise, God help me! Amen,'[1] (even if in this form it has long been shown to be legendary) has rightly become the symbolic expression of all that made Martin Luther, with the heroic submission of his will to the demands of faith, so dear to his nation. Yet the history of these days, the internal, political relation of the individual events, is still disputed in many points. Nevertheless we may say with certainty, that the official of the Archbishop of Treves, Dr. von der Ecken, who led the proceedings against the heretic, both on the first and the second day of the proceedings (April 17th and 18th) intentionally phrased his question thus: whether Luther would not retract something from the writings, which

---

[1] Only 'Help me God,' is supported by historical evidence.

were before the court (not if he would retract them in toto). Behind this, of course, lay the intention of the imperial estates which we have already discussed—namely to use the dogmatically unexceptionable part of his polemic for their own political ends. It does not, however, appear probable that the Elector of Saxony had any influence on this formulation of the question, or in fact in any way on the course of the proceedings. The behaviour of Frederick the Wise in these days gives the impression that he was completely helpless. Torn this way and that between his concern for his professor, who even now was much too bold for him, and the fear of bringing the wrath of the Emperor upon himself, he preferred to keep quite quiet, to assume an attitude of complete neutrality, and to commend Luther's affair to God, 'who will without doubt not abandon the cause of Justice.' The idea of himself assuming the leadership of the pro-Lutheran imperial estates, and carrying the Imperial Diet with him to a decisive reform of Church government, never occurred to him. And his councillors learnt nothing of what was going on behind the doors of the imperial suite, of the consultations between the papal nuncios, and the imperial ministers, about the form of the proceedings with the Grand Inquisitor. It is therefore improbable that Luther had been advised, as some would suggest, by the cunning politicians of the Saxon court to give an evasive answer on the first day, in order thereby to protract the proceedings and so to gain time for the more basic discussions of the estates and to force another session in the larger hall (instead of in the small courtroom of the Elector Palatinate). It can all be explained quite simply, as it has indeed always been understood: the monk came before the great lords of this world, without any political instruction, and without an idea of what lay before him. He believed from his reading of the summons that he had been called to a discussion of his writings: it had only spoken of informing the Diet and had contained no word about damnation and recantation. Now

HERO OF THE GERMAN NATION (1521)

all at once, in threatening, scolding tones, he is ordered to recant immediately without an opportunity of explanation or defence, indeed without even a precise indication of what it was that was heretical in his writings—and all this in a strangely new way (if he would not reject a 'part') which led him to suspect some ulterior motive. How could all this have failed to have disconcerted him in the first moment? The happy confidence with which he entered the hall was replaced by a certain confusion; with a quiet, timid voice (so the report runs) he asked for time to consider the matter. He simply needed time and reflection in order to be able to do justice to his affair. It was certainly not fear of men, which oppressed him. This could in no way be inferred from the reports of the Spaniards and the Italians of his appearance: how he came in with a 'laughing expression on his face', greeted old acquaintances in the hall and even while he was standing directly before the Emperor, turned his head this way and that in order to be able to survey the assembly without fear. His truly German lack of outward form, of Spanish *grandezza*, of any pose or pathos in his appearance, was highly offensive to the Romans ('He will not make me into a heretic,' the Emperor Charles is supposed to have said), but particularly pleased the Germans in their prophet. In any case he cannot have wavered for a moment in what concerned the root of the matter, in what was his duty. Not an iota would he retract, so he wrote immediately after his return to his inn.

We can see how carefully he prepared for his appearance on the next day, not only from the written sketch of his speech (of which a portion has been preserved to this day) but above all from the actual text itself: with its cleverly thought-out division of his writings into purely edifying treatises, attacks on the Papacy and purely personal attacks on private persons, whose form he would willingly abandon, without, however, abandoning the substance of the quarrel with the papal tyranny. None of these three groups could be in any way offensive to the imperial estates; but the real source of trouble, the dogmatic heresies, above all of more recent times, was cleverly passed over. It is most probable that his friends, more likely Spalatin than anyone else, had advised him in these matters of form. Nevertheless, in essence his appearance was in no way influenced by these advisers. Rather he chose just this moment to remind his listeners of a saying of Christ which he was so fond of quoting: 'I have not come to bring peace, but a sword.' It was for him no great cause of sorrow that God's word should cause such storms in the world, but on the contrary, a highly delectable sight. So his reply to the Emperor and Empire this time developed into a self-defence of unforgettable boldness: with the warning cry to the imperial youngster not to stain the beginnings of his reign with injustice, for God could overthrow him, and, above all, with the firm and clear confession that he would only accept his own conscience, advised by the Word of God, as a yardstick for his own action; all words which were worthy of the highest sense of the historical moment in which they were spoken. When he again returned to the inn, he threw up his hands with his fingers outspread in the gesture which the German knights and mercenaries used to make after a well-won fight: 'I have won, I have won!'

In truth by far the most difficult part of his task still lay before him. The really decisive negotiations took place not in the public assembly before the whole world, but in the privacy and quiet of smaller meetings. It is true that the Emperor issued a formal statement after Luther's second hearing, to the effect that he would use all the means at his disposal to root out this heresy. Yet even then the imperial estates did not abandon all hope of winning over the most typical of all Germans for their particular form of opposition against Rome, and of reaching, in one way or another, some means of compromise on the disputed questions of dogma: perhaps by an open discussion before a jury of disinterested judges or by the decision of a council. So for a whole week he had to endure the cross-fire of political threats and enticements. His room at the court of the Knights of St. John was never free from the visits of princes and lords. A committee of the Diet, which contained a lord as important and apparently as friendly as the Archbishop of Treves, the political ally of Luther's Elector in opposition to the Hapsburg and who had indeed been proposed by the Elector as the arbitrator in Luther's affair, went into his case with great patience. They urged him to entrust his affair to the imperial estates, who would see to it that honourable and just arbitrators were provided. At least, then, he should agree that certain particularly heretical articles should be selected from his writings and submitted to the judgment of a council. They urged him for God's sake to consider what would happen if the old structure of the Church was ruthlessly destroyed; revolt, war and strife would be unavoidable. The path he was treading led straight to chaos. Such arguments were not without their effect on Luther. The whole terrible weight of historical responsibility lay on his soul. Once again an honourable way out seemed to be opened up to the heretic, condemned to death and excommunicate as he was: had not he himself appealed often enough to the Pope—in fact only a short while before— to summon a council to deal with the matter? Was there not after all a possibility of a settlement? There were times in these days in which he seemed uncertain in himself about the way out of the confusion of political culs-de-sac in which they tried to trap him. At one time his nerves seemed near breaking-point: he was close to tears. In a state of great excitement he made his confession to the Archbishop of Treves, though what he actually said we do not know. Yet he never for a moment took a step backwards. In the hours of decision there often came into his mind the saying 'You shall not put your trust in princes, nor in the children of men, in whom is no salvation.

He declared that he could submit to no judge's decision which was not based on the Word of God. He did not abandon the least part of his teaching.

There are still to-day critics who reproach him with this as his most fatal mistake. Indeed, who will deny that these hours of decision were hours which determined the whole course of the German Reformation? In that he rejected all the offers of reconciliation which the estates made, he almost compelled them to abandon him as an obstinate heretic. The bloody edict of Worms, with its disastrous consequences, was the immediate consequence of his refusal to co-operate: in it the outlawing of the heretic was proclaimed, a penalty was imposed on the reading and publication of his writings, a spiritual censorship was imposed on all German literature and a radical ban on all libellous writings against the Pope. It was the first step on the way to the later Counter-Reformation. Was it completely inevitable? Could not Luther with good conscience have left a part of his writings to the judgment of a future council, in the sure knowledge that the Pope would not allow this council to take place for a long time, so that meanwhile he could gain time for the spreading of the Word? Yet these thoughts are more typical of the modern power-politician than of the Reformer. He and his faith were one. How could he deny it without abandoning himself too? How could he give credence to the idea of priestly mediation in the sacraments and protest against indulgences, once the internal relation of the two had been demonstrated? He could never for a moment have reflected whether any faltering in conviction would in fact anyway have been fatal for the mission of the religious prophet. 'If you had faltered at Worms,' Muntzer wrote later, wildly exaggerating, 'the nobles would have had you assassinated.' Yet for him the approval of men was of no importance. His responsibility before God was everything. In the end he was proved right against all the 'power-politicians' of his and our time—at least in their sense. The history of the reform councils teaches us perfectly clearly what was to be expected from a reform of the Church which did not start at the very heart of the matter—with its doctrine of salvation itself—but which set about cutting out external abuses without having first dealt with the deceased roots. Yet it was to this that Luther would inescapably have been driven step by step, if he had once held out his hand in peace. In any case was the offer of the committee honourably meant? Even if it was, would the negotiators in the estates have been able to maintain their honourable intention of peace against the obvious intention of the Emperor and Pope to destroy him and in face of the hesitation of the estates which remained faithful to the old creed? In any case Martin Luther would not have been himself if he had denied his past at this moment. He left Worms unvanquished in every sense: indeed as the true victor over all the endeavours of the politicians—'mad' in the eyes of men, but borne along by the proud certainty of an unbending conscience.

6. *First Signs of the Storm*

Martin Luther did not find it easy to agree to the game of hide and seek which the Saxon councillors organised to save him from the imperial wrath on his return from Worms. A feigned attack by armed horsemen was arranged; they dragged him out of his coach and brought him to the electoral castle, where he was allowed to disappear and so was afforded protection from the imperial executive. Luther did not protest. And yet in his hiding place on the Wartburg he was never free from the uncomfortable feeling that he had made too much of a concession to the politicians, by leaving the front instead of fearlessly 'baring his neck' to his opponents. However, he had to agree that the objection of his advisers was right; that to sacrifice his own life now would serve no useful purpose and would mean the end of his Gospel; the all-important thing now was to win time till the new teaching had gained ground and had taken so firm a hold in the heads of the Germans that it could never again be rooted out. The hope which he had expressed in his address to the nobles, that the Empire would carry out the great reform of spiritual life which even the Church could not achieve, was cruelly disappointed; scared and helpless, the estates who were opposed to Rome had had to leave the Diet in order to avoid having to participate in the decree of the imperial ban on the heretic and his followers which by now had become inevitable; and in so doing they made it possible for the rump of the Diet to adopt the truly brutal tones of the Aleanderan draft of the edict. Luther thought back with scorn to the behaviour of the princely nobility which he had observed in Worms: drinking, gambling, hunting and jousting, while the whole time it was God's Word which was under discussion. But the less he expected from human aid, the more he trusted in the silent activity of the Word: 'Look now, spread and help to spread the holy Gospel. Teach, talk, write and preach, as if the law of men were of no importance. And if you will allow us two more years, then you will see what has become of Pope, bishop, cardinal, priest, monk, nun, bells, towers, masses, vigils, cowls, hoods, tonsures, rules, statutes and the whole rotting, seething mass of papal government; it will disappear like smoke.'

When he looked out of the little window of his small room in the castle down on to the dark sea of treetops which spread out across the Thuringian mountains, he could see here and there the bluish columns of smoke rising from the kilns of the charcoal-burners. 'The smoke oversteps itself, becomes self-willed in the air, and behaves as if it thought it could put out the sun and storm the heavens. But what is it after all? Come a little wind and the wonderful thick layer of cloud is dispersed and disappears, so that no one knows where it has gone.' In this mood he looked out from his 'Patmos', 'from the kingdom of the birds' who every day give praise to God with full-throated song, back on the excited happenings at Worms. It was the secret of his inexhaustible energy that even in the tumult of battle he always retained a region of peace and quiet within himself. Nevertheless it was a great advantage, even for a man of his disposition, to be able to withdraw from the world for many months, to be alone with himself, with his books, his thoughts, in the depths of the peaceful countryside, which awoke a thousand memories of his boyhood, and whose quiet tones can be heard in countless images and moods in his writings from the Wartburg.

It was a time of recuperation; but clearly anything but an idyll. This stormy soul knew nothing of the repose in God, in the sense that the mystics did. Only an enormous amount of work was able to stifle the feeling that he was idling his time away here, while outside his life's work was in danger. Often he was compelled by physical sickness to call a halt for hours or even for days. It was just at this moment that he began to be afflicted by those physical ailments (above all chronic indigestion and insomnia, the consequences of inordinately strenuous mental activity) which from then onwards tormented his body and almost drove him to despair. For he tortured himself with the most bitter self-reproaches about his lifelessness: dull, stupefied, exhausted, he lived on: capable neither of prayer, nor of writing, nor of carrying on the struggle; as soon as his soul ceased to sparkle, his life became a burden to him. It was in the fight for the cause that he felt most sure of his divine calling; but in his solitude, in the sleepless nights when the storm howled round the walls of the castle, then he was tormented by dark thoughts and misgivings. 'They flee the light like bats, and like the night-ravens cry "Uhu Uhu" in the dark, and think that they can scare us like that.' With the unconditional honesty which was so typical of him, he could avoid none of these tormenting questions. 'What if you are wrong and are leading so many people into error who will all be eternally damned?' Often the devil tormented him, so he related later, with one such question so much that he could find no way out and could no longer find the slightest error in all Papistry. 'It was then that I really broke out into perspiration, and that my heart began to tremble and to beat fast. The devil knows how to present his arguments and has a hard, direct way of speaking; and such disputations are not carried on with any time for thought or consideration, but rather the answers come and go in a flash. And I have learnt how it is that one finds people dead in bed. He can throttle the body—that is one way; but he can also make the soul so frightened with his disputing that all at once it is forced to flee the body.'

But he always found his footing again: 'so long as Christ has assured and strengthened me with his one true Word, my heart shall not falter, but shall stand against the arguments of the Papists, as a rocky bank throws back the waves and scorns their threatenings and ragings.' His polemics from the Wartburg strike a far more confident tone than ever before, so that they sound almost arrogant. His answer to the news that his name was to be added to the list of heretics read out in all churches on Maundy Thursday evening was the 'Bull on the Last Banquet of our most holy Lord, the Pope'—one of the most coarse pieces of writing ever to come from his pen. In a completely unprecedented way he, the outlaw, compelled the Primate of the German Church, the Cardinal Archbishop of Mainz, by means of a formal ultimatum under time-limit, to renounce his new trade in indulgences, his 'idol at Halle', and

FIRST SIGNS OF THE STORM

to make a vow of his intention to do better in humble, submissive tones. He knew his power over the minds of the German people and knew how to use it.

But now, of course, was the time when he could throw himself wholeheartedly into the work to which he felt he had really been called. Now that the fetters of the old Church had been completely cast off, the time had come when the spiritual life of the new community of the handful of God's warriors must be built up anew. The profusion of pastoral writings which he produced in these months is astounding, and was achieved in spite of illness and 'trials', which in truth never really hindered his work but rather served to keep his inner conviction aglow within him. Here in the Wartburg, he laid above all the foundation of the two works by which he was to have by far the deepest and most permanent effect on his Germans: of the great collection of his sermons on the Epistles and Gospels for the festive (winter) half of the Church's year, 'the Church's sermons', and of his German translation of the Bible. The collection of sermons he considered himself to be his best book. For centuries it has been the model of the Evangelical Sunday sermon, and the household treasure of countless families in Evangelical Germany: the inexhaustible source from which the religious thoughts and experiences of the Reformer overflowed untainted into the hearts of his Germans. If the secret of his religious achievement was above all that the New Testament tradition was remoulded in the depths of a German soul, it is in just this respect that we can best see the appeal and greatness of his translation of the Bible. Over and above the literary genius of the artist and poet, the first creative master of the new High German literary language, stands the religious genius, the prophet of the Germans, who discovers with amazement the remarkable similarity between his own religious experiences and those of the heroes of the Bible, and who has a remarkable talent for presenting the stories and sayings of a distant oriental past in German dress, while yet maintaining their naïvety and force of expression in the same way as the German painters of that time: Dürer and Grünewald, Schongauer and the Cranachs, and so many others. Never again has such a perfect fusion of German and Christian sensitivity been achieved as at that time; the whole of the unbroken religious power of the German Middle Ages lives in the glowing colourful language of the translator of the Bible.

In his enthusiasm for the work, which he set about with an almost excessive zeal (he began the translation of the New Testament without adequate philological aids at the end of December and completed its first draft by the end of February!), the events in Wittenberg receded temporarily into the background. Yet it became clearer from day to day that the ' little band of Christians at Wittenberg ' was quite unable to look after itself without its prophet. It was an extremely critical moment. The foundations of the new Evangelical doctrine were now essentially complete. Now it was a question of putting this new insight into practice: of building up a new, more perfect life in the Church, instead of the old one which had been seen to be contrary to the Scriptures. In the numerous long letters which he sent to his friends, above all to Melanchthon, the exile tried to direct affairs according to his own understanding from his retreat at the Wartburg. But his patience was tried again and again as he encountered the lack of resolution, the fearfulness, the weakness of will in all questions which required a firm, determined decision, and this even in the most talented of his helpers, the clear-sighted Melanchthon, for whom he had so much admiration. At this time thousands of such questions were crowding in on him. Priests were preparing to draw the practical conclusions from his doctrine of the objectionableness of celibacy; monks were leaving the monasteries; the Augustinian order began to dissolve; and shortly Wittenberg would be invaded by a horde of released nuns, all on the lookout for a possible match. Where was now the sanctity of the vows which they had taken on their entry into the nunnery ? Luther had declared the priestly sacrifice of the mass at the altar to be blasphemous; now it was for him to reform the whole ordering of divine service and indeed the concept of the priestly office and thousands of everyday matters of church life down to its economic basis. What was to take the place of the mass and what was to become of the countless votive masses and masses for the dead which had been offered, and what of the people who earned their living thereby ? What was the sense of the monastic clergy (particularly of those who were not of noble birth) when their only spiritual function, the maintenance of the choral services, had been shown to be of no value ? What was to become of the property of the monasteries and the cloisters; what of the wealth of the ecclesiastical orders; what of the countless benefices which had lost their original meaning ? In what form should communion be received in future, and how was one to set about the whole question of reforming the services, so that they were simplified but still equal in unity and beauty of form to the old services ? What should be done about the innumerable pictures and carvings with which the churches were filled to overflowing ? Should they not be done away with as soon as possible as works of idolatry ? Further, the abolition of countless processions, festivals, pilgrimages, and of the church offices from matins to vespers, all this demanded a new ordering of services which must go right to the heart of the everyday life of the people. Not all these questions were of equal urgency, but as soon as one started to rebuild at one point then one thing followed necessarily out of another and it was impossible to see an end to the practical difficulties.

Admittedly Luther treated all these things with the supreme magnanimity of spirit typical of a man who knows himself set far above all the petty legalities of the external ordering of life.

He did not understand the importance which the Wittenbergers attached to these worries; all these things would find their own solution, just as soon as the preaching of the Word had created men anew, free from the compulsion of the old law, imbued with the power of faith in their hearts. Was it too difficult till then to bear with the continuance of the old order for the sake of the weaker members? Luther's unconditional trust in the power of divine grace finds its logical counterpart in his equally unconditional mistrust of all the inventions of human wisdom and human will and energy. Any attempt to rebuild the Church starting with the alteration of the ceremonies, the abolition of vows, the redistribution of ecclesiastical rights of possession, the organisation of the congregation, and so forth, was to him merely the work of men. There was nothing worse than that the old wine should continue to ferment in new vessels, i.e. that a tumultuous reconstruction of external church life should be undertaken, which would distract the people from the fact that nothing had been altered in their true spiritual disposition. Luther fought continuously and with great passion for the genuineness and purity of the spirit of the reformation—against muddled demagogic enthusiasts, against the ravenous hunger of the secular powers for the property of the Church, against the vanity and ambition of scheming Church politicians, and against all those whose desire for freedom meant no more than the removal of certain uncomfortable ecclesiastical restraints. For himself he did not entertain the thought of throwing away his monastic vows. He had not even abandoned his private masses with the elevation of the host, but had only reinterpreted it in the sense of a priestly self-communion.

But are the external forms of spiritual life really so completely unimportant? Does not every new religious standpoint require an exactly corresponding symbolisation in its services? Does not the actual contemplation, the continual experience of this symbolisation, form a very essential part of the religious life itself? Is church-fellowship possible at all without a clearly defined form of service? Would pure doctrine and right-mindedness really have been enough to solve the thousands of complicated questions about the external forms of life which confronted the adherents of the new dogma? If the new Church really wanted to be the true continuance of the old universal Church and not merely a band of chosen men and a sect, then it could hardly dispense with the establishment of new external rulings by a new spiritual authority. But who, apart from Luther himself, possessed such an authority—and possessed at the same time the inner certainty to meet the onrush of so many confused questions, wishes and demands. It was certain that the timid young Master Philippus did not. Instead, more rowdy, fighting spirits came to the fore: the Augustinian monk Gabriel Zwilling, a gifted mob-orator with a heated temperament, and Luther's colleague Professor Karlstadt—an unhappy, fated figure, who had dogged the footsteps of the greater man ever since the Disputation at Leipzig. As so easily happens to lesser men, who have their greatest moment in the train of a genius, so it was with them; what Luther only gained by hard struggle, fell easily into their laps; and now they made it their one ambition each to outdo the other by the strict and unrelenting application of his principles. The insights of Luther's genius and his religious institutions became in the hands of Karlstadt a new, sternly biblical set of rules, and out of the freedom of the Christian man he made straightway a new law. Soon the new form of his communion service in the Castle church, in secular clothing and without any ceremony and without the canon of the mass but with the distribution of the chalice, became a sensation for the curious; and the radical tenor of his preaching attracted all the unruly elements, particularly from among young students. Luther had not been away from Wittenberg for a year, before they started to destroy church pictures and communion vessels, and to declare fasting and confession not only unnecessary for salvation but sinful. They prevented the holding of mass with force of arms, broke down the altars, threatened to storm the monasteries and listened to the new teaching of Karlstadt, that whoever only received the host in the communion service commits a sin, that whoever puts up pictures in churches sins more grievously than he who steals or commits adultery; and that no priest may be appointed until he be married and blessed with children. It has been said in Karlstadt's favour that by his determined action he set in motion the hesitant inner development of the Lutheran Church order; and this is not entirely without justification. But how sorely did he confuse the ideas of Luther's reformation with muddled, irresponsible fantasies! A late and uncertain source reports how he used to go round the houses in the town and ask the simple lay-people to explain to him, the professor of theology, the meaning of obscure passages in the Bible, since God enlightens the unlearned and blinds the wise; he advised his students to go home and tend the fields (which he himself did immediately), for human teaching was of no account in the sight of God; and the Warden of the boys' grammar school is said to have sent his pupils home for the same reason. Even if these later stories have been elaborated, misunderstood and in part invented, it is nevertheless very probable that Karlstadt was then already well on the way to that mystical enthusiasm, which a very little later he was openly preaching: a purely lay religion, which had no possible use for theological study and which rejected all ecclesiastical offices, all external church services, the sacraments and indeed all ecclesiastical institutions and universities *in toto*. How could such an unsteady and mercurial spirit fail to throw men into the greatest confusion? The unrest was increased when at the end of 1521 the first followers of the ' new prophets ' and the Taborite Anabaptists arrived in Wittenberg from Zwickau: the godly clothmakers Storch and Drechsler and the writer Marcus Stübner—friends and fellow-travellers of the radical preacher Thomas Müntzer. They were sinister heralds of the coming revolution, filled with the burning spirit of the Bohemian revolution, heirs of every possible sect of the late Middle Ages, with that most dangerous mixture of religious enthusiasm and social hatred, which had already provided the explosive force for the preaching of the Taborites. They were men from the working classes of society, without any cultural heritage of their own, without traditions, and above all without any inner relation to the wealth of religious experiences, ideas and traditions of the Church, which had been built up over the centuries and which Luther had studied and examined for half his life. They based themselves purely on the naked word of the Bible naïvely and literally interpreted, or even on the direct inspiration of the ' Spirit ': and even in this they seemed to be the fulfilment of the Lutheran reformation, although in fact they were nothing but caricatures of it. Even a man like Melanchthon was helpless when faced with the confident appearance of these false prophets. When the Elector asked for the opinion of the university on the activity of Karlstadt and his followers, their judgment was divided and indecisive. By far the greatest practical sense and firmness of purpose was shown by the town council, which by proposing a new set of Church regulations attempted to keep the uproar within legal bounds and which suggested fruitful ways for the future by its plan (on which Melanchthon and Karlstadt worked) for a civic coffer for the administration and development of the moneys which had been released by the abolition of masses, etc. But its efforts for the preservation of public peace were all in vain. It was therefore with even greater anxiety that the council looked to the electoral castle at Lochau: for it was there, with the political power, that the last decision lay. A Zwingli (and later too, a Calvin) would have become the political leader of the State by dominating the town council. In these north German territories everything hung on the decision of the ruler himself. But Elector Frederick, who was called the Wise, was this time completely at a loss. The intention of the strangely confused letter which he wrote to Luther at that time is still disputed among scholars; only one thing is patently obvious: his intention, as helpless as it was generous, to submit everything to the judgment of the theologian, who 'has knowledge of these higher matters'. Sorely pressed by the imperial government and by his cousin the Duke of Leipzig because of his friendship with the heretic, there seemed no other course open to the ageing ruler, but to seek peace at all costs for the sake of his small and powerless state. So he had instructions sent to Wittenberg to suppress any stormy innovations and simply to restore everything as it was before— an order which was immediately seen to be impossible to carry out. Nevertheless he would not shrink from bearing the cross of Christ himself for the sake of the Gospel—if only he knew what God's will in this affair was. Everything now depended on this purely personal readiness to allow himself to be forced into one course or another—and in the last resort, on this alone depended the salvation of Luther's life-work. But the whole decision was eventually passed on to Luther. For better or for worse there was no one else who could take his place.

Luther himself was far from being oppressed by the pedantic anxiety of his colleagues in Wittenberg, who cried out in distress to the Elector for help as soon as a mob of students smashed the windows of a building where the priests were singing the hours. He was even less disposed to delay necessary reforms of the Church because of the political anxieties of the Saxon court. 'Are we to do nothing but talk about the Word of God and never act?' he answered angrily to the misgivings of the worldly-wise Spalatin. Full of scorn he answered the complaints of the courtiers about the bad reputation which was beginning to be attached to Wittenberg and about the disturbance of public peace. But of course! The preservation of public peace was a fit task for the disciples of Christ, in fact one on which one could stake even all one's hopes of eternal peace with God. What a wonderful reputation Christ and his followers had enjoyed among the children of this world! 'Should we then expect to be the only ones dogs never even so much as growl at?' His method was one of struggle, not the Erasmic ways of mediation and compromise; he explained this with classic clarity to the then most world-wise of all court theologians, Capito, at the court in Mainz: 'The Spirit of Truth is offensive and does not flatter. But it does not merely offend this man or that, but the whole world. And so our wisdom is to offend all, to annoy all, to confound all and to spare nothing, to make no concessions, to excuse nothing, so that truth may stand free, pure and upright, for all to see.'

Many of the Wittenbergers liked to think the man who could be so determined when he saw the purity of his message endangered would also take up arms along with Karlstadt and his companions for its ruthless enforcement in the practice of Church life. But he did not let himself for a moment be confused by the storming of the image-breakers and the enthusiasts. None of that could affect the depth of his religious principles. When he learnt, in his isolation in the Wartburg, of the extent of the confusion which they had eventually reached in Wittenberg, he felt as if an abyss had opened up before him. 'I was so overcome by grief,' he wrote to the Elector, 'that if I had not been sure that we have the pure Gospel, I would then and there have abandoned the whole affair. All the harm which has been done to me in this affair so far is as nothing in comparison with this. I would willingly have paid for it with my life, if it had been possible.' What was it that disturbed him so deeply? It can hardly have been the sight of the image-breakers alone. For the first time in his life it must have become clear to him how great was the distance between the ideal demands of his conviction, the renewal of life by means of the power of the Gospel alone, without its being regulated by laws at all, and the miserable reality of the human race, to whom his message was directed. Was this the community, in which the pure word had now been working day in and day out, and on which the Reformer was to build his new church: this wild, mad, student youth, these townspeople who allowed themselves to be taken in by every tempter, who misinterpreted the Gospel of the new freedom as an incitement to tumult and destruction; these theologians and scholars who were thrown into confusion by the fantastic inventions of cheap demagogues; this government, which seemed to be able to conceive of no higher task than the preservation of the old state of affairs and the opposition to every new reform and which was unable to reach any firm decision because of its extreme caution ?

Satan had indeed fallen on his fold, as he wrote to the Elector, and he could wait no longer before he met him in person. He had already once been to Wittenberg, in secret and disguised as a knight and without the Elector's permission; that had been his answer to Spalatin's attempt to suppress the manuscript of his pamphlets and to turn a deaf ear to the pleadings and threatenings of the captive in the Wartburg. 'This I cannot accept,' he had thundered. 'I would rather drag you and the princes and all creatures into perdition.' Even now Luther knew that he was acting against the wishes of his ruler, that he would cause the latter great political embarrassment, if he, who was under the ban, should again appear as a free man in the state. But his congregation was calling him, and there could be no hesitation. Duke George, their angry neighbour in Leipzig, could thunder against the prophet of the Lord as he liked. 'Even if things were the same in Leipzig as they are in Wittenberg, I would still ride in, even if it rained Duke Georges for nine days on end, and even if each of them was nine times as angry as this one.' Shortly before, in almost mocking tones, he had congratulated the Elector Frederick, the relic-collector, on his new treasure which God had given him in the form of the unrest in Wittenberg. 'Without cost or effort, a complete cross with nails, spears and whips.' And with the same highhandedness and pride he now cast aside the protection of the Elector:

> Your Grace must know that I come to Wittenberg under the protection of one much greater than the Elector. Indeed I think I could offer Your Grace more protection than you could offer me. Therefore if I knew that Your Grace was ready and able to protect me, I would not come. The sword can give no advice nor help in these matters; God must act alone, without any human cares or activity. So whoever has the most faith will afford the most protection; and while I still see that Your Grace is weak in faith I can in no way consider Your Grace as the man who can protect and save me. If Your Grace had faith then you would see God's glory; but since you have as yet no faith, then you have seen nothing.

This therefore was the spiritual disposition in which Martin Luther resumed his work in Wittenberg: in spite of all his disappointments, with an unbroken confidence in his eventual victory; with a deep contempt for the designs of the politicians, 'who think that my Lord Jesus Christ is a man made out of straw'. From his Elector he hoped for nothing more than that he would not himself arrest him, as the Emperor's 'jailer'. But if the Emperor and the Empire should seek after him, then that would be no reason for the Elector to revolt. It was much more in Luther's interest to be able to act freely on all sides without having to take political considerations into account, than merely to enjoy the protection of the mighty. Only a few more years and the Word must surely triumph, one way or another. His preachings after his return had always this object in view: to still the troubled waters, to demand love instead of force, patience with the weak, who were not yet free from the misuses of the old Church, to wait till God had created new men for the building of his new Church. The effect of his appearance worked powerfully on the troubled congregation. All at once the disturbances were at an end; Karlstadt again retired into the background and soon left the town angrily to seek a new ground in which to sow the seeds of discontent. Shortly after Luther's return the Church in Wittenberg showed all the external traits of its catholic ancestry. Its shepherd was quite confident that, bit by bit, it would of its own accord fall away from the old usages and that in the unploughed ground the tender plant of the new Church would shoot up gaily without any artificial help from men.

But what if human impatience and the mighty concatenation of earthly circumstance, what if the stern compulsion of political and social upheaval, should undo the peaceful work of the man of God and should deny the new Church the peace it needed for its gradual development and growth into a powerful tree, which would be able to withstand the storms of these angry times without flinching? Must not the reformer begin to question his confidence, when he saw to what degree everything in this congregation depended on his own personal presence and activity?

7. *The Storm (1522-5)*

At first it seemed as if the happy confidence which he drew from his faith would be proved right in spite of all the doubters. In his old age these years of the first sowing indeed seemed to him the most successful and finest of his life.

THE STORM (1522-5)

> *Summer is nigh at the door,*
> *Winter is long since gone,*
> *And the tender flowers come forth;*
> *What He has begun,*
> *He will perfect.*

This was the almost jubilant folk-ballad with which he sang the death by fire of the first martyrs of the new Gospel (in Brussels 1523): an event which deeply shocked him, more because of the proof it afforded of the living power of the new faith than because of the human tragedy. Indeed the power of the Word of God seemed stronger than all the political strength of his mighty enemies. All the designs of the 'little red hat' at Worms, which had seemed so successful at the beginning, had eventually come to nothing. No sooner had the Emperor and the Pope reached a political alliance, than the great European war between the houses at Hapsburg and France broke out again more violently than before; for years it claimed all the efforts of the Emperor and prevented him coming to Germany. But it was not only the war. Remarkably enough, even Charles's first great, and, as it seemed for the time, decisive, victory, the capture of the French King at the battle of Pavia, estranged him from the Pope's favour. What a misfortune for the Roman see that the successor of Leo (after the unimportant interlude of the imperially inclined Hadrian), Clement VII, was also completely unable to see farther than the boundaries of the politics of the Medici family and the Italian Renaissance! In his attempts to protect the world of the Italian Renaissance from the Spanish threat with his pitifully inadequate forces, blinded as he was by his fear of the overwhelming power of Charles, he brought upon himself complete disaster: German mercenaries, among them hard-headed Lutherans from Swabia, full of hatred of the priests, carried out in the pay of the Emperor the terrible sack of Rome (1527), which is usually considered to mark the end of the Renaissance. It was a strange turn of fate that in precisely those decades when the Lutheran heresy could still have been stamped out by force, the two protectors of the hierarchical traditions again and again exhausted all their energy attacking one another; that the Papacy was itself so far estranged from its spiritual vocation that it itself helped to blunt the only practical weapon which it had for the preservation of ecclesiastical unity! While the Pope was protecting Italy against Spain, he lost Germany to the heretic and thereby lost the universal dominion over his Church.

First of all, the edict of Worms proved to be impossible to put into practice. It was only since the days at Worms that Luther had really become the national hero of the Germans. The number of pamphlets and polemics written by his supporters began to assume monstrous proportions, as did the number of popular wood-carvings (among them pictures of the Reformer with a halo round his head!), of satirical songs, poems and caricatures with a Lutheran bias. They flooded the whole land —and there was nothing that the strictest edict of censure could do about it—while on the other hand writings which supported the old Church were hardly read at all. The German printing presses were hardly able to keep up with the demand in spite of countless reprintings. In the first five years after 1518 production increased three to seven times. Everywhere, particularly in the cities, the evangelical preachers emerged as the main advocates of the movement; serious, competent men along with hotheaded innovators, in whom the unrest of the times was strangely reflected. But also the world of the laity began more and more to take an active part in the movement; and not merely isolated circles of men whose interest was theological or humanistic, or literary groups, but the whole people in all its classes; nobles and bourgeois, lawyers, town officials, academics, artisans, artists, workers and peasants: in workshops, in guild-halls, inns and spinning-rooms, in the schools and town halls, everywhere the great question of the Church was discussed, everywhere were heard the new catch-words of the new freedom, everywhere men cursed the priests and monks and the sinful Babel at Rome and praised the bold reappearance of the monk from Wittenberg. Of the state governments none possessed any longer the power to suppress the movements, as had been demanded by the edict of Worms, namely by the destruction without examination or legal trial of those who showed Lutheran tendencies. Moreover the powerless committee of princes and of estates and imperial councillors, which sat in Nürnberg, to govern in the Emperor's absence, was disposed, under the influence of the Elector of Saxony, to let things take their own course. Already the evangelical message had penetrated to the extreme boundaries of the German-speaking area: to the Netherlands, to Holstein, Prussia and Livonia, and indeed even beyond, to Sweden and Denmark; in the south to the Tyrolean mountains and Austria, while in Switzerland a new centre for the Evangelical movement was established. By 1518 a first edition of Luther's collected writings in Latin had been produced in Basle, and then the non-German-speaking countries, particularly France, greedily absorbed the new, exciting heresy. It was even smuggled into Spain and Hungary, again partly in translation. The fame of the Reformer was constantly on the increase, and with it grew the flood of questions, requests and complaints from followers all over the world, which daily assailed him; everywhere he had to give comfort and advice, to help by sending off preachers, and yet all the time he remained convinced that it was not himself who was doing it all, but ' a greater man who drives the wheel'. If one compares how later Zwingli and Calvin in similar situations used all the arts of political calculation to further their life's work, then we can see clearly the extraordinary character of Luther's approach. It was enough for him to co-operate in the preaching of God's word, as he understood it, in all the world; to avail himself of temporary advantages in the political situation to build up a strong Church party could not have been farther from his intention.

On the contrary, nothing caused him more concern than to have to see how the movement, the more it developed, became increasingly involved with political, economic and social aspirations. The precipitate avarice of the nobles—'that bunch of knaves', as he called them bitterly—to appropriate the secularised property of the Church, without assuming the same degree of responsibility for the upkeep of the churches and schools and for the care of the poor, and the indifference of many town authorities for the care of Church institutions, once the rich possessions of the town clergy had been transferred into worldly hands and its privileged position had been abolished—all this provoked him to great anger and nearly to despair, without his being able to do anything more about it than to warn, scold, threaten, plead and preach. For us who live in a later age it is not at all easy to understand the total extent of the crisis, and the greatness of the danger to the continuance of any form of church life which arose with the dissolution of the old Church. All the centuries-old authority of the Church rulers had begun to disappear since the German bishops and prelates, anxious for their position of worldly power, had taken up their stand against the reform. This meant the end of any respect for diocesan boundaries, ecclesiastical means of punishment and spiritual courts. While the wealth of the Church was falling into the hands of the laity, the normal sources of income of the Church were drying up with a terrifying rapidity; no longer would anyone buy indulgences or butter letters, go on pilgrimages, worship at shrines, reverence relics, donate altars and carvings, vigils and masses for the dead, or give money to the ecclesiastical orders; the monasteries were emptying; the 'cheese-chasers', the mendicant monks, were turned angrily from the door by the peasants, and many priests went hungry because their parishes refused to pay them their tithes. Church buildings fell into disrepair. Schools and universities became terrifyingly deserted or even completely ceased to exist; for why should one study, when it was no longer desirable—indeed rather reprehensible—to become a priest, and to seek ecclesiastical sinecures and benefices? Did not Luther himself rage against the 'whore Reason', who had perverted the true Christian doctrine in the false teachings of the Scholastics and did not now 'poor peasants and children understand Christ better than Popes, bishops and doctors'? Of course this exposition and application was a crass misunderstanding of the Reformation doctrine, and Luther, deeply concerned by all these matters, attempted in his 'appeal to the councillors of all towns in the German territories' to explain to his Germans how much he himself owed to his studies, and that the supposed enlightenment of the 'heavenly prophets' like Karlstadt and Zwickau was of no worth. But who fully understood the whole depth of his teaching in this or indeed in any other question? Even the more perceptive of the popular preachers elaborated his ideas within the whole range of ideas of late medieval apocalyptic, and the mystical concepts and the social teaching of the Franciscans. The common man understood no more of all this than that the time was now come to shake off the domination of the priests: for him the Gospel meant relief from all kinds of Church commandments and duties; what did the oppressed craftsmen, labourers and peasants care about the doctrine of justification by the pure Grace of God?

There could be no doubt about it: the doctrine of the universal priesthood of believers was in extreme danger, not only of being misused for secular ends, but at the same time of being responsible for the total decay of the Church. If it did not prove possible to bring the new community of true Christians into existence very soon, then it seemed conceivable that it would have to be sacrificed or very largely redefined and limited, in order to save the German Church from floundering in the general chaos.

Luther had been intensely active in these years trying to find a form which would give it suitable practical expression. Since his hope for a general reform of the Church with the help of the Empire (which was to have broken the resistance of the old church hierarchy and thereby to have made possible its internal renewal) had been dashed in Worms, the emphasis was laid all the more on the building up of the new individual congregations. Their organisation was in every way to be suited to the gradual spreading of the evangelical piety among their members: a gathering of true believers at first in small circles, a reorganisation of church finances, a new order of church discipline, the building up of a new clergy, everything was planned and in part tried out in practice. We shall have to speak later about the reasons why these attempts met with no permanent success; but certainly the decisive factor was not lack of organisational ability on the part of Luther. His basic tenet of putting all the emphasis on pure spirituality and of beginning all reconstruction from within, from the spiritual creation of new men, rather than from without, clearly made it impossible for him to found a new 'law' as did Calvin (and also Zwingli) and to pursue questions of Church order with the same zeal as the Word of God. He was prepared to leave many things undefined (if they were not essential for the faith), much longer than was practically desirable. But then one must consider the ground on which he had to build—barren and arid and at the same time volcanic. The Swiss reformers lived and worked in highly developed civic cultural centres, in easily controlled, free, self-determined communities, among men who had for centuries been accustomed to governing themselves and developing their own communal life. Things were very different in Luther's world. If one follows the history of the congregations which Luther founded, one receives the gloomiest picture of the dullness and indifference of the Saxon and Thuringian peasants and farmers, of the roughness and greed of the German landed nobility, whose rights of patronage everywhere obstructed the new order. It is certainly no mere chance that he found most satisfaction in the congregations in the larger towns: and yet even there they presented a sorry enough picture. Only one of these foundations developed more or less as he would have had it: the one at Nürnberg under Lazarus Spengler.

But his daily ejaculatory prayer that God might grant new men for his Church had hardly time to wait for an answer. Already he could feel how the ground of German society was becoming daily more unsteady beneath his feet. This Germany on the eve of a social revolution in the grand manner was not the land in which the ideal realisation of religious principles could have been carried through by practical organisation, or in which the ideal form of the binding of individual freedom to the order of a legally ruled society could easily have been found. The preaching of the freedom of the Christian man necessarily became the war-cry of social discontent.

For years he had seen it coming. Even when he was at the Wartburg. Into the calm of his room in the castle must have penetrated dull, deep murmurings from the villages of Thuringia, the sound of 'poor Conrad' sharpening his knife in secret, and the forgotten echoes of furtive speeches by nameless agitators. His prophecy had given Germany a movement, which no one would be able to stem. 'And if it is stemmed it will become ten times more angry. For there are plenty of peasant lads in Germany.' And not for a minute did he doubt that this revolt would cling to his heels. Nothing disturbed him more deeply. The prevention of this disaster was one of the most pressing reasons why he hurried back to Wittenberg. 'For we see how the Gospel is given to the common man as a wonderful gift and then how he only accepts it as something fleshly.' What a terrifying prospect: the Gospel of the true reconciliation with God dragged down into the filth of popular struggles for personal advantage and tainted with the smell of blood and burning from the people's revolt. He swore to the princes that he would prevent the worst from happening, that he would no longer restrict the preaching of the pure Word of God, but further it with all his power; for it alone might still the raging of the masses, while on the other hand if anyone tried to put out the light by force, he would only make men more bitter in their hearts and force them to revolt. But also the extortion of the poor man must cease or God would soon put down the mighty from their seat.

But when he considered the blindness and folly of the German princes, which became daily more and more clear, then he already saw in his mind 'all Germany bathed in blood'. No one disappointed him more bitterly than these nobles. It is a very typical picture; he seems to have been unmoved by any of the great hopes which the protestant politicians were then entertaining for the success of their tactical political moves, of their diplomatic influence on the imperial government and diet. He could only see the reverse side of the medal, the practical failure.

The institution of the imperial Estates government was one attempt to deal with the situation. If it could succeed in gaining firm authority during the absence of the Emperor, and if the protestant Estates could succeed in making themselves felt in the government and in the Diet, then one could perhaps hope, not only to secure the freedom of the estates for ever and to unite the empire more firmly on the basis of the estates, but in the end also to achieve what it had not been possible to achieve in Worms, the reform of the German Church by the Empire, as a unified political act. For years the scheming advisers of the protestant princes occupied themselves with hopes of this kind and even after the dissolution of the government (1524) they once again seemed near to fulfilment: the national assembly whose summoning to Speyer had been previously decided in Nürnberg was to be responsible for the regulating of questions

THE STORM (1522-5)

of faith in Germany until a general council should meet together. In this the great movement for political Church reform seemed at last to be once again in sight of its goal, and it seemed that it might be possible to make good the failure at Worms.

But of course all these plans were to meet with no success. For it was above all in the meetings of the imperial government that the disunity of the German princes in questions of religion became most clear; the religious policy of the committee changed as often as did its members. Apart from the Elector of Saxony (who anyway continually denounced his protégé in public), hardly more than one or two of the other princes were prepared to entertain the task which Luther had allotted to the ruling class, namely of protecting the preaching of the Word. It was only fear of the threatened revolt, in Luther's judgment, which forced them to make one tame compromise after another in religious questions. Already the proceedings were seriously prejudiced by the preponderance of the spiritual princedoms, that unhappy political legacy from the German Middle Ages, which from now on for more than a century (till the Thirty Years' War) was to be the curse of the nation's history. Not without reason did Luther hate the spiritual princes, who barred the way to the Gospel for the sake of their worldly power, perhaps more than any of his other enemies. Although they showed themselves far more favourably disposed to his affair than many other later Diets, he could not but consider the achievement of the two Diets at Nürnberg (in 1523 and 1524) to be pitifully inadequate. He could only see what had not been achieved: he saw the genuine zeal for reform of some of the Estates shipwrecked on the stupidity and resistance of the others. Indeed, these Estates who stamped and shouted so stubbornly against Rome in the last instance proved completely incapable of following their grand words with action. In their eagerness to band together to protect their 'liberty' against the

Emperor and to support the newly created estates government against any monarchical ambitions, they were prepared not only to deny the imperial government obedience, whenever its edicts conflicted with their own particular interests, but even to appeal to the Emperor for help against them (as did the imperial cities against the plan for an imperial tax): a policy to whose short-sightedness the rapid miscarriage of the plans for a council at Speyer can be attributed. It was a time for rapid decisions and for exploiting the situation in Europe to the full before it took a turn for the worse. Nor did the active diplomacy of the Pope give the Germans time to ponder over their decisions in their normal way; hardly had the assembly of the estates at Speyer been authorised to decide the question of the Church, than the papal legates had succeeded in uniting the south German estates in the Ravensburg League under the leadership of Bavaria, from which Ranke dates the formal confessional division of the German nation. It marked the first beginnings of a conscious Church reaction and of the efforts of the counter-reformation in Germany. The consequences of all this were soon to be seen. As had already happened in the home-territories of the Emperor in the Netherlands, now again here and there in Bavaria, the Tyrol, West Austria and Upper Silesia, the flames of the stake shot up, the blood of heretics flowed and persecuted preachers fled from place to place. Moreover the struggle between the confessions, which was now just beginning, rapidly assumed wilder forms. While in Dithmarschen drunken peasants barbarically tortured Luther's friend and envoy Heinrich Zütphen to death and in Halberstadt the suffragan had an evangelically-disposed Carmelite castrated, on the other side the people of Stralsund tore a monk of the old faith from the pulpit and nearly lynched him. On the Rhine, Sickingen embarked on his adventurous march on Trier, in order to win himself a princedom, despite the imperial government and its ban; on the sleeves of his horsemen, it is said, stood the fine words:

'O Lord, thy will be done!' Driven on by evangelical preachers and Lutheran nobles (among them Hutten), he disguised as a religious struggle, as a war on the priests, what was at heart only the work of brutal, unenlightened hunger for power in the style of the German dynasts of the fourteenth and fifteenth centuries, or perhaps, to be more exact, in the style of the Italian Condottieri. It was the nobles' curtain-raiser for the peasants' revolt.

In the midst of all this raging activity rang out the voice of the man of God from Wittenberg, Martin Luther; this time more excited and more shrill than ever. To his horror he heard that the statesmen at Nürnberg knew no better in these times than to renew the edict of Worms; that in fact this was by way of a political compromise, that the renewal had more of a formal character, that it had only been passed with reservations, was of no interest to him whatsoever. 'The princes must all be mad and drunk. Ah well, I suppose we Germans will always be Germans and the asses and martyrs of the Pope. No amount of complaining, teaching, begging or pleading seems to be of any avail.' 'Just look at the poor mortal worm of an Emperor shamelessly boasting that he's the true supreme protector of the Christian faith.' 'May God deliver us from them, and of his grace give us other rulers. Amen.'

In unforgettable words, in phrases of enormous historic import, he preached the freedom of the conscience, of the inner conviction of faith, from all state coercion. 'God can and will let no one rule over the soul except himself alone. Therefore where worldly power takes it upon itself to make laws for the soul, it interferes with God's government and only leads the soul into corruption.' 'We are not baptised in kings, princes or in the people, but in God and Christ themselves.' 'Everyone is responsible to himself for his own belief and he must see that he believes what is right. For just as it is impossible that someone else should go to heaven or to hell for me, neither can he believe for me or not believe, nor can he open or shut heaven for me and nor can he force me to believe or not believe.' 'One can never present heresy by force, it needs another weapon.' 'It is God's Word which must do battle here; and if that is not sufficient, then no amount of earthly power will be of any use, even if it filled the whole world with blood. Heresy is a spiritual thing, which one cannot strike with the sword nor burn with fire, nor drown with water.' But who listened to such warnings? Already the reaction from the Church had penetrated as far as the immediate neighbourhood of Wittenberg. In the Duchy of Saxony the Evangelicals were cruelly suppressed; and just across the border from the Electorate they had Luther's New Testament burnt by the public executioner. While he himself had to steal through the land in disguise to visit his congregations, the bishops of Meissen and Merseburg were allowed to make Church visitations in the Electorate quite openly. His bitterness grew inordinately. Careless of all the political anxieties of the Elector, who was seriously threatened by the dangerous plans of the Hapsburgs in league with their cousins in Meissen, he gave full vent to his anger and scolded the fat Duke George for a bubble which thinks it can scorn heaven with its big belly: 'I wouldn't put it beyond him that he wants to eat up Christ as a wolf eats a gnat.' But above all he raged against the landed bishops, 'the unlearned, idols, images, ghouls and loungers, who know so little that they could not even say what a bishop is called, never name what his office is about'. 'All who stake body, possession and honour that the bishoprics may be destroyed and the government of the bishops effaced are dear children of God and true Christians, keep God's commandment and fight against the reign of the devil.' 'It were better that all bishops should be murdered, all monasteries and cloisters uprooted, than that a single soul should be corrupted—certainly that all souls should be lost for the sake of those useless images and idols.' Did not that sound like the fanfare of a war on the

THE STORM (1522-5)

priests, on which Sickingen promptly embarked? Yet his anger found scarcely less violent expression in his attacks on the godless rulers of this world:

> I'll have you know that since the beginning of creation a clever prince has been a rare bird, but a pious one still rarer. They are in general the biggest idiots and the most arrant knaves on this earth. They can do nothing but scrape and scrounge, levy one duty after another, one tax higher than the last, and let loose here a bear, there a wolf. And so now God has made them all mad and will make an end of them and of the spiritual Junkers. For the common man is coming to his senses and the plague of the princes which God calls *contemptum* has become powerfully active among the rabble and the common man. One cannot and will not put up with your tyranny and petulance any more, my dear princes and lords, so consider well, for God will bear with it no more. We no longer live in a world where you can hunt the people like game. So let God's word have its way. And if you think to reach for your swords, be on your guard lest anyone come and tell you in God's name to put them up again.

Was this a call to open revolt? Certainly Luther did not see it as such. It was the cry of anguish of a heart which saw its highest aims in life in danger of being dragged down into the dust and smeared with the dirt of common humanity—the angry outburst of a man who was struggling with his trembling conscience and with the powers of doubt, to fulfil his mission in life. In spite of all his revolutionary words, he was no revolutionary as the world would have understood it. Indeed, the essay in which these passionate outbursts are to be found deals with 'the higher powers and to what extent one owes them obedience'—namely in all things which are not spiritual; and even in these matters 'one must not resist wickedness, but suffer it—yet neither must one condone it, nor serve it.' That was its real message: to comfort the persecuted brothers in the faith, to show them the way in which they could remain true to God's commandments and yet avoid revolt, and at the same time to give the heir to the Saxon throne (to whom this accusation was dedicated) a clear picture of the ideal Christian prince. If he called on people to use force against the bishops, then it was because he no longer considered them to be rightful rulers; nor did he appeal to their worldly inferiors, but to the 'higher powers' of this world, to the princes, nobles and towns, as instruments and executors of divine justice. He soon realised that Sickingen was pursuing unworthy ends and that he was not the Ziska that he had for a while hoped he might be, and saw in his sudden fall the (truly remarkable) judgment of God. Yet how could he have thought otherwise without abandoning the foundation of his life and doctrine, the principle of true spirituality, to the arbitrary will and passions of man? The true Christian must suffer tyranny: and he can do this because he is inwardly free from all the power of men. Such was his unshakable conviction. Strangely enough this man with his fighting spirit made no attempt to avoid the harsh unconditionality of the commandment of love of the Sermon on the Mount. But of course God will not allow the tyrants to remain firmly seated on their thrones. The teaching of Christ only takes hold of a very small handful of true Christians, and God will use the anger of the others—and this was often a source of great (although admittedly rather remarkable) comfort to him—to destroy the rule of the tyrants. So he saw the coming disaster as the just judgment of God, carried out by the sins of the godless world. He who himself no longer entertained any hope that he might disperse the dull hatred of the mob by his preaching (being indeed inwardly convinced of the justification of this hatred) himself accused and threatened the guilty rulers, and yet was not ready to preach revolution. In his agitation he could

THE STORM (1522-5)

in the same breath provoke the masses and exhort them to suffer patiently: a phenomenon which was as paradoxical as the message which it proclaimed: in its true meaning, wonderfully logical and in the eyes of the world full of the most remarkable contradictions, indeed a complete mystery.

No politician could have any doubts about how the masses would understand him. It is true, of course, that in its substance and origin the great Peasants' Revolt from 1524 to 1525 was nothing but a renewal of the social disturbances of a religious and economic character which now for more than a generation had again and again shaken Germany. But even the course of these disturbances had been influenced by religious ideas. This became now even more clear. It is still one of the most notable facts of German history that the greatest purely spontaneous rising of the masses which we have seen till this day bore such a strongly religious character. The economic and political demands of the insurgents were made up of a confused mass of conflicting local interests of countless groups of widely varying local and social background. On one point, however (at least after the beginning of 1525), they were all agreed. They proclaimed the 'heavenly kingdom' of the poor man and exploited the Christian idea of the equality of all men before God to establish a programme of social justice. This was certainly no idea of Luther's (who thought much more in the patriarchal terms of the teaching of Paul and the Church of the Middle Ages about the God-willed inequality of men)—but was more akin to the ideas of certain medieval sects. Yet the extent and course of the Peasants' Revolt cannot be understood without taking him into account. Just as the French Revolution is symbolised in the figures of its great orators and political philosophers on the one hand, and in its military tyrants and world-conquerors on the other, and as the Civil War in England is symbolised by its great practical statesman Oliver Cromwell, similarly at the centre of the German revolt stands (even if very unwillingly) the figure of the religious prophet.

Now of course not all the men who took it upon themselves to bring the evangelical teaching right into the middle of the ferment of social chaos were true Lutherans in spirit: least of all, those rabble-raisers and hot-heads, who had long learnt the way of turning the teaching of the new Gospel into ready-made slogans, of misusing it as the instrument of social ambition and greed. These wildly mixed old and new together, and invoked the whole confused mass of prophecies and astrological calculations for the end of the world, of social utopias after the model of the old Jewish state and of the ancient demands of natural law, garnished with supposed doctrines of the New Testament —in short the complete armoury of ideas of the traditional demagogue. But the purer ideas of the baptismal enthusiasts who now began to expand, particularly among the large class of the common people, also departed from the true spirit of the Wittenberg Reformation, to which in the last resort they owed their spiritual birth and a good deal of their basic concepts. How far was Luther's agreeable and spontaneous manner from that of the North German and Swiss Baptists: this combination of sober legalism and rationalistic interpretation of dogma with the enthusiastic and pretentious features and the spiritual narrowness of a sect of the chosen people! It was perhaps the most disastrous act of the unhappy Karlstadt that, by his agitation in Upper Germany and Switzerland, he caused Luther from the start to see Zwingli's doctrine about the Communion, and indeed his whole person, in the light of the radical wing of the Baptist movements, and thus made his ideas appear more foreign to Luther than they really were. The majority of these Baptists, whose ethical strength lay in the heroism of their suffering, were never revolutionaries; they never preached revolt, they were only temporarily associated with the peasant movement and then only in a very modest way: only so long as they hoped that it might help to assure their freedom of belief. The new kingdom of God for which they suffered and died was by its nature of a purely spiritual character. Even if they often saw the worldly state with its powers of coercion in the light of the Apocalypse, as the ' monster from the pit ', they never thought of using force against force. But on the volcanic ground of the upper German peasantry the preaching of these chosen people had the effect of sharpening the religious self-consciousness of the masses, and strengthening the tenacity of their resistance against the reactionary Catholic rulers much more than Lutheran doctrine could have done. Indeed Luther was considered in these circles, even before the outbreak of the revolt, as a blind reactionary, as ' the new Pope and Anti-Christ of Wittenberg ', whom they used to reproach with all the spiritual pride of the sectarian, for his harmless pleasure in good company and lute-playing, terming it a ' wild and godless life '. It was only gradually, under the guidance of such noble and deep spirits as Hans Denck and Sebastian Franck, that a purer spirituality was able to shake itself loose from the pedantic biblicism of the smaller minds.

Still louder, and sharpened with passionate excitement and bitter jealousy, rang out the accusations of Thomas Müntzer; the Thuringian prophet who from the beginning stood out as the most original and hence most effective mind among the German Baptists. Wherever really revolutionary thoughts are found at work among the enthusiasts, it is not difficult to trace their origin to him. A mysteriously gloomy figure, stormy and turbulent, with a constantly burning passion and, in spite of his disturbed and confused outward appearance, with a strong power of suggestion. For the modern reader who has not had the benefit of a thorough theological education it is admittedly difficult to form anything like a clear picture out of the ponderous emphatic sentences, packed full of images, of his ' warning against the unspiritual soft-living flesh at Wittenberg '. Only one thing is clear: that he wished with all his heart that the devil might come and ' cook the tough meat of this ass in his own boiling-pot' and then make a meal of him. Even his contemporaries, the theologians from Wittenberg and Basle, had the greatest difficulty in making any headway in this whirlpool of thoughts and images. No one would deny that there is a genuinely primitive power in his use of language. Behind the palisade of his strangely dark speech lies hidden a firm, consistent core of religious thought: the constantly repeated injunction of the necessity of the indispensable, true, once-and-for-all conversion under the cross, and the appeal to the ' inner word', to the direct illumination through the ' Spirit ' instead of to the external witness of the Holy Scriptures. Both these fundamental ideas of his preaching have had a great historical influence: in the development of the ideas of the medieval mystics and in the intensification of the ideas of Luther into a religious subjectivism, which thanks to its inherent bias from now on had unforeseeable possibilities of development. Yet it is fantastic how even here genuinely Lutheran and post-Lutheran ideas are woven together with a brooding late medieval apocalyptic: a wilderness which no one has ever properly charted! For this mystic never attained true spiritual clarity. Moreover if one then considers the defects of his character as they have been unambiguously laid bare by recent research into his life—his boastful and cowardly mendacity, his consuming hatred for his nearest rivals, his conscious goal in life to overshadow the fame of these rivals, the irresponsible unscrupulousness of his demagogy, which was so pitifully inadequate in any danger—then one finds it hard to believe in the genuineness of his prophetic vocation at all. In any case, the most characteristic traits of his teaching, the trust solely in the uncertainly flickering light of the inner word, the self-righteousness of the man who has been converted once and for all, the fantastic venture of building up here on earth the Community of the

THE STORM (1522-5)

Saints as a visible reality, with its consequent scorn and judgment of the rest of the godless world, all this was as far opposed to Luther's spirit as possible. The latter already found the politically much less harmless mysticism of Müntzer's comrade Karlstadt, (who, in his praise of the spiritual gifts of the peasant, forgot his chief duty, namely to punish them strictly for their sins), as highly repugnant to his moral gravity and prophetic thinking. So one can imagine what he thought of the revolutionary teaching of Thomas Müntzer, who appealed to the spiritually awakened to free the Gospel by force, to destroy the worship of idols and to cast down the godless tyrants, the princes and lords, with all their 'learned biblical scholars', from their seat, since Christ alone is our Lord; to restore to the common people the power which was by right theirs—the appeal, in a word, to social revolution with a religious goal! As soon as this preaching began to have its first practical effect, Luther's attitude towards it became clear: this muddle-headed Karlstadt, who with feigned demagogue humility himself played the peasant and raised the spiritual arrogance of his parishioners at Orlamund to an intolerable degree, and with him, moreover, the 'Satan of Alstadt', Thomas Müntzer, must be driven from the land, if everything was not to be spoilt which God's Word had achieved up till now in Saxony. They fled into exile and everywhere preached hatred against the new Pope and servant of the princes at Wittenberg.

From the very beginning the polemic of the Old Protestants has maintained that these false teachers and not Luther should bear the guilt for the outbreak of the revolution, or at least for its later disastrous religious trend. But one can only say with certainty that they hoped, and in practice tried (although with very little practical success), to assure the victory of their reformation ideas with the help of the great revolt—as opposed to Luther, who never considered using such means. But the factor which controls the development of history is not so much our intentions, but much more the unintentional effect of our actions. We have long since learnt that there is no sense in inquiring after individual guilt in questions of suprapersonal, historical destiny. But who could fail to recognise the great, tragic pattern of these events? Here is a people overflowing with natural, but as yet unformed and unbridled, power; as a political whole almost completely crippled by an unhappy chain of circumstance and guilt, of historical burdens, external restraints and the incompetence of its rulers; no longer able by peaceful means to resolve the internal social tensions, which had long since assumed intolerable proportions. On the horizon appears the enchanting vision of a more happy future within easy reach: the rapid solution of all these tormenting questions by means of a powerful political and spiritual resurgence of the whole nation in the storm of a religious movement, which breaks the chains of a thousand centuries and arouses thousands of new hopes, plans and ideas. But only for a moment; for scarcely has this new growth shown itself to the world than the old powers set about its destruction with a will. For a moment it seemed as if the reform party would nevertheless win the day; then it became suddenly quite clear that the old structure of the national State, long since cracked and rotten, could no longer stand this test of its strength and with an enormous crash it burst apart before the eyes of the whole world. A general battle began between the religious parties, waged on the side of the supporters of the old religion with all the means of power of the State. Nothing seems to have been gained: only more disappointed hopes, new oppression of the masses and new despair. What would be the result of all this? To ask the question is almost to have answered it. 'As soon as the constituted powers become confused,' says Ranke, 'falter, estrange themselves and *simultaneously* insist on enforcing ideas which are in their essence opposed to those which hold sway, then the greatest possible dangers arise.'

Was it seriously thinkable that even now it was possible to prevent the flaring up of radical ideas, which denied the whole existing structure of society and whose first flickerings could in 1522 still have been extinguished? According to medieval doctrine, revolt against unchristian authorities was permissible. Was it possible to suffer the rule of this hierarchy (at whose head, according to the Lutheran view, stood the Anti-Christ himself) as Christian any longer? Was it thinkable that the traditional idea of the right of resistance by subjects could be banished so quickly from men's hearts and minds?

In any case they did not succeed. A local uprising in the south of the Black Forest, which had no specifically religious aims, was of the usual kind, and had quietly smouldered at first for some months, being put down here and there, was suddenly fanned into a bright scorching flame (in the spring of 1525) which swept over the land as over a field of dry stubble. Soon all Upper Germany from Alsace to the Main was in flames, and then Thuringia and Saxony and the Alpine regions; Allgau, Tyrol, Salzburg, Steiermark and the region above and below the Enns. Recent research has given substance to Ranke's opinion that the enforcement of the Edict of Worms by the governments at Regensburg must bear a great deal, if not the main part, of the responsibility for this sudden outburst. The story of the evangelical town-clerk at Kenzingen, who in the sight of his wife and children was made to kneel in the glowing ashes of Bibles and Luther's writings while the executioner cut his head off, and whose blood worked on in silence as the seed of the revolution, seems to be typical. Here in Upper Germany, Church reaction and the ruthless insistence on the rights of the nobles clung inseparably together. It was easy for the outside observer to demand that the spiritual and temporal realms should be sharply divided from one another; but to the man who was in the middle of the battle, things appeared quite differently. The man is fighting for his life is not likely to ask too anxiously where his help is coming from. The peasants from Klettgau, hurried into revolt against their Catholic rulers, were certainly only too willing to subject themselves to the religious mandates of protestant Zürich, in the hope that they would thereby gain the intercession and support of the powerful council at Zürich. Conversely, the bold preacher Balthasar Hubmaier and his foresters, who had to protect the freedom of the Gospel with their lives, could not possibly dispense with the help of the rebel peasants, who were fighting in their immediate vicinity against their taskmasters and common enemy, the archducal house of Austria; it was in itself remarkable enough to what extent and with what energy the man of God of the foresters nevertheless held fast in principle to the Lutheran teaching of obedience. It was the pressure of the Church reaction itself which forced the revolt, the longer it continued, more and more into the ways of religious opposition. Then it was that it first lost its local character. Suddenly everywhere the peasants began to remember their old grievances against the spiritual tyrants; and wherever the nobles supported the latter, they immediately attracted the wrath of the masses. In 1525 a broadsheet was published which originated in Memmingen in Upper Swabia, entitled the *Twelve articles of the peasantry in Swabia*. This, above all, with its convincing and cleverly thought-out marriage of evangelical and socio-political demands, gave the tendency towards a general movement irresistible force. Now at last they had a clearly formulated goal, a programme which could carry all before it. The flames of revolt burnt most fiercely in the struggle in Franconia, where the rebels threatened to overrun the powerful bishoprics. Here, too, the radicalism of the exasperated lower middle classes was at its strongest; and it was here that Karlstadt eventually found some support for his teaching of spiritual freedom, as, from the sure protection of Rothenburg, he fanned the flames with a will. In Thuringia, Müntzer announced the beginning of the great marriage of blood which must directly precede the advent of the heavenly bridegroom. He exhorted the peasants of Allstedt and the miners of Mansfeld to establish immediately the new theocracy in the sign of the sword and the red cross, with the threatening war-cry of the mercenaries: 'On, on, on. Have no pity if Esau tries to dissuade you with soft words. Consider not the plight of the godless; spare them no pity. On, on, on, while the fire is hot. Let not the blood grow cold on your sword. Play out a merry tune on Nimrod's anvil, and cast down his tower to the ground!' Terrible words even if they were not immediately followed by bloody deeds; for the Thuringian peasant with his basically sober and good-humoured nature could at first make little of the fantastic ideal of this apocalyptic Kingdom of God, whose nature even the prophet himself could only paint most indistinctly. Nevertheless it was in him that the element of the uncanny in the movement found its most powerful expression: and who could say to what deeds this fanatic might one day stir up the angry masses? Till now little blood had flowed in all the raging and burning, but who would guarantee that it would always be so? What had happened and what was happening now meant nothing but the beginning of complete universal chaos.

Of the opponents of the revolution in Thuringia and the Electorate of Saxony, Luther was the only man who was likely to meet with any success. The whole success of his affair was now at stake and he was never more magnificent in his anger than at such moments. In April, when the twelve articles came to his notice, appealing to him among others as arbitrator in the cause of the peasants, he thought he might still be able to urge both sides to seek a peaceful outcome of the matter. But what an injunction it was!

> Firstly we have no one on earth to thank for all this uproar and shambles but you princes and lords, and particularly

you blind bishops and mad priests and monks, who never cease to rant and rage against the Holy Gospel. . . . The sword is at your throats and yet you still think you are firmly seated in the saddle. . . . You'll break your necks with such arrogance, you mark my words! I've warned you many a time before. . . . If these peasants do not do it then others will. . . . It isn't peasants, my dear good lords, whom you are up against, it's God himself! . . . And if I felt like avenging myself on you, then I'd just laugh up my sleeve and let the peasants go their own way, or even join forces with them and help to make things worse. But the Lord prevents me from such things, as he has before.

It was not his teaching which was responsible for the revolt, which he never advocated. So he urged them to repent and to accept the demands of the aggrieved peasants in so far as they were justified. Then he turned on the peasants with no less venom. Did he not stand in danger of drawing the hatred of the people on himself for ever? 'Then I ask no further, for it is enough for me if I can save the few true-hearted and upright men among you from the danger of the wrath of God.' Even at this hour he remained true to his calling as the pastor of the nation. He preached love instead of revenge, patience instead of revolt—the commandment of the Sermon on the Mount, as if there were no command of fate which was stronger than the minds of men. He set himself forth as an example of the rebelliousness which is always ready to make peace—completely unaware that he also, in the last instance, had helped to unleash the powers of the deep. In vain he attempted to separate spiritual and temporal issues from one another in the twelve articles—clearly aware that his life's work now stood in grave danger of being once and for all swallowed up by the devil. 'Well, if he eats me, I'll give him a rare belly-ache.' But he was not the man to calm the storm—he who in all seriousness now recommended flight to the peasants as a legal means of self-defence against tyranny. A few weeks later his last hopes, if he had ever seriously entertained them, were disappointed. Higher and higher rose the flames as the revolt rolled on from cloister to cloister, from castle to castle. The common man from the towns had long since joined the ranks of the peasants. The government itself began to totter. Elector Frederick, on the point of death, tormented himself with the thought whether God had not desired that 'the common man should reign', to punish the many sins of the princes. For the while it would be best 'to play as little part as possible in this affair', and to let God hold sway. His brother John, who was soon to follow him to the throne, was even more pious; without military skill, and waiting resignedly for the 'destruction of the princes', he was still uncertain whether the communists were not in the last resort right, and so spent his time collecting proof-texts from the Bible. The Count Mansfeld was on the point of giving in. And what of Luther? At this moment he was in the midst of the mob in Stolberg, in Mansfeld, in Nordhausen, going from village to village, preaching and exhorting the people at the risk of his own life. When he was preaching from the pulpit at Nordhausen, they rang the storm-bells 'and it only needed a little more to set the whole thing off'. What a disaster if they had killed him then! But he was still as fearless as ever, warned the men of Mansfeld to stand firm, and wrote the most terrible of all his polemics, 'the little book against the plundering, murdering bands of the peasants'. It is only a few pages in length, but it earned him the universal hatred of the Germans, and still to-day those people who do not understand the nature of his religious genius shake their heads over it. 'You've got to smash them and strangle them and stab them secretly and openly, whenever you have a chance—just as if you had to put down a mad dog; and if you don't break them, then they will break you and the whole land with you.' 'Whoever dies on the side of the authorities is a true martyr in the sight of God, and whoever falls on the side of the peasants will burn for ever in the fires of hell.' 'These are indeed strange times, when a prince can more easily deserve heaven by shedding blood than by others saying their prayers.' Later he did indeed try to justify his 'severe book' by a new tract. But how did he answer the reproaches of his enemies? 'A rebel does not deserve to be answered reasonably, for he won't take any notice. You've got to answer their loud mouths with your fist, so that the sweat runs out of their noses. The peasants wouldn't listen either, wouldn't be told anything, so one had to prise open their ears with musket-fire, which blew their heads off. But such pupils deserve that sort of beating. Whoever does not hear God's Word when it is spoken gently will have to listen to the hangman and his noose.' What sort of language is that! Is it still the voice of the liberator of the Germans or is it the hard angry tones of the new spiritual tyrant thundering out his decrees of excommunication? It is in fact nothing but the cries of distress of a man who is gripped by terror. 'I think there can't be any more devils left in hell, but that they have all gone and taken up residence in the peasants. Mark well how much the devil feels the nearness of the last day, for otherwise he would never have undertaken such an unheard-of task. It's as if he had said " It's our last effort so we'll make it as terrible as possible," and wants to stir up the mire and to tear up the earth. For we wrestle not against flesh and blood but against the spiritual powers of darkness in the air which must be attacked with prayer.' Was this the hour which the prophetic books of the New Testament had foretold in which all the power of the Evil One would be united together for a moment to establish the kingdom of Satan ' as a prelude to the Last Day, which will not be long—to destroy all order and authority and to throw the world into wild confusion'? If this was the fate which was to overcome Martin Luther's life-work, then he had good

THE STORM (1522-5)   171

reason to be seized with terror—but he could not let it cripple him: he wanted at least to 'go to meet his fate with a good conscience. That's why there's no cause for sleep. Nor are patience and pity of any avail here; the time has come for the sword and wrath and not for mercy.—Before I would condone and justify what they are doing, I would lose my head a thousand times rather than that God should come to my aid with his mercy.'

He remained true to himself in every trait. Yet he must have appeared to the world as one who gives in in the hour of danger. When the revolt collapsed in the face of the armoured and well-drilled columns of spearmen of the German rulers, and when the rabble-raisers were chained to the trees and slowly roasted to death to the shouts of the drunken Junkers, when dozens of them had their eyes put out, when hundreds, thousands and even tens of thousands of prisoners were slaughtered at a time—then the hopes of the masses for an 'improvement of the Christian estates' were for ever at an end. But the nation had lost its heroes. What was the use of his thundering against the 'furious, raging and senseless tyrants', the 'wolves, swine, bears and lions', these petty Junkers thirsting for victory, whose reward would be 'fires of hell, and wailing and gnashing of teeth in hell for eternity', if he now also added to this the injunction that they should patiently bear their raging as God's punishment for the evil world? The great masses could no longer understand him. Indeed had they ever understood him? His voice rang out like the voice of a preacher in the wilderness, over a vast field of corpses, over endless ruins and rubble. It was not like the revolution of more happy people, tragic but elevating, relieving the atmosphere; the greatest social rising in German history ended sadly and depressingly, in defeat and bitterness. The mercilessly subdued peasant could greet only with apathy and indifference the message that the divine grace was the only power which can make men blessed. 'What is that empty priest saying about God now? Who knows what God is, or even if there is a God?'—was how they scorned him in the villages of Saxony. The time of great hopes was over, to be replaced by the grey realities of everyday life.

8. *Founder of the Evangelical Churches*

For more than two decades Luther shouldered the weight of this everyday work—an enormous burden which continually increased and which often seemed to suppress completely his human feelings and instead brought out all the more strongly the sharper, more offensive traits of his character. Yet it was never able to stifle the confidence of his faith, nor the many-sided richness of his character, the inexhaustible humour and goodnaturedness of this great and childlike soul. 'I hope they will not rob me of my courage and joy,' he wrote in the middle of the Peasants' Revolt. Of course, as a natural man, he was grieved to be the object of universal hatred; for 'it is something which is deeply rooted in our nature that we should be pleased when people are favourably disposed towards us.' But this did not for a moment distract him from his vocation; he was only plagued by the spirit of his conscience. 'All their blood is on my hands. But I can lay it at the door of our Lord God, who ordered me to say that.' Again, the way in which he countered the hatred and contempt of men was typical of Luther: with supreme defiance for all the blasphemers and to the overwhelming horror of Melanchthon, he chose this precise moment, which was in fact earlier than he had planned, to embark on marriage with a nun who had run away from her order. So, right at the beginning of this last great period of his life, we find an event which almost suggests symbolically to us what will distinguish the work of these decades from that of all previous ones: the monk and man of God who had been so withdrawn from earthly matters, now settles into an earthly life; the Titan, without betraying his ultimate aims, is content to work at first only in small circles; to erect by faithful but outwardly modest work, a limited and so more solid building and at the same time a cell of the new communion of saints, after the bold outlines of the first plan had proved far too ambitious to be able to find any firm footing in the cracked, volcanic ground of Germany. Faust builds dykes to win back a little firm ground from the eternally fluctuating sea. That he found courage at this moment, and indeed time and time again, is—in spite of all the trials and tribulations of this late period of his life—the unforgettable historical achievement of the ageing Luther.

The catastrophe of the Peasants' Revolt did not prevent the continuance of the Reformation, and perhaps did not even seriously hold it up; but it gave the movement another character. It did away for ever with the confidence that one could achieve a reform of spiritual and secular life all at once. The nation as a whole lost not only its hope in this transformation, but also its chance of internal participation in public life—that tempting prospect in which they had followed and applauded the breaking away of the Church from Rome as the beginning of a better period for the Germans. From now on the future of Germany was left entirely in the hands of the victors and oppressors, the German princes and their advisers. If they wished now to continue the struggle with the Emperor and the Pope, then the people obeyed blindly and apathetically. This was the situation which Luther had to reckon with from now on. But a great division between the parties had occurred.

Luther's teaching preserved its purely spiritual, fundamentally unpolitical character; it had withstood the severest test of fire; and now it must carry on in its own way: by the inner transformation of men. The revolutionary fanatics, who had wanted to renew everything all at once, at the risk of invoking chaos, were overpowered. Their rash courage was broken for ever; they became submerged in the peaceful, suffering movement of the Baptists, who were now subjected to a merciless persecution—not least because they were blamed (in the main unjustly) for the disaster of the Peasants' Revolt. Everything which was not of the Roman Catholic or Lutheran faith was driven underground into concealment and bigotry; oppressed, harassed and hunted, they were ineradicable and could boast of thousands of brave martyrs. But Luther's life-work was saved from the whirlpool and could continue to hold up its head in public.

But one of the strings to his bow had been broken; no one who had ears could mistake it. Ever since the 'tract on the severe little book against the peasants' there had been mixed with the deep, heart-felt pathos of his voice a new, sharper and at times clearly disharmonious tone. His polemics were always passionate and terrible; but now they were sometimes malicious and bitter; the contradictions of his opponents not only aroused his anger, they made him impatient and irritable; suddenly one saw a nervous man who was no longer in complete control of himself. Even now his battles were in the grand manner: he was always pursuing some great and pertinent aim; he always rose above the level of petty intrigue, of personal enmities, which surrounded him in Wittenberg, right up to the very last days of his old age. But, for the first time, in that 'tract' he brings himself to threaten his opponent with external force: 'Beware: the sword could strike even you!' One does indeed feel that his faith in the effectiveness of the mere Word on men is no longer what it was. He does not doubt the power of

FOUNDER OF THE EVANGELICAL CHURCHES 175

the divine Word, but their good will to accept it and their ability to follow the better insight. Basically this was nothing but his old notion of the complete sinfulness of natural man; but the power of Satan must have seemed greater and greater to him, the more disappointments he experienced, and the sad pessimistic attitude of the religious in regard to this sinful world turned into contempt of mankind. The severe physical illnesses which consumed him more and more, and at times plunged him into unconsciousness, may have done their share towards making the struggle more difficult, but they could never break the power of his spirit; the amount of work which he produced even in his worst weeks is almost unbelievable. But this battle which was carried on without ceasing for decades, and which he alone—for that was what he felt—had to wage day by day against a whole world of merciless enemies, gradually embittered him. Throughout his life he could never allow himself to retire from the forefront of the battle, where he struggled on with ever-increasing vigour. All his actions show this, not least those of his old age, when we see him leaving Wittenberg in a furious temper, refusing ever to return to a town where there were so many enemies and false friends; and it was at this time that he gradually began to estrange even the closest of his friends with his overdominating will, while they in turn at the end no longer dared to tell him of all the setbacks in the Church struggle, for fear of his outbursts of anger. Always he longed for the peace which he had left behind him, and always his fighting spirit drew him into fresh conflicts.

Indeed, the colour and tonality of his manner had changed appreciably. But the theme remained the same. Anyone who thinks he can find a deep-seated break, a formal contradiction between Luther's attitude before and after 1525, has never properly understood the depths of his character. It is true that whereas before he had put all the emphasis on the preaching of the Word and the inner transformation of men which this would effect, he now allowed more room for the gradual, educational effect of Church institutions on the masses. What was previously for him of least significance, the creation of external forms and organisations, now came to assume more importance after so many bitter experiences. His marriage was the first external sign of this change of view; it was high time to make an end of the separation of the clergy, which was manifest to all. Even in this he was led on step by step by the internal logic of these matters; from the gradual establishment of external forms of worship to the formulation of a confession of faith, of a new dogma which he developed more and more fully, and which he had to define more sharply against the spiritualism of the Baptists. Out of the free preaching of the Word there arose a new Church. And he had never been of the opinion that men could do without Church order. It was precisely because the inner sanctuaries of his faith occupied him so exclusively that it never occurred to him to dispute the divine institution of the Church, the necessity of external institutions for the education of men. The reformation tract, 'Address to the Nobility', written at the peak of his activity, shows this clearly. Melanchthon's *Loci communes*, the first protestant attempt at Dogmatic theology, was produced in the year of the Diet of Worms. He did not intend to destroy the old Church but to restore it in its pure form. But even the freedom of conscience which he preached was not a mere arbitrariness; it was always bound to the Word of God, and over and above this he was much more attached to many of the traditions of the old Church than one could have expected at the height of the battle. Everything which he renounced had to be torn away from his soul with great pain and suffering. True, what he effected was a revolution, but at the same time it was a historical development. It was here that we have already seen part of his genius, and by no means the least. Everything which in the last decades of his life seems like spiritual obduracy and even like reaction, is at heart nothing of the kind at all: he is only strengthening his continuity with the Middle Ages, which he had never given up. If here and there (as is undoubtedly so in his doctrine of the sacraments) this forces him in some of his theological formulations to go against his own earlier statements, it did not mean that he abandoned anything of the essence of the Reformation doctrine: on the contrary, that essence now gains its ultimate depth and maturity, its true systematic consistency. Immediately after the Peasants' Revolt, appeared the deepest and scientifically most searching of all his writings; his discussion of Erasmus's views on the freedom of human will and original sin, on divine omnipotence and predestination ('Of the Unfree Will', 1526). In the rough emphasis which he lays on all the supra-rational elements and irrational elements of primitive Christian teaching, it announces the final and conscious break with all Catholic attempts at reform, and with all the rationalism of the Renaissance theologians; but it is just out of this delimitation, which he carried out less by polemical attacks than by patient, searching inquiry, that the Reformer was able to arrive at the maturest formulation of his concept of God. Still richer and more varied is the wealth of ideas in his great course of lectures on the first book of Moses, which he worked on for fully ten years (1535-45), and which is a truly inexhaustible source of his theological ideas.

Yet, for all that, there had been a transformation in his life-work. At first sight it is disappointing, almost tragic, to see how the stormy, open-hearted enthusiasm of the early years gradually changes into dogmatic rigidity: how in his struggles and disputes with opponents on both sides the immediate testimony of his living experience of God is withdrawn behind theological definitions and ecclesiastical formulations of doctrine. But the cause of this change was anything but a cooling of his original enthusiasm. It was not determined from within but from without; for he was forced by external pressure to change his role of religious liberator for that of a Church Father—to become the canonical authority for a new theological school, so that as a teacher he had to define his conviction on all sides. It was just in the same way that he had previously been forced by external circumstances to develop the revolutionary impetus of his own new understanding of God: step by step with greater clarity and power.

By far the most important task which now lay before him was the refounding from within of an evangelical Church. This presupposed above all one thing (as we have already noted): the re-establishment of an effective spiritual authority. But where could such an authority be found after the decline of canon law and of all priestly and hierarchical powers of coercion, except in the congregation? For Luther had indeed even in his address to the nobility recognised the right of the 'common will and command' to judge the doctrine of their clergy and to appoint and dismiss them. But in this congregation he had from the beginning counted on the 'Council or Authority' that is the secular powers in the late medieval sense, as the most important members. He even included the rulers of the state, although only in so far as they subscribed to right doctrine. And on the whole (as we saw) he had more confidence in these secular rulers than in 'Messrs. Omnes' from whom he expected wild tumults and the blind destruction of their traditional inheritance rather than the calm reconstruction and clear insight. This did not exclude certain practical attempts to organise the congregation on an ecclesiastical basis: the laity were to take part in the administration of Church possessions; indeed Luther wanted to see the voluntary establishment of a Christian rule of life with 'house-fathers and house-mothers' with certain means of discipline, with a greater and lesser excommunication. But his constant worry in all this was to prevent this new rule of love becoming a new spiritual compulsion, or even a new canon law. Before he would allow this to happen he would rather leave the establishment of external order to the secular authorities as a 'service of love'. Nor would he grant any purely spiritual authority to the 'congregation' in the sense of a compulsory rule, because of his deep conviction that it was impossible to separate the pure, true Christians from those who merely seemed to be Christians, from the camp-followers and the busybodies. He had thought at first of gathering together a small congregation of living witnesses and disciples of the new doctrine round the communion table in the chapel of the Black Cloister, as a core from which the new communion of the saints would gradually develop. He would preach to them himself, while 'outside' in the town church his chaplains would preach to the 'great mass' as missionary preachers. But this was to be no more than an outward means to an end; and it should in no way lead to a sect-like separation of the 'Elect', still less to any special position of privilege for the inner circle in church government. The true church of Christ was for him always the invisible one. For this reason the plans for the systematic development of the Lutheran congregation were never properly put into effect and Luther contented himself instead with the formula that the Church is everywhere to be found where the pure Word is preached and the sacraments are properly celebrated. For the time being he was himself the living central figure of this new congregational and ecclesiastical formation, as the spiritually most powerful witness and preacher of divine truth.

But in this way the problem of a new form of spiritual authority was not solved but merely shelved. Could it in fact be solved at all? Or was it for the Lutheran way of thought, which only recognised the 'pure Word of God' as the final authority and which feared that any human authority might bring with it the falsification of that Word, basically insoluble? Was it not a paradoxical task which Luther had set his church: to build a community not of this world and yet for this world and in this world—invisible and yet visible—a community not based on outward laws but on the inner conscience, and yet again not a sect, but a national church, an organised community of baptised Christians? Unquestionably there is reflected in these contradictions something of the paradox of Lutheran theological thinking, which in the last resort is a consequence of his ruthless renewal of the paradox of the preaching of primitive Christianity. As a community in love of like-minded men, the new Church needed no external order, while as a national Church, on the other hand, it did; for as such it embraced true believers and apparent Christians alike—and Luther had no intention of leaving the affairs of Church government in the hands of such a motley crowd. The practical consequences of this were the endless trials of evangelical Church order which till this day have not been overcome, but rather (in a largely non-Christian world) have been considerably increased; and this is particularly true of the Lutheran Church. Zwingli, the sober, practical, humanistically-minded Swiss, helped himself out of this difficulty by building his church ' goers' from Zurich into a form of Christian community, a type of theocracy, in which the preachers of the reform were in fact assured that the majority of the Council were dependent on them, and so were able to bring secular politics for a time completely into the service of the new community of the faithful. This was a political and so purely temporal solution. Calvin, who attempted the same thing in Geneva, had to withstand a long and difficult struggle in order to gain a majority in the Council. He had, therefore, to form a militant and purely ecclesiastical organisation, which could maintain itself and hold sway, even without—or, indeed, against—the secular authority; a community of chosen, fanatically convinced adherents which excluded all half-hearted and weak members or mere hangers-on, by excommunicating them, and which then created its own order and its own means of government according to ' biblical norms', in the executive committee of the presbyters and consistories. But this was not possible without the creation of a new legalism: official Church trials of conscience in situations of acute danger with inquisition and consequently trials for heresy and the erection of a new canon law, which instead of the old books of canon law used the Bible in the New as well as the Old Testament as a law-book for external ordinances. Luther rejected both these ways on grounds of the deepest conviction; and he had to as the preacher of a purely inner religion which recognised no code of 'divine' ordinances and also no visible community of the Elect. He was left no alternative but to substitute the respect for secular authority for the ecclesiastical authority which he was unable to obtain by the creation of new ordinances; thus, to a very great degree he entrusted the fate of his Church to the 'secular sword'.

This step, to modern thinking with its clear-cut distinction between Church and State, seems very risky, and its dangers have been amply experienced by the evangelical Church since the eighteenth century. At the time of the reformation there was scarcely anything remarkable in it. Already long before the appearance of Luther the internal collapse of the Papal Church had made it necessary on all sides (not only in Germany) for the 'Christian rulers' to take more and more responsibility for the reform of Church life. A formal law of secular assistance for the Church in emergencies had been developed; and so Luther was only completing what had for a long time been practised everywhere—only, of course, his mighty blow against the Papacy considerably increased and accelerated the process of development (for a time on the Catholic side, too!) and, too, the 'state of emergency' in his own Church which required the interference of the authorities was not of a temporary nature but was indeed one of its characteristics. We have already seen how little it occurred to him to release the authorities, which had now been freed from their spiritual surveillance by Rome, from their Christian duties. He knew nothing of the modern distinction between 'State' and 'Church', as autonomous forms of community independent of each other. He only knew of an admittedly secular, but nevertheless Christian authority as an estate of Christendom among others. He knew the 'State' only as a Christian community which has essentially moral and religious educational duties to perform. Like every other estate the authorities are duty bound to serve the Kingdom of God—the prince firstly as a private person, out of a duty of love, as the most respected member of the Christian congregation, but also by virtue of the duty attaching to his estate, as the bearer of his office of government, 'which as such belongs to the Christian congregation and is of use to it'. It is not for his own sake that God has given him so much riches, power and outward splendour, but only for the sake of his subjects, whom he has to serve in his office—even if it means sacrificing all his personal political interests and even those of his dynasty. Luther speaks of this duty of the Christian father of the State in complete agreement with the medieval law-code of the princes; only his understanding is more fundamental and radical, and above all (at least after 1522) he suffers from no illusions about the demonic powers of political reality and so discards the traditional servile hypocrisy. The most noble of all the duties of the prince is the care for the salvation of the souls of his subjects by the establishment, preservation and protection of true Christian doctrine and discipline. Even if the 'spiritual government' of the preachers is responsible for making man devout and just for eternal life, not by the power of the sword but by the proclamation of the Word alone, it must nevertheless be complemented by the secular government; for the real Christians who do not need the power of compulsion are always in the minority compared with the great mass of those who are not Christians or who merely seem to be such. So the secular government has the duty of seeing that all those who do not wish to become devout and just for eternal life should be yet compelled by the sword to become devout and just in the eyes of the world. Both spiritual and temporal government are under the same law of God and serve the same highest moral and religious duty.

Luther held fast to those basic insights (whose origins we have already seen in the 'Address to the Christian Nobility') unerringly in spite of all his many changes of outward approach. It made it easier for him to dispense with the determined enforcement of the 'principle of the congregation'. In practice he never even had the time to build up those closer circles of committed Christians as the core of a much larger community. One lesson had been made unmistakably clear by the catastrophe of the Peasants' Revolt, and that was that no time must be lost in building up a new and stable form of Church order. In this task Luther could less than ever afford to dispense with the help of the State authorities; how else could he have saved the few and have built up again the pitiful ruins of the beginnings of a new form of Church organisation which had been left by the storm of the revolution? In the larger towns it would still be possible to continue with the attempt to build up the new Church on the basis of the congregation; in the country all hopes for the success of this plan had been destroyed. These wild, ignorant, religiously indifferent peasants ought not even to be entrusted with the choice of their own pastor; while the remains of the old clergy—who to a certain extent had now lapsed into unworthy occupations, as publicans or exorcists—were in serious need of spiritual rehabilitation, as was the wild confusion of the half-ruined organisations of the old Church. Even the imperial Diet recognised (at least, the imperial dismissal of the Diet of Speyer in 1526 could in emergency be interpreted in this way) that the secular heads of state, who alone of all the imperial Estates had successfully calmed the storm, were also the only ones in a position to create new forms of Church order, even if this was only a temporary measure. They all, north and south, Lutheran and Catholic alike, vied with each other to exploit the favourable situation of the next few years in the sense of the imperial direction from Speyer. While their Emperor and Pope were at open war with each other, and the imperial mercenaries were engaged in sacking the holy city of Rome, they sought to strengthen their own power by Church reforms carried out within the boundaries of their own territories with the use of secular force. The foundation of the German State Churches which had been prepared since the previous century was now finally realised and became one of the most important factors in German history. While it formally put the seal on the political divisions of the nation, it also determined the character not only of the Church life but also of the political life in the individual states. The Reformation, which was one of the spiritual roots of modern political democracy in Western Europe, also contributed substantially in Germany and the countries which came under the reforming influence of Lutheranism, to the victory—which was admittedly inevitable in any case—of absolute monarchy.

However great Luther's historical responsibility for this course of affairs may be, particularly with regard to his role as founder of the Reformation movement, it would not be fair to say that he really determined its further development. As always in history, as soon as a spiritual movement has advanced beyond the battleground of pure ideas and has come into the spheres of political struggles for power and of material avarice, its founder loses all power over it. The force of historical circumstance and the interplay of political interests wins the upper hand. What good was it that the Reformer was at pains to make a careful distinction between questions of the ministry of the Church and of its external order, between occasional and temporary legal assistance (in the visitations) and the permanent government of the Church, between the service of love of the prince as the most respected member of the Church and his duties as secular father and lord of the State, if he never spoke at all of the rights of the princes in Church government but only of their duties? The constantly growing influence of State bureaucracy on the inner life of the Church could not be withstood for long, particularly once Luther had made the decision to undertake, with the help of the officials of the princes, a great visitation of all religious foundations and parishes for the correction of the countless abuses and emergencies which had arisen (1526-8). This gradually developed into a formal 'church police'. Even the electoral instruction to the Church visitors in 1527 undisguisably laid claim on behalf of the State rulers to the spiritual government of the Church. Even if Luther himself sighed and at times raged over the claims of the government lawyers, his fellow-workers, above all Melanchthon, Bugenhagen and Amsdorf with their theologico-juristic formulations, consciously prepared the way for the State consistories and helped them to create a new evangelical Church law (not without considerable leanings towards the old canon law) which had in practice become indispensable. But in this Melanchthon, the humanist, considerably watered down the Lutheran doctrine of the spiritual duties of the rulers greatly in favour of the supreme power of the State. At first, that is as long as Luther's powerful personality dominated the court of the Wettins, there was little practical danger in the Electorate of Saxony of a misuse of the new Church government for the ends of secular power. But beyond the Saxon borders his personal influence was much smaller; and would his successors ever be in a position to withstand the political independence of the German rulers? The Reformer himself was soon able to see what course things were taking when the pious and easily-led Duke was succeeded by the theological dilettante and absolutist John Frederick. His generation and the one which followed took up its responsibilities for true doctrine in a highly personal way and with a zeal which seemed for a moment as if it would turn the complicated and purely dogmatic disputes over the doctrine of the Lord's Supper into the most important issue in German territorial politics. In this development opposed points of dogma and the territorial interests of the states became entangled in each other in a truly disastrous manner. The more petty the power of the princes, the more petty and malicious became the squabblings of their theologians. The misfortune of the small German states was made even worse by the half-spiritual authority of the German princely courts; and in reverse effect this multiplicity of states succeeded finally in really hardening and exacerbating the theological bickering.

So the historical development of Luther's life-work wandered far from the point where it had begun. In the orthodox court-preachers and theological faculties of this later period there was nothing to be seen of the coarse, bold defiance of the Luther who had ranted against the German princes as the 'biggest fools and the most arrant knaves on earth', because they put obstacles in the way of his preaching—the preaching of the pure Word of God. But did he not himself play a part in accustoming the State authorities to making decisions on purely spiritual matters? Did he not himself set the secular sword in motion, in order to destroy his spiritual opponent with it? What could one say if he who had poured so much scorn on the art 'of overcoming heretics with fire' himself advised the ruler of his state to prevent the preaching of the Baptists by exile or even by execution? Is this not a gross betrayal of the principle which he had wrung from himself of the freedom of the conscience? Indeed it is not!—if in the place of our modern relativism of all values, on which our concept of freedom of conscience is based, one substitutes the religiously bound conscience of a medieval man, who knows that he is in sure possession of absolute truth: a truth whose possession arbitrates over this life and the next! Here as everywhere in Luther's thought, the idea of God stands in the forefront and explains associations of ideas which would otherwise remain obscure. If he demanded freedom of conscience, he was not concerned, as we are today, to allow more scope to the human personality, with its subjective claims to certainty, its convictions and prejudices; he was much rather concerned with something which excluded this—to clear a way for the working of the Word of God in the hearts of men. Only if the individual comes before his God immediately and with full responsibility for himself, without the sacramental mediation and guidance of the priests, can the mysterious struggle with God be broken off and that blessing of grace be experienced which lies at the centre of all Luther's religious thought. But only in this sense, in the sense of the responsibility of every individual before God, could he come to a knowledge of what we call (and in most cases also fundamentally misinterpret) his 'autonomous conscience', which in no way means that man is now free to think up his own arbitrary ideas about God and divine things. For man's thinking is just as much subjected to God, and so fundamentally unfree, as is the human will. The *content* of divine revelation was for Luther as sure and as certain as it had been for the old Church; it has been laid down once and for all in the Word of God, which Word and its contents one must know and whose interpretation is not in any sense a purely arbitrary matter. Any doubts about this are the works of devilish powers and the prophet fights for the Lordship of his God, when he battles against Satan, who blinds men to God's clear revelation. There is still more: God's purpose of grace, revealed in Christ, is not a mere gift to men: it is our sacred duty to prostrate ourselves to it unconditionally, and to accept grace willingly; whoever resists this, whoever makes reservations for the freedom of the human will, blasphemes and brings down God's just wrath upon himself. That there were many interpretations of the revelation was plain for all to see; but that he the reformer had with God's help again discovered the true one, and that every other exposition was idolatry and devilish error was for him never in doubt: how else could he have accomplished the gigantic task of standing alone against the whole world ? Only a man who has the sure and certain conviction that he is proclaiming nothing but God's will and meaning can withstand such tensions in the soul. All the strangely wild and terrifying aspects of Luther's character in the eyes of modern men, and also the heroic greatness of his historical achievement, are most closely bound up with this conviction.

Yet it is not true to say that the Lutheran belief in revelation led to the same outward constraint of conscience as in the inquisition of the old Church. God's spirit blows where it will and we men should not presume to interfere in its work, or to compel its activity by outward means. God wills that his Word should be preached, pure and unhindered by false doctrine, and that all men should hear it; for this reason the authorities must employ the true teachers and prevent the false ones from preaching, and ensure that their subjects attend the schools and churches. But the working of God's Word in our hearts is not our affair but God's. No one may be forced into a state of mind or a decision of faith; in the last instance everyone stands immediately before God. The unity of the Church which so much preoccupied Luther was a unity of the spirit and not of external Church order—of the Word, not of the hierarchy. The Spirit of God must have a free path, but no blood, no inquisition, no trials for heresy; not the Church, and still less the secular authorities, are responsible for the eternal salvation of the individual soul, but every individual himself; because no one can or may take away his immediate responsibility before God. It is not for the sake of human freedom that the consciences are free, but only for the sake of God: then the individual who turns away may go to the devil on his own responsibility—if only the preaching of God's Word is unhindered.

From these basic concepts we can understand Luther com-

FOUNDER OF THE EVANGELICAL CHURCHES 189

pletely. Their interrelatedness was clear from the beginning; there could be no question of any fundamental alteration. Yet he does not always seem to have defined in quite the same way the outer limits of what was to be regarded as immediate divine truth. A certain basis of dogmatic propositions, as they had been developed up to the Council of Nicaea and formulated in the so-called Apostolic creed, was for him, as for nearly all his contemporaries, inviolable, and any attack on it would have been tantamount to public blasphemy. Naturally he was firmly convinced that the core of his new Gospel, man's justification through God's grace alone and through the redemptive act of Christ, was to be found in these propositions; and he could without further ado brand justification by works as blasphemy. But the longer the fight with the Baptists lasted, and the more the danger of a pure spiritualisation of the concept of revelation became clear to him—the danger of the dissipation of all dogmatic traditions in favour of a purely subjective arbitrariness—the closer he came to the idea that every deviation from his understanding of Christianity was to be seen as false teaching and idolatry. At the beginning he had been prepared to tolerate such false teachings so long as they did not preach revolt against secular order; one must let the spirits fight it out together in an honourable contest, he wrote when Karlstadt and Müntzer first appeared before the lords of his state, then it would become clear of itself, which was the true teaching of God. After the experience of the Peasants' Revolt (which he, too, unfairly blamed on the Baptists) he became sterner—the more so since in Thuringia the dominant form of Baptist movement was of a particularly fanatical nature which denied the power of the sword to the secular authorities. Now he wanted to banish public false doctrines even if they were only preached 'in corners' by unofficial preachers, and to punish public denial of the basic truths of Christianity and the preaching of revolt even, if circumstances demanded it, with the death penalty. For now the Gospel had been preached long enough and had been established on all sides, so that no one could any longer with justice plead ignorance of the true faith. From now on toleration could only be afforded if false doctrines were kept locked in the heart; for no one can or may compel the working of the spirit by external means. Indeed even this narrowly limited 'toleration', which was soon limited even more by the circumscribed zeal and nervousness of the Lutheran rulers and by the narrow-minded misunderstanding of the orthodox followers of Luther, was an enormous step forward for those times; even the permission of unhindered departure for reasons of belief which became law first in the Protestant territories and then in the whole of Germany, was then felt to be an unheard-of innovation. Nor can it be denied that the freedom from Roman dogma which Luther won for himself and for his Church was able to be used against his will for the general destruction of dogma: the split in the Church, purely as such, had infinitely wider consequences than he had intended or even realised. But Luther was not, and did not want to be, a forerunner of the modern idea of freedom of conscience. On the contrary, the new fire of religious life which he kindled in the world countered most successfully and powerfully the rationalisation of religious thought which was even then beginning to spread from Italy.

So we too may perhaps attempt to understand the last great crisis of his spiritual development—his much criticised dispute with Zwingli, his Swiss fellow-reformer—in its proper context. It has often been pointed out that in this quarrel, which split the two men, there were more fundamental contradictions at stake than theological formulations for the interpretation of the sacrament of the altar. The Swiss stood opposed to the North German, the secular priest to the monk, the born ecclesiastical statesman to the purely religious prophet, the son of the Renaissance to the founder of the German Reformation. If Luther's education had been purely governed by scholastic theology,

FOUNDER OF THE EVANGELICAL CHURCHES

Zwingli had only come into contact with theology very late, when he was already in office as a secular priest. Originally he was exclusively a pupil of the humanists and an enthusiastic admirer of the ancient writers, and had in these early studies been steeped in the moralism and rationalism of the pre-Christian world of ideas—admittedly as they were presented in that narrow mixture, which was peculiar to German and Erasmic humanism, of Christian, Platonic and Stoic ideas, in which the ancient world was seen through Christian eyes, but which was nevertheless entirely foreign to Luther's deepest feelings, which indeed appeared antagonistic to them. For this was precisely Luther's aim; to restore religious life to its naïve originality, to free it from the bonds of natural reason and moralising legalism which had fettered and crippled it under the domination of ecclesiastical and scholastic thought and which now threatened to become more dangerous than ever in the age of the tame, delicate and somewhat pale edifying religion of the humanists. That these radical contrasts in their spiritual outlook should be fired off over just this question of the Lord's Supper was of course no mere chance: the sacrament of the altar was the central core of medieval worship and stood even at the time of the Reformation (unlike today) right at the centre of the evangelical divine service. On its understanding depended not only the form of all church services but, in the last instance, the position of the ministry of the Church in relation to the congregation. It was inevitable that at this point men should begin to differ passionately.

This is not the place to attempt to expound in detail the religious depths of the Lutheran doctrine of the Lord's Supper; fundamentally Luther was moved here by the same simple but powerful religious thoughts which we saw in his struggles in the monastery: the immeasurable omnipotence of God, for which no miracle is too great, and which alone is active in this sacrament, while man can do nothing but receive in humility.

The Lord's Supper is seen then not as a self-elevation of the soul in a common ceremony of remembrance of the congregation's founder, but as God's gift to the individual believer, the surest and, for the doubter, indispensable, token of his grace, in which (in a wonderful way) he makes a gift of himself. Yet this does not come about in a merely miraculous and primitive way as the Scholastics had commonly taught, but in such a way that the deeply and passionately felt need of the religious spirit for 'Frau Hulda', the 'whore Reason', has to keep completely silent. It is in such a way that we (to put it into Luther's own words) find consolation in the sacrament, not merely in a meal of remembrance, ' not in the bread and wine, nor in the body and blood of Christ, but in the Word, which in the sacrament offers, presents and gives to me the body and blood of Christ which was given and shed for me ', a formulation, as one can see, whose religious intention is clear, but which makes the sacramental process for the first time really enigmatic.

To Zwingli's clear good sense this was all nothing but a relapse into the Middle Ages; he could not understand why the man from Wittenberg should torment himself with so many mysteries. Sufficient for him was the celebration of the pure meal of remembrance, at which, of course, Christ the founder was present in the spirits of the celebrants; and this too was testified biblically in Jesus' words of institution. While Luther longed above all for a visible, tangible comfort for the distressed soul, he considered the sacrament as a sort of solemn confirmation of the covenant of love which had already been made, of the spiritual communion with the risen Lord which had already been achieved. Behind this stood a different understanding of man, who is seen not as a self-assured being (as has been exaggeratedly said more recently), who needs no grace or redemption, nor as an eternally tempted one, who stands always in fear and trembling before the omnipotence, the wrath and the mysterious elusiveness of God, but rather as a happy, confident person, sure of God's clear purpose of grace and convinced of the reasonableness of this will and of the justice of the divine government of the world—which is also clear to the human reason—and so inspired by a strong confidence in the importance of human reason. Of course Zwingli recognises, too, that the human will has been corrupted by the ' imprint' of original sin and is unable of itself to find salvation; but faith is as sure of itself as every other clear insight which man wins, and so fundamentally it needs no strengthening, no external confirmation and assurance of the divine purpose of salvation by visible signs. So it is just for this reason that Zwingli can only allow the sacrament as a divine gift to the true believers, while Luther was principally concerned to include also all those who were tempted in their faith, independent of the result of their psychological self-examination. This was the central question of the whole dispute, although of course it became involved in all sorts of theologico-metaphysical questions about the omnipresence of God and the two natures of Christ, which to us (in spite of their very real importance) seem in some ways purely scholastic. At heart, however, the dispute reaches right down into the realms of the purely religious, to the question of the true understanding of God. For it is obvious that the God whose grace is assured for ever by my insight of faith into his being is different from the hidden God of Luther, if the Lutheran Christian cannot be sure of his own salvation without the constantly renewed help of the sacrament.

But in spite of all this even Zwingli was separated by a huge gulf from the shallow moralism of the Humanist reformers. A pupil of Erasmus, he was latterly deeply influenced by Luther; and more than this, he had also been through a period of intense religious upheaval, which had admittedly not penetrated such depths as had Luther's, but which had nevertheless reached into the roots of his soul. He reacted as violently to the legalism of the Catholic doctrine of merits as had Luther, and followed

Lutheran theology in the doctrine of justification and original sin—even if his statement of them is less radical. At least at the beginning it did seem perfectly possible that they would be able to reach agreement in nearly all the disputed points of doctrine except on the interpretation of the sacrament of the altar. Even if it were not possible to gain complete agreement on this point, could they not have tolerated each other's differences over this? Was it so completely necessary to make precisely this issue into the cause of such violent struggles, and on top of everything to do it with the help of scholastic formulations which previously had not even been mentioned in Luther's own writings? It would be idle to waste too much time on these questions. Only one thing is clear beyond all doubt. Luther was always sensitive to the dangers of this alliance and never to its necessity. Was it personal pride as so many of his best friends asserted then, and as even today many of his admirers admit with resignation? Was it his boundless vigour which blinded him in the dispute and which ran away with him in extreme situations, so that he could not find his way back again? Or was it simply that the ageing man lapsed back into the Middle Ages? Indeed his writings against the ' sacramentalisers' are among the most terrible of his polemics; and in spite of their deep insight their manner is in places intolerable. The most powerful conviction in the rightness of one's own conviction cannot justify such excesses; even Calvin later showed how for the sake of the unity of protestantism certain differences in doctrine may well be tolerated, without in any way abandoning one's own teaching. But even the example of Calvin makes it easier for us to understand Luther's stand; for he had the greatest horror of the political battle which Calvin directed with such skill. One can understand the course of affairs only in the context of this situation where Luther and Zwingli faced each other as the leaders of the two main groups of Protestantism.

FOUNDER OF THE EVANGELICAL CHURCHES

For a long time it had been shown that it was impossible (as we have already seen) to restrict the Gospel to the spheres of a battle purely of ideas. The extent to which countless worldly and particularly political interests depended on it had become clearer from year to year. After the foundation of the State Churches this fact gained its true prominence. And with this the political tension between the two religious parties increased in the same degree. Again and again confessional dispute began to destroy old political relationships: it dissolved the old community of interest between the city states, it reached out over the political borders of Switzerland, softened old feuds between princely houses of an Evangelical disposition, broke up political friendships of others, and began slowly to make itself felt in the religion of the European coalition—in short, it created a new political world overloaded with tensions. Luther's Gospel, which had been intended to release religion from its entanglement with earthly powers, had now been brought to the stage (this tragic contradiction confronts us again and again), when for the first time in the history of Europe since the days of Islam (and in a much more remarkable way than at that time), religion assumed a position of central importance in the political struggles of a whole century. The words of Jesus which Luther had so often used (what an ominous and yet unsuspecting prophecy!) found their literal fulfilment: 'I have come not to bring peace but to bring a sword.' New feuds produced new alliances. North and south of the Main the estates which remained true to the old faith began to unite; against them stood Philip of Hesse and the Elector of Saxony, who were soon joined by other north German princes; in the south the Evangelical imperial cities of Upper Swabia, in Switzerland the friends of Zwingli in the Christian Civic League under the leadership of Zürich stood against the Catholic alliance. Immediately these alliances became of immense actual importance. In the summer of 1529 Charles V had at last managed to safeguard his rear by treaties with the Pope and France, so that he could turn his attentions to fighting the hated German heresy and to asserting the supremacy of the Hapsburgs in the Empire. The long-awaited change in German fortunes seemed to be imminent; without armed resistance against the Emperor and the Empire which was supported by the majority of the estates, it would be impossible to withstand the forces of reaction any more or to save the work of the Reformation from destruction. If both parties were true to their intentions then there seemed no longer to be any way out; it must inevitably end in a war of religion.

What a prospect for Martin Luther! Where was he being led by his God, with whom he had wrestled in his monastery cell at Erfurt! Was this the end of the way on which he had then unsuspectingly embarked? In these months, it has been suggested, the most splendid of all his hymns was written: those verses on the 'sure stronghold' which are the pithiest and most virile in all German literature, and which have long since become a symbol of this whole human existence and even a national song of defiance. But it is again typical of Luther that we should not (according to the results of recent research) think of them as trumpets of war: they were most probably composed on the death of an evangelical martyr as early as 1527. For that is how he felt: he sang the hero not of a political struggle but of a spiritual one. His true mood in all the political confusion of these years is far better shown by the fine saying when he was at the Coburg in 1530: 'When I looked out of the window I saw the stars in the heavens and the whole beautiful vault of God, and could nowhere see any pillar on which the master could have set such a vault; and yet the heavens did not fall down and the vault is still secure.' In all the vicissitudes of politics he remained unchangeable; and nothing was further from his thoughts than to support the vault of his heaven on the pillars of earthly might. He could not and would not see that,

FOUNDER OF THE EVANGELICAL CHURCHES

independently of himself, the fate of his own Church had become inextricably entangled with the fate of the German states; that the only choice left now was either to fight with all the tools of political force for the preservation of the new doctrine and its ecclesiastical organisation, or else to perish. Wherever possible he had thrown himself against the policy of revolt against the imperial authority—for that was how he saw it—even against the very policy of alliances and military agreements in itself, with the clear foresight that if it was carried to its logical conclusion it would one day lead to 'unspeakable murder and misery'. 'How could one's conscience bear such a thing! The devil would delight in such a game, but may God preserve us from it!' At this point the real greatness of the man who remains true to himself to the last becomes clear, but so also do the limitations of his influence on the world. The only effect of his warnings was to make the politics of the Lutherans internally uncertain, to rob them of their good conscience and to hamstring their powers of action, without in any way averting the disaster. He is not without his share of the blame for the tragic outcome of the Schmalkaldic war. It is here that we can see most clearly where he differed from Zwingli.

Their meeting in the castle at Marburg (October 1529) was the meeting of two foreign worlds. Zwingli, the true civic republican in the Swiss manner, with that remarkable mixture of the narrowness of outlook of the small state, and international perspective, which attaches itself so easily to politicians of the Swiss confederation, lived and moved in the world of politics, and spun thousands of plans, great and small, for the salvation of the Gospel from Rome and the Hapsburgs. Only just before, the evangelical princes and the cities from Upper Swabia had for the first time formed an alliance against the threatening forces of reaction. Now Philip of Hesse and Zwingli were planning to enlarge the League by the addition of the Swiss protestant city-states, and further of Venice and many of the north German and Danish territories. Glowing with zeal they had painted themselves a fantastic enough picture of the new buffer of Protestant powers which would stretch from coast to coast. The agreement on the question of the Lord's Supper was intended to facilitate the forming of a general Protestant alliance: the theological discussions were entirely subservient to their political aims. A remarkable discussion! Everything seemed to be hinged on the theological formulations, whereas in fact, the two leaders of Protestantism were fighting each other for the dominating influence on the new Church. Who would determine the spirit of the new Church and who would take over the political leadership? Only Zwingli was prepared to form a purely political alliance without absolute agreement on the theological issues, and he was virtually driven to this by the danger of his isolated cities, which as it seemed, at least for the time, were most immediately threatened by the Hapsburgs. He had good reason to burst into tears when the attempt at unification failed. Yet he could never have considered the possibility of submitting to Luther's ideas. Such weakness would have cost him his political position in Switzerland; he even refused to accept a formulation which was outwardly much more moderate, although still essentially Lutheran, to which Luther allowed himself to be persuaded in private consultations in the last few days. Only later after his death did it become important. If the alliance had succeeded he would certainly have devoted all his efforts to dominating it. For what else could he have done? Would it have been possible to carry through what he was planning, namely the powerful self-defence of the Protestant cause with all the weapons of the politician, if Luther had retained the leadership of the Germans? Luther himself did not indeed see through all the political plans of his opponent, but he could sense clearly enough that there was another spirit abroad there. Was it not inevitable that this energetic Swiss (whose strange dialect annoyed him for a start) with his cheerful openness and impudent self-confidence which won all the politicians over to his side, with his intelligent and somewhat sharp features which betrayed no sign of religious trials and temptations, was it not inevitable that this man should appear to him as the tempter sent to him from the Prince of this world, to drag his work into the immeasurable whirlpool of higher politics and thus into sure destruction? Did not his seductive arts become all the more dangerous, the nearer one came to a theological agreement? Even Luther sensed, as did all the participants, that a storm was gathering in Europe over the young plant of the Gospel: even he sensed the magic spell which was drawing all the Protestant estates, princes and cities alike, into the net of higher politics. Again and again the feeling must have overwhelmed him that he was sitting at the table with the emissary of Satan. He lifted up the velvet cloth on the table and wrote with powerful strokes in chalk the saying which was the shibboleth of his conviction: 'This is my body.' 'They can leave that saying as it is whether they like it or not.' He was not to be persuaded, for he did not want to be persuaded. Long before the meeting at Marburg the Wittenbergers had regretted the first Protestant alliance of Speyer; Melanchthon for fear of the imperial wrath and in his human weakness; Luther because of his hatred of the 'sacramentalisers', 'the wanton enemies of God', and because in principle he rejected all fleshly alliances. We now know that shortly before the two theologians went to Marburg, the Elector of Saxony and the Margrave of Bayreuth had formed a secret alliance on the basis of a confession of faith, in fact the first evangelical one, which intentionally emphasised the Lutheran standpoint. It was intended to help break up the League of Speyer and perhaps also to insure that from the start they were running no risks with the discussions at Marburg. So the outcome of the discussions at Marburg was hardly in doubt even before they began. Luther would not allow himself to be tricked out of his leadership in any way; he treated the Swiss with all the imperious consciousness of his own religious superiority. A few years later Zwingli's political career ended in disaster and he sealed his fate with his heroic death on the battlefield; his opponent in Wittenberg, however, rejoiced that God had now judged the heretic and blasphemer as he had once judged Thomas Müntzer, and only regretted one thing: that the successful Catholic cantons had not immediately attended to the task of rooting out the heresy which he had sown. He was in no doubt that it had been none other than Satan himself who had been the loser in Switzerland.

Strangely enough, for the time he was right about all this. Once again peace was preserved in Germany: to all appearance 'without human agency', that is to say by virtue of new changes in the eternally uncertain fate of Europe. Zwingli's great plans for defence turned out to be nothing but an empty political bubble, and all the fears of the industrious Melanchthon and all his efforts to exorcise the danger by cleverly thought-out statements of reconciliation at the new Diet of Augsburg in 1530 were in vain.

It was at this point that Magister Philip, as the leading theologian of the Protestant estates, thought to gain acceptance for his own fainthearted policy of reconciliation, while the exiled Luther, who since 1521 had been under the imperial ban, did not dare to leave Saxony, where he was protected by his Elector, and was thus forced to remain in the fortress of Coburg, right on the extreme borders of the Saxon domains. The Lutherans should testify to their true faith, in the sense of the oldest and purest catholic traditions, before the Emperor and the Empire. And so their 'Augsburg Confession' (Confessio Augustana), which set out their doctrine of faith in detail in the form of separate theses, and which till today still holds as the foundation of dogma of all Lutheran churches, was made to appear as near to the old faith as possible, and moved markedly away from the 'sacramentalisers'. Every possible offer was made in the dis-

FOUNDER OF THE EVANGELICAL CHURCHES

cussions in order to come to an agreement and reconciliation with the representatives of the papal party. In the last event, of course, it was all in vain. The unification with the old Church failed as it was bound to fail, and yet the Reformation was again granted almost half a generation to develop undisturbed. All the enemies of the Hapsburgs, now France, now the Turk, played their part in averting the danger from it, and in the curious game of European politics there were moments when the Papacy, wedged between France and the Hapsburgs, secretly assisted the opposition of the Lutheran heretics against the Catholic Emperor; moments when the principles of the Renaissance, the politics of purely secular interests, broke through the system of confessional differences almost by force. But the process of the souring of all political life by the party hate of the various confessions could no longer be withstood. Least of all in Germany, where after the departure of the Swiss, the political unification of all the Protestants was eventually achieved in the Schmalkaldic League. Saxony assumed the leadership; the confession of faith of its theologians was taken as a basis for the alliance. But Luther did not play a determinative role in these affairs. The timid spirit of the Confessio Augustana was as foreign to him as was this whole world of political negotiations. He could not prevent it and so he left the matter to God, to his friends and to the lawyers, who tried to convince him that opposition to the Emperor was not revolution but a legitimate action in accordance with legal procedure. At all the Diets and at all the many religious discussions and attempts at reconciliation Melanchthon appeared in his stead: a delicate little man with the fine, thin face of an academic, a product of the study and by no means a happy figure on the stage of politics, as no one realised more deeply and painfully than himself. Yet he had made himself indispensable with his agility in theological debate in finding clear formulations for opposing theological points of view, and had thus become the true representative of the ecclesiastical policy of the Electorate of Saxony with its constantly uneasy conscience. Among the members of the league, above all in the Upper German cities, there now arose a vigorous new breed of theologians, which spiritually already stood on the shoulders of Luther. The perfect example of this type was Martin Butzer, a much experienced man from Alsace, a born diplomat and negotiator: the reformer of Strasbourg, the city on the border of the two nations which was then of more importance for the course of German history than ever before or since, and in whose council chamber the strands of political interest from all sides were intertwined. He was the confidant of the Landgrave Philip, the most active of all the Protestant princes, and the friend of John Calvin, in whom the particular qualities of these political theologians and theological politicians were united with a religious life of true original genius and depth, and who gave the Reformation a new direction which was of immense importance for the history of the world.

These were the men to whom the present and the immediate future belonged. Among them Martin Luther looks like a piece of the Middle Ages in another age. He was beset by an increasing feeling of inner loneliness, by sickness, and by a deep resentment at the course of affairs which ever remained a mystery to him. So he buried himself in the spiritual tasks which had always been dearest to him, and to which, so he himself thought, he was best suited: the translation of the Bible into German, on whose constant revision and correction he spent an immeasurable amount of time and energy, the creation of a new evangelical service, of a new evangelical hymnody, of a new type of church music, and finally in his favourite work of all, the catechism for religious instruction in schools and in the home. He even took pains to continue his academic writing; and as the tutor of his students, as the counsellor of countless people and as the father confessor and pastor in particular of the Protestant princes, he daily accomplished a host of small tasks. The benefit of this work is greatest where Luther was most faithful to his mission. Once only did he seem to betray it, and that was in the unhappy bigamy of the Landgrave Philip of Hesse, in which he confused spiritual and secular law, responsibility before God and before men in a truly disastrous way. The Landgrave, one of the most important princely patrons of the Reformation, appealed in his (alleged) trials of conscience to Luther as his father confessor, and asked whether he could not take a noble young lady as his second wife in a secret marriage, since she refused to submit to him without a marriage ceremony. He based his appeal on the fact that otherwise (if his proper marriage were to break up) he would be in danger of falling into the sin of extra-marital intercourse, and had pointed to the double marriage of the Old Testament. Luther clearly honestly believed in the trials of conscience of the Landgrave (who in actual fact had committed adultery several times before) and so equally (with a biblical justification) gave his 'penitent' dispensation. But it was never more clearly shown how fatal any compromise with sinful reality would be for the religious rigorism which he preached, what calamities would be wrought by any compromise, no matter what theological sophistries were found to justify it. That Luther then tried to cover up the step, once it had been taken, for motives which the world neither could nor would understand, with 'a good, honest lie', only served to make matters worse. It is difficult to say which was worse: the moral or the directly political damage of this princely failure: in any case it decisively crippled the Protestant party at the moment when they were most sorely pressed by the Emperor. As a result of his bigamy the Landgrave came into contact with the punitive laws of the Empire and had to woo the Emperor's favour in order to avoid being deposed, which favour of course could only be had at a high political price: Philip had to break with his allies in the further negotiations of the imperial estates over the questions of faith and had to promise the Emperor that he would hinder their alliance with foreign powers. So the disastrous bigamy led to the first division of the evangelical party.

In this case, as in others, one can sense clearly the limitations of Luther's genius. It is not so much lack of worldly wisdom, which caused him to miscalculate so seriously (the worldly-wise but all too active Butzer was even more embarrassed by this match-making), but he lacked that calm calculation, that certain political intuition, without which it is not possible to take successful action in the world of secular affairs. The more difficult and incomprehensible the tasks were which fell to him as head of the Reformation movement, the more obvious did this become. Instead of assuming the confidence and assurance of a long-tried ruler, we see him becoming more and more passionate in his outbursts, more and more heated in his rage. The tone of his polemics does not become milder as he grows older, but more and more violent and uninhibited. Alongside his theological opponents there now emerged more and more strongly new enemies of the Gospel: Turks, heathens, Jews, Catholic potentates. On many occasions he worked as an 'army preacher'; he considered the war against the Turks to be a Christian duty—no longer a spiritual exercise, a crusade, but a secular undertaking for the protection of 'Christendom'; and he further considered the Emperor Charles to be the appointed leader of all the Western powers. He urged the Germans to throw their last energy into this battle—with a belligerent patriotism which would not allow itself to be outdone by the zeal of the Humanist propagandists. It is most remarkable to note the change in his attitude to the question of the Jews, and it is most characteristic of the older Luther. Before the Peasants' Revolt, in the period when his hopes were still high, he had still expected that the light of the refurbished Gospel would also attract the Jews and lead to countless conversions; for this reason he had urged people to 'treat them in a friendly way' and not with 'arrogance and contempt'. His disappointment now drove him to the extremes of bitterness. In his later writings, particularly in the notorious battle-cry 'Of the Jews and their Lies' (1543), which has since become the stock-in-trade of anti-Semitism, he unleashes against them a whole flood of popular hatred and evil rumours about their secret abominations. It is clear that as a foreign people they appeared to him to be repulsive and uncanny. Nevertheless his attitude was not determined by any racial political points of view (of which he had no knowledge), but by moral and religious considerations: as obstinate liars and enemies of Christ he wanted to impose exceptional laws on them. The authorities were forcefully to prevent their public services by destroying their synagogues and houses (as also happened in the case of heretics) and to restrain them from usury by dispossession and forced labour, indeed at best they should expel them from the land (which did happen in Saxony and Hesse). He did not want to compel them to believe in the Christian faith, 'for we must leave that to every individual's conscience'; nor did he give up hope that individual Jews might be converted to Christ and thus escape destruction; but as a whole the Jewish people stood under the wrath of God as a result of their religious obstinacy, and the Christian preacher believed that his rulers (and clearly in no way every private individual) are called to carry out the divine judgment on the damned. So one sees the Reformer at the end of his life assuming more and more the role of the wrathful prophet proclaiming the woes of the evil-doers of the world and announcing God's coming vengeance. He even assumes a more threatening tone with the rulers of this world and again and again pours out polemics against such powerful potentates as Duke George of Saxony, the Cardinal Archbishop Albrecht of Mainz, King Henry VIII of England, or 'against that Tom-fool', the bellicose Henry, Duke of Brunswick. He attained a last extreme of coarseness in his maliciously bitter pamphlet 'Against the Papacy at Rome, Fonnded by the Devil' (1545), with which the last echoes of his life's struggle die away; appended to them was a series of caricatures drawn by Cranach, on the 'Ass and Swine of a Pope', which Luther furnished with some extremely coarse and indeed lewd verses. That Luther could have written this on the eve of the Schmalkaldic war, with the intention thereby of coming to the aid of his Emperor against the renewed insults of the Papal Curia, shows once again only too tragically how little understanding this religious prophet had of the tactics of higher politics.

Undeniably all these later polemics bear the highly personal stamp of Luther's own nature and cannot simply be explained and justified by the boorishness of the times. For in them the wild, boundless anger of a warlike spirit finds expression. Yet whoever seeks to characterise Luther's later years in the light of this alone has failed to see the riches of his personality. For immediately behind the terrible anger, one finds, to one's constant surprise, the good-natured man who wants to be loved, the poetic spirit with its warm joy in everything beautiful, in all the fresh life in the woods and fields, in the garden and in the house; the intensely musical creator of the Evangelical hymn, seeking refreshment in singing and playing on the lute, and working on the rewriting of a German mass with astounding zeal and technical skill; and finally the father, friend and tutor of his children, whom he cares for lovingly and tenderly. There is a sickly form of hero-worship which has often romantically transfigured the characteristic sobriety of old German family-life with its unquestionable patriarchy and its over-emphasis on the woman's place in the home and presented it to modern German sensitivity in the form of sentimental pictures of families and saints. Yet now one can see clearly how the reformer could unfold for the first time, in the warmer atmosphere of his own household, the warm and homely side of his character, which would have withered away in the monk's cell; and one also sees how much this is a true part of all that is deep and beautiful in his rich personality. It is in just such a way that one can see right into the heart of his piety, which in fact penetrated the whole of his personality, lending everything a distinctive tone. Whoever listens to the sharp, unsophisticated yet penetrating conversation of the master at the round table in 'the Black Cloister' at Wittenberg, whoever follows him in his study, in Katie's garden, playing music with his friends, taking counsel with fellow preachers, in the pulpit, in the lecture hall and at the sick-bed, will again and again recognise the greatness of the man in the spontaneity and informality of his actions. Indeed he will not be able to rid himself of the impression that here a great soul was burning itself out in the fetters of triviality. His genius was of the kind that can only breathe freely and stretch out its wings on the heights of great historical developments, in the regions of the great storms, and which in the lowlands of monotonous daily routine, hemmed in by the blank and narrow walls of political realities, beats its wings like a trapped bird trying to escape. But even now there were moments of great historical importance, in which great fundamental decisions had to be taken; then once again he reached up to his full height before us, and in a trice all the others seemed like pitiful accessories beside the one great hero. He was at his most magnificent in the Coburg in 1530. While Melanchthon, nearly overcome by the weight of responsibility, was coming dangerously close to the borderline where he would have betrayed the Gospel in his Erasmic offers of reconciliation to the representatives of the old Church, Luther alone in his fortress looked up to heaven with a heart sure in the knowledge that God was on his side alone and that all the offers of compromise on the part of his opponents were nothing but lies and deceit. 'The One who lives in heaven laughs at you, and the Lord mocks you.' He stood as firm as a rock in the storm, while the others nearly lost heart.

'The way of the ungodly will perish. But it will endure for a long while yet. So be steadfast!' These are the words which at one time he wrote on the walls of his room in the castle for his own comfort. His steadfastness was rewarded. It happened as he had always prophesied: that all the power of this world could do nothing against the preaching of the pure Word. When, in Augsburg, the representatives of the Protestant estates were allowed to read the Evangelical confession of faith to the imperial assembly, and to the very same Emperor who had once sworn in Worms that he would stake everything, his crown and his life, in the attempt to root out this heresy, Luther had the sure feeling that 'the Gospel has been established.' Not entirely without the help of the sword, and yet in the majority of cases by peaceful means, one bulwark after another had been wrested from the Catholics in Germany over the last thirty years. Meissen, Saxony, the Electorate of Brandenburg, Anhalt, Pomerania, the Palatinate, Wurtemberg and Brunswick, and over and above that, many cities in all parts of the Empire; even in Bavaria and Austria and other no less spiritual dominions, the Evangelical message began to gain ground, and eventually it seemed as if even the Archdiocese of Cologne would become Evangelical. No matter how little Martin Luther understood the younger generation, they still flocked to him in large numbers. As he neared the end of his life it seemed as if, given a little more time, all Germany would be won over to the Gospel, as he had once hoped in his happiest days. 'The reign of the Pope has lost its glory; both his eyes have been put out.' Of course, he could still hear the roll of the drums recruiting for the imperial regiments, which were being raised for the fight against the heretics, and still hear the Spanish troops delivering the first blows on the Lower Rhine which heralded the outbreak of the great storm of war. Yet he was allowed to close his eyes (February 18th, 1546) just before the disaster broke over Germany, which had so long hung over his life like a dark cloud, and which had passed over so many times before that many had ceased to believe in it. If he had lived to see it, it would have deeply troubled his conscience; yet even this would not have cowed him. He gives his own testimony to this in his 'Warning to his dear Germans':

> If it should come to an outbreak of war, then my God and Lord Jesus Christ can save me and my people, just as he saved Lot at Sodom and as he saved me in the last revolt when I was more than once in the greatest danger of my body and life. And if he does not wish to save me, then let us give him praise and thanks. I have lived long enough and well deserve death, beginning at my baptism honestly to avenge my Lord Christ. After my death they will all feel the true Luther for the first time just as if I were now to be murdered in an uprising of the Baptists or the priests. Then I will take a whole crowd of bishops, priests and monks with me so they can say that Doctor Martin was brought to the grave by a great procession; for he is a great doctor above all bishops, priests and monks, and so they shall go with him to the grave so that men will sing and tell of it. And if they, the Papists, should feel like making a little pilgrimage together to their God of lies and murder in hell, whom they serve with their lies and murders, then I will go to my Lord Jesus Christ, whom I have served in truth and peace.

9. Luther's Historical Importance

But the battle-cry of the warrior was not Martin Luther's last word to the German people. If we look for the enduring and positive results of his life and particularly for what he has to say to us, then we must turn back to the reflections with which we began our study. The most general and permanent achievement of his life lies in his own personal secret: in his life with God and in the direct relationship of all his thinking and willing with him—in this particular respect, that with Luther everything which is external springs as it were automatically from a faith which bursts the bonds of the human imagination. It is in his simple religious insights that we find the true meaning of the man. The key to his ethics is his proclamation of the supremacy of the eternal, the law of God, over all human action, and his consequent rejection of ecclesiastical authority or of any considerations of man's own happiness. He strove constantly to establish the idea of man's direct, personal and inescapable responsibility to God firmly in men's consciousness until it completely dominated men's lives, so that they might experience again the release from the intolerable tensions which had been set up by casuistry and teleological ethics. He gave men a new vision of the exaltation of the human self, regardless of its limitations, of an exaltation which can only be experienced as a gift from God and which man can neither bring to pass nor truly understand. Just as a flame, once it has been lit, will warm and illuminate everything which comes close to it, so the true attitude of the heart in which eternal life beats strongly will transform and ennoble all outward action as it were automatically. It was this vision which inspired all his teaching on individual and social action. The development of this religious message was the true fruit of his literary work, and it owed its power to the fact that Luther's message did not derive from any personal opinion, but from the depths of his fundamental religious experience: from an experience which was indeed of a highly personal nature, but which was intended in no way to be individual, original or in any sense new, but rather a reliving, a faithful acceptance of the earliest Christian revelation. The West has indeed produced in plenty saints and founders of religious orders and of new ideals of piety and of new religious communities (from the Church Fathers to the days of the Pietists and beyond), in whom the purity of the religious impulse was certainly no less genuine than it was in the case of Martin Luther. Nor has it been lacking in reformers before, since or even then; bold men of great determination who were genuinely grieved by the ruins of the worldly Church grown cold in the grip of its hierarchy, and who created new forms of spiritual life—in part with more skill and outward success than the monk from Wittenberg. But not one of these penetrated so deeply into the heart of the message of primitive Christianity as he, and no one before had been able to transform Christian life so completely from within. So no one has as much right to the title of the renovator of Western Christianity as has Martin Luther. He, and no other, stands at the end of an age which is passing away, and at the beginning of a new religious epoch.

This is of infinitely greater significance than his negative achievements, infinitely greater than the destruction of the universal dominion of the Papacy. For this was only partially successful in spite of the misery which was inflicted on European humanity by a century of religious wars, in spite of the irreparable split in the German nation which must (though this is only partly justified) be laid to his charge. Since then the Roman

Catholic Church has shown a thousand times over that her power to come to the aid of men was by no means exhausted but merely slumbering. Admittedly, it required a man like Luther to rouse it by his attack and this is not the least of his historical achievements; but even many Protestants would be inclined to admit that the political form of Christian community which is the essence of the Catholic hierarchy and which Luther was so eager to destroy, does still have its particular, if limited, value in the world of today alongside the free preaching of the Word. Should we applaud the chorus of those Rationalists and religious neutrals who since the sixteenth century have seen the real achievement of our hero in the destruction of the 'medieval outlook' (by which they understand nothing but Christian dogma in its scholastic expression, which is then censored as 'dark' and mysterious); indeed in an (unconscious) victory over the Christian concept of God, according to the most recent discoveries? Whoever approaches him from this side will always be disappointed by him; for he did not destroy the world of ideas of the Middle Ages as a whole but the Rationalism of a much later age whose first modest forerunners in Erasmus, the enthusiasts and 'sacramentalisers', he persecuted with all the bitter hatred of a medieval heresy-hunter (although admittedly without his sword and fire). He transformed, purified, deepened and renewed the thought and sensitivity of the Middle Ages but he did not abolish them; it was others who came after him who undermined and destroyed them. Or should we fête him above all as the founder of Protestant church order? Our study has already shown over and over again how little we would touch the core of his being in this, how little we would show the ultimate significance of his work. His achievement would appear scanty beside that of the other reformers. For it was just the Lutheran state church which was always the weakest and most insignificant of all; it has never (except in Sweden) thrown off the traces of the oppressed and miserable world of the small German states in which it grew up. But just as Luther's weakness as an organiser was inseparably bound up with his greatest qualities, so it was with the Protestant churches. Even if their earthly appearance bears something of the character of a temporary structure, this appears to be the inevitable complement to its radical rejection of any claim to worldly power, which is an essential part of its character. No, the foundation of the German state church is by no means adequate to convey the significance of his historical achievement. Way above all confessional, ecclesiastical and national limitations, his religious message, in which we find the true fruits of his life's work, spread its influence for the remoulding of Western culture in all the great ferment of the sixteenth century. The world-wide effect of the Reformation far surpasses the spiritual horizon of even its founder himself. Without at first suspecting it and without later realising the extent of its possibilities, he had by his action helped to determine the spirit of a new epoch in history.

It is (or at any rate was) a widely accepted error to consider his work, the Reformation, as a part of a more general phenomenon, which we usually call the Renaissance of the West—that great spiritual movement which destroyed the veil, 'woven out of faith, prejudice and fancy', which lay on the 'dreaming, half-sleeping' minds of the Middle Ages (Burckhardt). However, the German Reformation was not merely part of the Renaissance, nor even a parallel phenomenon, but to a much greater extent it was its counterpart. It trundled along like an enormous block of stone flowing from the Middle Ages to the general secularisation of thought and sensitivity of the modern age. It was in fact the most powerful restraining influence on the tendency to distort and to sweep away the spirit of Christianity. It was Luther's real historical role to rekindle this spirit, this most valuable inheritance of the Middle Ages, and so to make it fruitful for the future history of Western civilisation. Even the rekindling of medieval piety which shortly afterwards began to spread across the whole of the West from Spain in the age of the Catholic Counter-Reformation would not have achieved its universal importance without his action. The old Church had first to be shaken to its very foundations by the falling away of the Germanic peoples, before the way was made clear for the spirits which even there had long been active under the cover of the hierarchical tradition. Renaissance, Reformation and Catholic Restoration—these were from now on the three great spiritual forces whose conflict gave birth to the modern world, by whose tensions the spirit of the modern national cultures was everywhere, and everywhere quite differently, determined.

Yet, if we should seek to calculate the significance of the spiritual heritage of Luther as an active agent in this process of development and ferment, or to discover the ways by which ideas and tendencies of Lutheran origin have continued to bear influence on the many ramifications of modern culture within Germany and far beyond its borders, and with what success, then we shall find ourselves dealing with highly controversial questions, towards whose serious solution only the very first tentative steps have been taken. Our chief concern is to approach the question from the side which is easiest of access for us as Germans; we shall be able to see Martin Luther's importance for the world most easily reflected in our own example; indeed it was in Germany that his work came nearest to having its desired effect; and it is surely true that in his whole manner and character he is far more easily accessible and familiar to us than to other peoples, simply because we can feel that he belongs to us as a German. There was a time when our young students used to fête him with overwhelming enthusiasm as a 'German hero', as the ideal of German manhood—those youths who went off to fight in the war of liberation against Napoleon and who returned home with high ideals of a new, free, unified, but also devout, Germany, liberated from the false faith of the Italians. Today we have moved far from the excesses of early German nationalism; yet why should this prevent us from recognising certain characteristic traits of the German national character with its strength, its weaknesses and dangers, in Martin Luther?

It is only since the time of the Reformation that German spiritual life has begun to assume certain clearly recognisable traits of its own. The medieval man and Christian, as we saw, was always in a certain sense a European. It was the age of the religious wars which first gave the modern nations their sharply defined characteristics, and it is one of the most tragic facts of German history that the nation should have been split in two by the confessional struggle. Yet German Rationalism and German Idealism both attempted to tone down the differences and to do away with them. Who would deny that they have extensively influenced the spiritual disposition of even the Catholic part of our nation? And who would deny that their spiritual home was in Protestant Germany? So it is not in the least to disregard our Catholic fellow-countrymen if we attempt to understand ourselves in the light of Martin Luther's character. We will be concerned with very natural things. In what form and pattern did he bring up his people? For centuries every family in Protestant Germany went daily or at least every Sunday to church, where the deep and rich thoughts of the Reformer, which were offered in his book of sermons, were preached from the pulpit either in his original words or else in a thousand attenuated and varied forms. There they sang his vigorous tunes and the heroic verses of his hymns, from which the German people has from generation to generation in its recurring tribulations drawn new comfort and courage to hope and to stand fast:

And should it last throughout the night
And still be there at daybreak,

> Yet will my heart in God's great might
> Its courage ever take.

Then, not infrequently, the head of the family would question the children and the servants on the Little Catechism: 'that the old Adam in us should, by daily remorse and penance, be drowned and should die with all his sins and evil lusts'. Finally, in every house there was Luther's Bible, whose sayings, in his deeply poetic translation, became a real part of our national heritage, and whose incomparably sonorous tones are re-echoed in the language of our greatest poets; and none of its books had more impact than the one which is translated in the most typically Lutheran way, the Psalms, in whose trembling and yet heroic trust in God he found his own spiritual life most truly reflected (and it is surely no mere chance that his academic lectures on the Bible dealt with this book remarkably frequently!). 'Whither shall I go from thy spirit and whither shall I flee from thy presence? If I ascend up into heaven thou art there: if I make my bed in hell, behold thou art there also. If I take the wings of the morning and dwell in the uttermost parts of the sea, even there shall thy hand lead me and thy right hand shall hold me.' Could it be otherwise than that this enormous educational programme which was undertaken by the new Church and which extended into every sphere of daily life and work, illuminating them in the light of moral considerations, should have gradually been infused into the blood of the whole nation and have become a permanent leavening in its nature? The more the mere presentation of the sacramental means of grace retreated in the Lutheran Church, by contrast with the medieval Church, behind the infinite and the religious and moral claim on every individual, the more intensive became its spiritual effect. Luther himself was at times surprised at the new spirit of the youth, which was growing up under his eyes. Of course, he was as unable to leave behind a fully competent heir to his spirit, as was any other of the great men of our people: but however little his followers may have understood the true and genuine Luther with their strict orthodoxy, and however certainly it involved a serious relapse into the theological scholasticism of the late Middle Ages—even in the miserable form of this orthodox Lutheranism there still lived on enough of his spirit, to carry on his work as he would have wished. It is as if for centuries it had lived on underground and yet again and again forced its way up into the light in the most penetrating minds in the history of German thought. It certainly did not happen as earlier generations liked to think—that is to say that the 'idealism' of our 'classical' period lay in the direct line of development of the Protestant tradition. It is one of the peculiarities of the history of German thought that its driving forces appear in a great number of combinations; yet at bottom they are all remarkably closely interconnected. This is brought out most clearly in the peculiar form of *Gesinnungesethik* which was Immanuel Kant's and in his theory of radical evil which—without being actually Lutheran—is not conceivable except as a product of the Protestant spirit. Even in the philosophy of Fichte and Hegel, which has been called the philosophy of pure inwardness, one can detect a certain relationship in spite of all its pantheistic and intellectualistic traits. But the deep-rooted influence of the Lutheran spirit is not confined to philosophical thought; it fertilised the widest areas of spiritual life, to a far greater extent than the thinkers and writers of our nation themselves realised. Whenever our culture was submerged under a wave of West European thought—in the nationalism and humanitarian ideals of the Age of Enlightenment, in the economic theories, the scientifically orientated positivism and empiricism, and the socialistic ideas of universal happiness of the nineteenth century—again and again one sees the German spirit taking up its stand against these intrusions and tirelessly renewing the attempt to interpret the foreign ideas in terms of Luther's ethic, to maintain the unconditionality of the moral demand against all the attacks of mechanistic theories of world enlightenment and against eudemonistic moral theories which would seek to establish material welfare, happiness and utility as the highest good in moral actions. In these exchanges it indeed becomes most clear to how great an extent the history of German thought and culture rests on the foundations of the Reformation teaching and through this on the Christian heritage of the Middle Ages. In recent times there has been a great deal of discussion whether Martin Luther belongs to the Middle Ages or to 'the modern world'. It seems more important to us to ask the question whether we ourselves belong, or want to belong, to the modern world—if by the modern world one means the spirit of an un-Christian world.

Looked at historically the great process of secularisation of European culture has occurred in two ways: in the world of the spirit by means of a slow dwindling of conviction in the Christian faith, which passed through the intermediary (or hybrid) stage of a Christian Humanism, of a belief in the power of human reason; in the sphere of political and social reality in such a way that the purely natural desire for power and recognition of the ruler and later of whole nations, burst all bonds which at the end of the Middle Ages still remained from the traditions of the community of peoples of the Christian West, and of Christian social ethics. In both instances it was a case of a world-view breaking through which took man as its starting point rather than God, and which either denied the existence of God or else banished him to the periphery of human consciousness. The full effect of this process of secularisation on practical life was not felt in its full force as long as those spiritual cross-breeds of a Christian Humanist culture still represented an active spiritual force and still kept the demonism of the struggle for political and social power within certain bounds. The final collapse of all these humanitarian compromises sets the seal on the dangers of our present cultural crisis; for now our primary concern is with the future of Christianity itself.

Luther himself only lived to see the very first beginnings of this great process of secularisation: in the person of Erasmus, the Renaissance theologian, in whom the great movement of Christian Humanism in the sixteenth century reached its first peak. But with his sure instinct he sensed that here for the first time he was dealing with an opponent whose polemic (in the 'diatribe on the free will') was of greater significance than the usual defensive action of the Catholic apologetes: that Erasmus 'has finally discovered the nerve of the whole affair and wants to have his opponent by the throat in this fight'. As we follow the actions of the Reformer as he makes his stand against this apostle of Christian Humanism, we become for the first time fully aware of the historical importance of Luther as the (at any rate up till the present) last great prophetic figure for Western Christianity.

What separates Christian Humanism from Luther is at heart a different concept of man and a different concept of God. Humanitarian thinking means respect for the natural dignity of man. Man is not evil by nature, but originally inclined to do good, and intended for good; a social and not an asocial being. Even if this original goodness has been darkened by his deserved and inherited sinfulness, yet it is still present at the very heart of his being and only needs to be reawoken (Renaissance). Since, in fact, the really spiritual part of man, which wars against his fleshly nature and exalts and transforms him, is his reason (as Plato had taught), then the really important thing is that he should be made aware, through his reason, of his higher purpose; that one should preach a moral idealism which brings out the contrast between the shining light of the pure idea, of the world of the beautiful and the good, and the obscurity of the sensual passions. By such an insight man will become pure and ennobled, since his will is in the last instance always governed by his insight. The human will did not lose its freedom of choice between good and evil either by the Fall or by Original Sin; for what then would be the point of the preaching of morals, which occurs so often in Scripture ? What is good, true and beautiful had already been taught by the great thinkers of antiquity; the teaching of Jesus only confirmed, deepened and intensified this teaching. Above all it is the natural virtues of companionship, conciliation, love for one's fellows, which we learn in Christ's Sermon on the Mount. They are realised in the institutions of human society, from the family to the state, which have already been prefigured in certain basic institutions of nature, and which are thus in some way present in the consciousness of all men as the content of a natural law. So one must only appeal to the true nature of man, to its natural conscience, and human society will assume the form of that same well-ordered cosmos, which is the true form of all nature. But God is the highest reason in the world. He rules it according to the same rational laws of goodness, justice and wisdom, which we can also find in our own spirit; indeed our own spirit is nothing but the reflected splendour and glory of the divine spirit, and so our spirit can perceive the internal natural order of the world. The Christian faith is only an insight of the same kind as we find in the great pre-Christian thinkers, but one which has been heightened and intensified by the teachings of Christ. All in all a highly harmonious picture of the world. We may trust man because in his innermost being he is good and reasonable, and God because he rules the world in accordance with the same principles of the highest justice which he has also planted in our reason.

This harmonious system of thought is completely and utterly destroyed by Luther's theology. One can see clearly how Erasmus's understanding of the world develops from his understanding of human nature and human reason, and how on the other hand his understanding of God is nothing but a translation of human ideals into the realm of the transcendent. Luther takes an exactly opposed position. 'If it is true that God by his eternal and unshakable counsel and will has foreseen everything and creates and brings everything to pass, then this thunderbolt brings free-will crashing down, and dashes it to pieces.' Luther knows nothing of the free power of disposition of the human reason over the free human will. The will of man is indeed not at all free but either possessed by God or by Satan—and really 'possessed' like a horse which is ridden by God or by Satan. 'He is a means between God and the Devil and allows himself to be ridden, led or driven like a horse or any other beast.' In all this he is never 'free or in control of himself, to choose which of the two he will run to and hold to; but the two strong men fight and struggle between themselves about who shall possess him.' The earthly world is not a harmonically ordered cosmos ruled by human reason, it is not a sunny carpet of flowers, like a Renaissance garden, as the humanists imagined it to be, nor is it a dark vale of tears and sorrow as the radical fanatics thought. It is the arena of a constant struggle between God and Satan, in which man, like Faust in the play, is torn hither and thither between the two. In the end, of course, everything, both the devil and evil, must be subjected to God. But for the reason that nothing can happen, not even the most insignificant thing, without God's foreknowledge and predestination, it is impossible to speak of the freedom of the human will in any metaphysical sense (i.e. 'freedom from God and freedom in matters which concern salvation and damnation'), but only in matters which are 'among men', i.e. which in the realm of morally neutral decisions of the will are subordinated to man's free power of disposition; but even here in the last instance, God makes his influence felt in all matters. What sort of God would it be whose decisions did not hold sway unchangeably and from all eternity, over things both great and small? What should we think of a foresight which did not foresee absolutely everything, including the tiny scrap of life which makes up one's existence, and in whose promises one would therefore not be able to put any trust? It is not we who choose God, but God who chooses us. If we want to take this power of election away from God, 'then God becomes nothing but an idol or one of those inconstant gods, such as the heathen called Chance or Fortune, with whom everything happens without following any particular counsel or design.' He becomes simply a God of the world to come, purely a 'prime mover' in Aristotle's sense of the word and indeed of all deistic believers in God till this day: a God who has set the world in motion but has then really left it to look after itself, looking on, at any rate in time of need, with the best of intentions and care, as the watchmaker looks at a watch. He refuses to reveal to men whether they will be blessed or damned, and yet will not fight for them himself, 'and has perhaps gone off to the land of the Moors for a drink, as Homer writes of Jupiter'. No, the matter is quite different: 'God is not sleeping or snoring,' as 'foolish reason' imagines, but 'does everything, acts, punishes and makes, is mightily present and fulfils everything powerfully in all creatures'—he is activity in its highest degree.

Luther thought out the idea of divine omnipotence to its extreme conclusion, to the abolition of the freedom of the human will. But in this way a rational understanding of the internal order of the world and its events becomes for the first time fully impossible. If God determines everything and causes everything, then how is it that the power of evil is so enormously great in the world? Why does he not prevent it? Why does God remain silent in the face of the most intolerable atrocities? Why does he not come down on them mightily with thunder? And why indeed does God harden the wicked (as is his way) by spurring them on in their wickedness, 'as the God who drives all creatures ceaselessly forward and who will not allow them to rest'? Does he not in this way himself become the originator of evil? How, then, can he threaten those who are possessed by Satan with his wrath, if they were from the beginning destined for damnation and were in no position to loose themselves from their fetters? Is this not the height of injustice? And is it not as unjust (adds Luther) if he has mercy on the sinners and rejects the just who have offered everything which lies in the compass of human virtue?

Yes indeed, comes the answer, for in the light of reason, God in his goodness, just as much as in his wrath, appears at his 'hardest and most tyrannical and seems to take pleasure in our misery, even though he could help us, were we so inclined'. Luther himself experienced these doubts as deeply as any man, till it brought him to the point of despair. Yet it is really so:

> The Lord God acts and rules in external matters in this world in such a way that if one were to look at it and judge it in the light of reason one would have to say either that there was no God, or else that there was an unjust God; as the poet said: 'I am often tempted to believe that there is a God.' If one considers how deeply God hides himself behind the events of world history, how apparently senselessly he allows one kingdom after another to be brought crashing down, then to be built up again, how all earthly fame dies emptily away, then it must often seem as if the history of the world were nothing but 'God's Punch and Judy show', his own tournament where everybody is having at one another, and where the only thing which goes is: who's down, is down and who's up, is up. . . .

Of course one sees from time to time how God raises up a great and worthy hero, a 'wonderman' with remarkable gifts, who brings back the sick world to order with his hard tyrannical fist, who champions right and sweeps away all that is rotten and builds it up anew; but in general the world is nothing but 'beggary and confusion', and it is impossible to distinguish any design or plan in the whole; we cannot penetrate the demonic twilight of this world's history. And more still: is it not the dreadful experience of all believers at all times, that injustice all too often triumphs while righteousness and piety are overthrown; is it not the relentless course of the world that again and again the good and the noble is destroyed by the physical supremacy of the masses—that even the greatest nobility of character is no protection against crass and senseless destruction? 'For this reason even the finest people, who have been endowed with the highest and most excellent reason, have come to grief at this point and have been led to say that there is no God and that everything is a matter of luck, just as things turn out; and we have to be contented with whatever chance brings us.' So the humanists spoke of the blind choice of fortune. The Deists, however, dreamed up a highest being which enjoys its blessedness far away in a quite different world from that of earthly history.

Once again as at the beginning of our story we stand face to face with the ultimate secret of Lutheran piety. It is the point at which even today men's minds are divided. How many countless explanations has man dreamed up in his attempt to unveil this mysteriously menacing riddle, or at least to draw its sting to some extent? How can the omnipotence of a good God be reconciled with the enormous superiority of the forces of evil in the world? Why is the way of mankind enveloped in such a terrifying darkness, if the glory of an immaculately pure light is shining down from eternity? Thomas Aquinas had attempted to relieve this darkness a little by finding in every man's spirit a small flicker of eternal light in spite of all that evil had done to obscure it, and by seeing that the world was already on the path from chaos to the well-ordered cosmos. Philip Melanchthon, after Luther's death, had in a private letter declared the latter's doctrine of the complete bondage of the human will and of the divine predestination even of evil, to be blasphemous;

his faith could only see the good God, the Father of the Gospels; had refused to look at the dark chasms of the hidden God and found consolation for the wickedness of man in the possibility of his education through the preaching of the faith; for faith, instead of revealing the moral impotence of man, as with Luther, effected his moral perfection. Later on, as Protestantism began to become more and more secularised, its philosophers devised all sorts of systems to show that the meaninglessness of world history was not without meaning, so that they could then go on to prove the existence of an all-mighty world reason. These efforts doubtless sprang from a need which is grounded in the innermost nature of man; from the longing of our spirit for a rational understanding of the nature of the world and from the desire to build up our social and spiritual environment on the basis of such a rational order. So the greatest systems of rational metaphysics and of 'natural law', in which the modern, late and post-Christian mind believed to have grasped the meaning of this world, do without doubt have their place among the greatest creations of Western thought, indeed of Western Christian civilisation. They rapidly outstripped the optimistic moralism of Erasmus. At the end, and indeed at the climax, of this secularisation of Western philosophy, Hegel discovered the 'self-realisation of Reason' as the ultimate content of world history; the dialectic process by which it is brought about needs evil as a counter-weight to good, in order to keep the process of development continuously in movement by the 'cunning of reason'. The idealistic view of history which arose from this takes account of the tragic shadows of history in the eternal conflict of 'Ideal and Reality'; but it passes over this by fixing its attention only on the lofty goal, on the most sublime phenomena, on the truly spiritual forces in human history, and by seeing these as its true content.

But what man who had been thrown into complete dismay by the senseless destruction of all that is most noble, by the blind rage of earthly battles, and by the demonic possession of the human race, and who had felt their consequences directly in his own life, could ever be seriously satisfied with these attempts at consolation? The question about the meaning of history and of world events in general becomes more and more obscure, the more seriously and ruthlessly man struggles to free himself from beautiful illusions. Luther can only point to one answer: 'Nay, but O man who art thou, that repliest against God?' (Romans 9, 20). 'God's mysterious will is not to be explored, but rather to be worshipped in fear and trembling as a deep and sacred mystery of his high majesty.' Who gives you the right to judge God by your own righteousness? In other words, how do you presume to speculate about the sense or nonsense of God's government of the world, when you do not understand the ultimate purpose of his Will? How can you dare to contradict him, because his actions do not please your human reason? 'If God's will was subject to standards or rules, laws, causes and origins, it would no longer be God's will.' Is God then a God of pure caprice, as the Nominalists saw him? By no means! The only standards which are referred to here are ones which have been imposed by men. 'If this justice were of such a kind that one could comprehend through our reason that it was just, then it would not be divine and there would be no difference between the justice of men and the justice of God.' So it must remain an unexplorable mystery. We have no right to argue about it; it has no need to justify itself to us.

Is God's will then like blind fate which pays no regard to what is just or unjust—and to which we must blindly submit ourselves? Luther does indeed again and again have recourse to the pre-Christian belief in the Fates, in the inescapable Fate of the heathen, whose superior power over even the best and strongest human will was confirmed by 'natural reason'. He names Virgil as witness to the power of this Fate even over the gods themselves, names the Parcae of the Greeks, whose strands of fate cannot be broken by any effort of the human will. More recently we have also been reminded of the belief in Fate of the early Germanic period, which Luther is said to have renewed in his own way; his fearless searching in the chasm of the irrational, by contrast with the nature of Roman Catholicism, which everywhere longs for rational clarity and order in its view of the world; the heroic will which cannot accept a comfortable seclusion in a clearly observable view of the world as its highest aim, and which seeks to overcome Fate by a cry of defiance in face of its incomprehensibility and inevitability; the cry of the tragic hero who believes that he has won fame and victory by inwardly affirming the inevitable and making the alien will of Fate into the object of his own free will. Indeed even Luther knows of such a cry. But it is the cry of the Psalmist: 'Nevertheless I am continually with thee: thou hast holden me by my right hand. Thou shalt guide me with thy counsel and afterward receive me to glory. Whom have I in heaven but thee ? and there is none upon earth that I desire beside thee. My flesh and my heart faileth: but God is the strength of my heart and my portion for ever.' The overwhelming and inevitable will to which the Lutheran Christian abandons himself is not, however, the blind Fate of the pre-Christian world. Luther knows it as the will of the merciful God, who seeks our eternal salvation in spite of the outward appearances of the darkest tragedy. The hidden God (no matter how it may seem to human reason) is the merciful God, the same who like a father shows mercy, not only to the sinner, but to all living creatures. *Once only* in the middle of the mysterious twilight of world history a bright clear light shone out: on that Christmas evening when the true nature of the hidden God was revealed to men in the son who was sent to all the world: a revelation which was really contrary to all reason! Admittedly this was a revelation of wrath as well as of love, which brought as much terror and destruction as it brought blessedness; for it was the revelation of the cross which precedes the resurrection. Man was to encounter this Christian God not as he encountered that Fate of the pre-Christian world, in dull submission to the unchangeable, or even with the proud gesture of the heroic warrior, who throws away his life in order to fulfil his destiny and so to win earthly fame. The boundless, humbly trembling prostration which befits this God is (paradoxically) a boundless trust; it leads to a fellowship which allows one to triumph over death and the devil and all human wickedness. In this fellowship man's selfishness disappears and with it his conceit. But in its place he is now driven on by an incomparably stronger will: 'One can see from practical experience how Christians and saints stand like iron walls, if one tries to force them to do anything else; indeed it only makes them happier, braver and more defiant; just like a fire, which the more the wind blows against it, only burns more brightly.'

Luther's heroic piety was far removed from the weakly Cross and Comfort theology of later orthodox Lutherans and even farther from the attempts of Protestant rationalism to tame and water down his concept of God; his consolation never led to an isolationism which would forget the darkly threatening mystery of the hidden God in the purpose of grace of the revealed Christ. His faith always remained an extreme risk. It was not a faith based on intellectual certainty (as it was with Melanchthon), but a faith based on ignorance. Even the theology of the cross can give no rational solution to the ultimate riddle of the world. But whenever it takes the form not of a mere theology but of true belief, of true experience of fellowship with God, then we are presented with the possibility of not seeing, and yet believing. Then the will is released from the agony of its vain struggle, from the eternal uncertainty of conscience, from the crippling experience of human failure, by the certainty that in the last instance it is a mere tool in a stronger hand. The dilemma of the eternal contradiction between ideal and reality, between the moral consciousness of man and the demonism of the concrete events of the world, of all the riddles and senselessness of our earthly existence, then gives way to the prospect of a future 'Light of Glory', in which will be revealed all that in the 'Light of Nature' is still deeply hidden.

Thus the vision of the secrets of the other world should make it spiritually possible for us to stand fast in this world. But is this steadfastness purely a matter of patience, of the creature forgetting itself and reaching forward from darkness to light, of the Christian transcending himself in his yearning to be free of the endless and merciless struggles of this age and to rest in the peace of God for ever ? Luther was—as we have seen again and again—not the sort of saint who shuts himself off from the world, but a warrior of great strength, with an indefatigable, and indeed ever increasing zeal for the struggle. It was not to find rest or to escape from reality that he transcended the earthly world in his faith, but to seek new strength for his daily battle: it is as if he paused to take in a deep breath of purer air of eternity. Luther was surely one of the greatest men of prayer in the history of Christian piety; but even his prayer was not mystical; less a pious abandonment to God than a constant, often forceful and bold struggle with his God, to win new strength and certainty. His religious experience did not lead him out of the world but right into the very middle of the world. However powerfully he was from time to time beset by eschatological premonitions (certainly to a far greater extent than the average adherent of popular medieval Catholicism), he was as little deterred by the expectation of the coming end of the world from the task of working in this world for the victory of his Lord, and from founding a lasting community, as were the founders of the first Christian communities. The conscious paradox of Lutheran theology is pressed to its furthest extreme and at the same time to its most magnificent conclusion, in the new interpretation which Luther gives to the Augustinian doctrine of the two Kingdoms, the Kingdom of God and the Kingdom of the world; they do not form a gradual progression as in the teachings of the Scholastics, in which the Kingdom of Nature is transcended and transfigured by God, nor are they set loosely and unrelatedly alongside each other (as is for the most part incorrectly supposed today) as two divided realms whose mutual relationship remains undefined, but rather interpenetrate each other at every point. There is no place for the Christian outside this world—no quiet corner in a church where he can flee from his imprisonment in this earthly existence with all the turmoil of everyday life and with its conflicting duties; but on the other hand there is no sphere of ordinary everyday activity which, no matter how ordinary and insignificant it may seem, does not at every moment bring the Christian face to face with God, in order to give account of himself. For God is Lord of the whole world and cannot be served with adoration alone.

So the Lutheran Christian is set the infinite task, which cannot be settled by any ecclesiastical casuistry, indeed for which there can never be any absolutely sure solution, of himself testing his own Christianity in the world and of bringing the Christian spirit to bear on all forms of secular activity. Yet at the same time he is not free to moderate in any way the sternness of the divine command by adapting it cleverly to the natural way of the world or to political reality (in the manner of medieval Church politicians or even of Jesuit confessors at princely courts); nor on the other hand can he ever entertain the illusion that one can transcend the sinful and imperfect nature of all human endeavour and so create a truly 'Christian world', or even a 'Protestant culture' on a clearly religious basis. It is the very nature of this problem which presented Luther and his Church with its greatest difficulties. They form an essential and central part of the story of his life, and till this day Lutheranism has not freed itself from the internal and external trials which have ultimately resulted from the commission of the evangelical Church to act as the leaven of the Christian spirit in the world without any claim to a position of power as the centre of a Christian world-order. But the Catholic solution which presupposes a divinely willed cosmos of natural ' orders of creation ', and also a ' Christian natural law ', which the Church by virtue of its divine supremacy in the world proclaims and ordains—a cosmos in which human insight and divine revelation, nature and grace, are in a wonderful way brought into harmony with one another—this solution was quite unacceptable to Luther's way of thinking. He did not believe in a ' natural theology ' which could present the same claims to absolute truth as the revelation of scripture, and so for him the whole Christian humanist culture of High Scholasticism is deeply suspect. Behind every claim for the validity of Christian natural law he senses a new attempt by the ' Papists ' to prop up the building of its world dominion with ' walls of paper '—that unhappy mixture of the sacred and the profane, which was most deeply responsible for the internal decline of the Catholic world Church. For him there is no Christian system of culture, because the Church of Christ can make no claims to secular power and dominion; at the same time, one could not arrive at a worse misunderstanding of his position if one were to read into this a fundamental antagonism of Lutheran Christianity to secular culture. Neither the Pietists with their pious self-satisfaction which finds edification only in the contemplation of the sufferings of Christ, nor the belief in the acceptability to God of constant busying in ceremonial and pious works, nor even the arrogant contempt or resigned despair *vis-à-vis* the world and its many-sided attempts to create a culture (which one then abandons to its own devices), are in any way representative of Lutheranism. For Lutheranism, in contrast to Calvinism and Calvinistic Puritanism, never prescribed any particular form of sanctity or ' inner-worldly asceticism ', by which the Christian had to cut himself off from the life of this world. For this reason the spiritual life and the sciences, writing, art and music bore much richer and more varied fruits on Lutheran than on Calvinistic soil. If one inquires about the historical effect of religious teachings on cultural life then the German Reformation has no cause to fall into second place behind the Calvinists.

But of course the question of the relationship of the Lutheran reformation to the development of European culture is by no means fully answered by such general considerations. Was it not Luther above all who preached in the baldest manner (by contrast with other reformers and above all with Ulrich Zwingli) a deep and fundamental mistrust of human reason? Would not this mistrust have to a very large extent the effect of crippling the development of culture? If all earthly activities, even including the most noble creations of the human spirit, are nothing more than an empty semblance of reality, in the sight of God, and if in the last instance they all stand under his wrath and judgement, what is the point of such enormous efforts? Indeed there was a form of orthodox Lutheranism (and Calvinism), in the past as well as the present, which was inclined to draw such premature conclusions: a 'theology of crisis' which either in despairing resignation, or else out of a feeling of superiority, turned (or seemed to turn) away from any moral duty to help in the great tasks of forming the mode of human existence. One cannot say often and clearly enough that this is in no way the true attitude of the reformers. Luther's mistrust is not directed indiscriminately at human reason, but against its claim to be able of itself to discover the ultimate meaning of the world and the secrets of God: above all he disputes its ability to establish of itself, i.e. without the Law and Gospel of God, without the total renewal of man in his encounter with God, a really enduring form of culture—a culture which like the mere humanity of unrealistic ideologies like that of Erasmus, could from one day to another be reduced to ruins by the stirrings of those demonic passions of the deeps, by the onslaught of those satanic powers of human desire for power and domination, which lie only too close to the surface of the cultural existence of civilised humanity.

Seen in this light Luther's theology is not a high-flown theology of crisis but a very sober theology of reality. He never had any illusions about the natural goodness of man; yet the relationship between the Lutheran Christian and fallen man is not to be governed by hatred or contempt but by the purest attitude of love, the attitude of the Sermon on the Mount. This again leads to new internal tensions which can be seen most clearly in Luther's social ethics and in particular in his thoughts about the Church and the State, the secular authority. They are as much determined by his central concept of God as any other Lutheran thinking; but again in this point Luther takes up a position which is radically opposed to the main stream of modern thought.

For it is the decisive mark of recent centuries in comparison with the Middle Ages, that the spiritual dominion of the Church is gradually undermined by the secular state. More and more the latter becomes the really decisive element in men's lives. This has much deeper causes than the destruction of the external forms of the papal world dominion by the Reformation. Long before Luther the political unity of Western Christianity had crumbled away into a system of national power states; and long before that, secular politics had assumed a quite different character. The demonism of power, which began to show itself in the struggle for power at the end of the Middle Ages —most brazenly in Renaissance Italy—was nothing but the expression of the purely natural and unsuppressible desire for recognition and influence of the fighting spirits in the world of politics, who had absolved themselves from the last ties of Christian morality. This by no means needed the blow of the Reformation against the authority of the Pope to set it in motion. However, this struggle for power no longer had the naïvety of the pre-Christian age; it was felt to be demonic because it was open revolt against the sanctity of the ideal of law, and a conscious emancipation from the traditions of the Middle Ages. It was out of the consciousness of this new and unheard-of development that the political theories of the Renaissance sprang up, which attempted to find rational principles to guide the blind caprice of the power lords and warriors. Machiavelli's political doctrine of nature interpreted this in the sense of a pure doctrine of intelligence, of pure technical skill in the use of power—even if it had the higher goal of a moral regeneration of decadent peoples by a system of State controls and by education in the use of arms and in the idea that it is the duty of all to stake their lives for the State. The political Utopia of Thomas More with its humanisation and domestication of politics attempted to tame men's lust for power by means of a new, rationalised, Christian Humanist morality in the manner of Erasmus's world-view. The one was directed towards the goal of the ideal rational but warlike power state, the other towards the dream of a fundamentally peaceful but equally rational welfare state. The one started with a picture of man with purely warlike characteristics, indeed in some ways more like a beast, the other with Erasmus's confidence (which we have already noted) in the basic goodness of human nature. The one sought to perfect the warrior, who ruthlessly destroys everything so that he can build it anew, the other sought a humanitarian sense of collective responsibility, and strict legality on which to base his peaceful society. Here the two basic types of modern political thought and modern ideas of the State are presented in literary form: and this in Luther's lifetime, one year before he posted his theses.

Luther as theologian never developed his own political theory; indeed in his world of small German states he was unable even to gain an adequate idea of the modern power State. He had no concept of the State as autonomous in its power and in its laws, but only of secular authorities and their deputies, and even to these he speaks purely as a Christian pastor: 'We are not now teaching how a secular prince should live, but how a secular prince should be a Christian, that he too may go to heaven.' 'And so I have no law to prescribe to a prince, but only wish to teach his heart how it should be inclined and disposed in all laws, counsels, judgments and actions.' This is quite different from Calvin, who knew how to organise his band of Christian soldiers even outwardly into a type of spiritual storm troop, and who passed highly pertinent judgments on secular and political questions. Luther kept himself well within the bounds of a purely religious appeal to men's hearts, and feared nothing more (as we have repeatedly seen) than that it should become mixed with political motives. We know too well the political tribulations which this has brought on his Church; yet we do him grave injustice if we say that he left the political life of this world to its own devices and preached a 'double morality' of the Christian prince, as Christian and as Bearer of his office, thus opening wide the gate to every caprice of political lust for power in the style of Machiavelli. Of course he has no concept of a priestly supervision of secular politics, and the activity of the court confessors is equally foreign to Lutheranism. Like every other estate the office of the secular sword is freed from ecclesiastical casuistry and from priestly supervision; this in no way means that the ruling powers can become a law unto themselves with the right to overstep the bounds of the moral commandment whenever it becomes politically expedient. No theologian ever addressed himself more sharply, more ruthlessly and with less respect, to the conscience of political rulers than this peasant son; we have already heard him speak, and know how little inclined he was to bend the knee in adoration to the secular authorities or even to grace them with a bow. It is again a grave injustice if one makes him responsible for the rise of princely absolutism in Germany while in England a Calvinistic revolution—although to be sure a hundred years after Calvin—destroyed the absolutist monarchy and developed the basic tenets of modern liberal political theory. After the First World War men attempted with such comparisons to prove to us the superiority of Calvinism over Lutheranism, which was reproached with having brought up its members as blindly obedient subjects without any political sense. After the catastrophe of 1945 these attacks were redoubled. Yet, for all that, they contained only a half-truth. It is true that the whole range of democratic ideas was completely foreign to the peasant son Luther, just as it was to the whole of the Thurungian and Saxon world around him; they are the product of a later time and of the culture of the west European cities. (The old feudal right of resistance of the Germanic vassals had long been in decline at the courts of the German princes.) But as such the Lutheran and biblical preaching of obedience (according to Romans 13) has nothing to do with any one particular form of state but only lays down the first and most general basic principle of all political authority as against anarchy and chaos. For the rest the princely absolutism was the necessary transitional form on the way from the declining feudal state of the late Middle Ages to the modern nation state; it became established in nearly the whole of Europe, in Catholic territories as in Evangelical ones, and reached its classic fulfilment not on Lutheran soil but in the form of the incense-filled godlike monarchy of the courts of the Catholic princes in the age of the Baroque. In the painstaking process of development which long after the time of the Reformation led to the founding of liberal and democratic states on West European soil, the political opposition of the Calvinist churches—and to a far greater extent of the sects!—was only one of the many contributive factors.

What then was the content of the Lutheran teaching to the princes and to the authorities? It is not directed towards their political actions (as we have already heard), but exclusively towards the attitudes which govern them. Just as there is no particular form of Christian action, nor is there any particular form of Christian politics. To be a Christian does not mean to act in this way or that, but means placing all one's actions before God. It means acting in the consciousness of one's constant responsibility before God, and acting for God's sake, not for the glory of men or for one's own glory—not to please men but to please God; acting out of that great and free love of God which we have already seen to be the true centre of 'the freedom of a Christian man' and which alone can make our actions truly spiritual. It is in this that the Lutheran Christian doctrine of authority differs most radically from the political concepts of the Renaissance: it alone contains the concept of a truly responsible statesmanlike action, because it alone sets a highest and inescapable authority over the rulers of the State, to whom they will all have to answer. The possession of power is not the enjoyment of power, but service; it is the commission of the Almighty to the strong men of this age. The prince is God's official—this old Christian doctrine is brought home to the rulers of this world with greater point and vigour. His task is never to look after his own interests, ' but only to help dispense law and order, that the wicked may be held in check'. But what is lawful in every individual case is not a matter for theological doctrine, and cannot always be found in books—either the Bible or the law-books—but is a matter for the natural conscience which is active in every man: a conscience which as 'natural law' is to be found even in non-Christians (even if it is often very much more pale and uncertain) and whose content is determined by the clear pronouncement of the biblical ten commandments, and the commandments of love and equity of the Sermon on the Mount which are so closely connected with them. 'For nature teaches, as does love, that I should do what I would have people do to me.' To act unselfishly and not out of self-interest, conscious at every moment of one's responsibility before God, that is without puffing oneself up, always ready to do penance—this is the true meaning of Christian ethics, which should guide the Christian prince in all his actions.

Luther is himself perfectly well aware that such demands can be fulfilled only where the Christian prince is filled with the true Christian faith and the true love of God, and that they stand contrary to the greatest passions in the history of man, that is to the natural ambition and desire for power of the politically strong and mighty. He knows that the expectation that they 'should withstand evil', not in their own interests, but in the interest of others, that they should never 'seek unlawful gain' nor use the power of the sword with the intention of serving their own interests, but in order to punish evil, 'is a strangely dangerous thing': that it almost involves a paradox. For he too knows the uncomfortably strong temptations of power. Again and again he stresses that politics is a dangerous trade and that a Christian prince is a 'rare beast in heaven'. But this in no way gives him cause to abandon the struggle against the demonic forces of political passions. He stands firm in the opinion that irresponsible action is a work of the devil in the eyes of God and he remains as far removed as possible from the purely amoral admiration of the modern world as such for the greatness of its boundless striving for power, and for its mastery of physical matter and intellect. 'Cursed and damned is all life which is lived and tasted for its own sake and for its own good, and cursed are all works which do not lead to love.' In all seriousness he expected the Christian prince in his political actions to work only in the best interests of the State, and always to dispense faithfully the authority which had been committed to him; not to seek his own glory, or to act for 'the sake of his beautiful yellow hair'.

Is it then hopeless to attempt to establish a perfect welfare state, a Utopia in the style of Thomas More, in which love for one's fellow men and reason shall reign instead of power—or an enthusiastic belief in the reality of the kingdom of God and of eternal peace on this earth? By no means! Luther does not believe in the natural goodness of men, as do the Christian Humanists, who only need proper instruction so that they can then follow the guidance of their own reason. He knows men better. He knows that Satan rides them if they have not been rescued by the miracle of divine election and faith. Their selfishness is so great, their actual store of moral consciousness so small, the light of the natural conscience so uncertain, that they cannot be kept in order without the strictest use of force. True fellowship, which needs no compulsion, is only to be found in circles of the true disciples of Christ, who form a minority even in the visible Church, and are in the world a tiny lost group among the mass of apparent Christians and non-Christians. Any thought of building up this fellowship, this kingdom of the children of God, into a visible dominion over the world (after the manner of the medieval secular Church or even of the Calvanistic city of God) and of providing it with its own means of coercion would have been pure hypocrisy or fanaticism. 'World is world.' And for this reason God established the sword of the secular authorities as an office of the 'hangmen, jailers, judges, lords and princes'— 'so that the necessary force should not be despised or flag, or go under; for they neither can nor shall dispense with it'. This force needs the power of the sword to punish the wicked and to protect the good; and in particular circumstances it will also have to wage war in order to protect itself and its land in the struggle against other rulers. For a lord and a prince is not there for himself but for others, whom he has to serve, protect and defend. In such circumstances Luther urges them to be bold: 'then hold back no longer but set about it with a will, be men and look after your armour. For the time for fighting with ideas is now over and you will have your work cut out to file down the teeth of these proud, angry, defiant iron-eaters so that they can't even bite through fresh butter.' If the cause is just (and Luther makes this a necessary condition) then the war is fought in God's name. 'For then the hand which wields the sword is not the hand of man but the hand of God. And it is not man but God who hangs, racks, beheads, strangles and wages the war. It is all his work and judgment.'

One could not speak less cautiously in defence of the moral right of the power of the sword in the world particularly with the world as it is at the moment. But one must be careful to note that all this is only said of force in the service of the law in its strictest interpretation! It has nothing in common with the advocacy of the uncontrolled use of power. Rather one could bring the very opposite sort of criticism to bear, namely by asking how anyone who is so deeply convinced of the corruption of the human race can write a princely code for Christian rulers, in order to warn them against breaking the ten commandments and to impose on them a duty of the highest unselfishness? Could he not see like Machiavelli that only a knave can rule among knaves, or at least someone who is ready at any moment to play the knave? Had he no concept of the impossibility in foreign affairs of even discovering what actually is right? Indeed it was true that the Wittenberg professor had no idea of the true nature of the struggle for power between nations; how could he have had, in this world of petty German states? His pronouncements about 'just' and 'unjust' wars kept closely to the pattern of medieval doctrine which had been laid down by Augustine, and were probably augmented by his experience of the German feuds which were always partly a legal battle and partly a battle for power. His Christian prince is essentially presented as the father of the State, and restricted in the main to his internal governmental functions; but in these internal matters he can in no sense rule in an arbitrary way, as a mere jailer and despot. For the men whom he has under his care

are indeed all sinners in the eyes of God, but this does not mean to say, humanly speaking, that they are all rogues. The Lutheran Christian concept of men does indeed have a certain outward similarity with Machiavelli's, but it is nevertheless separated from it by an enormous gulf. Certainly selfishness, whether it is open or hidden, conscious or unconscious, is the basic motive of all human action; and man's natural reason is of itself powerless ever to master this original sin to such an extent that the sinner can be justified before God by his own moral efforts, no matter how sincere. For all human efforts pale into insignificance before the true holiness of God. This humbles the natural pride of man, but in no way releases him from the duty of listening to the voice of the natural conscience which God has set in him and whose message has been truly revealed by his clear commandments. This impulse towards the good is nowhere wanting either in Christians or in non-Christians; and this is the point of contact which is offered to the Christian ruler, law-giver and judge. In other words, natural man has fallen from grace; he is ruled by his own selfish impulses; but in all this he has not lost his moral consciousness; it only needs to be ordered, established and educated by the revealed commandment of God. Men are all sinners, but they are not beasts; they can be educated—never indeed to moral perfection, but yet to the point where instead of constant fighting there is an established form of law and order. If they could not have been educated Luther would never have founded a State Church but would have contented himself with a mere conventicle. The establishment of law and order, the protection of the good, the punishment of the wicked and the education of men into a law-abiding community is the task of the secular rulers. If they are Christian then they will also accept the Christian preaching and doctrine, will help to keep it pure, will found churches and schools and thus ensure that there is every opportunity for the Word of God to work among his people.

This in no way means that the 'great mass' of the people will be transformed into a community of saints; but much will have been achieved if a true community can grow out of the dull and irresponsive masses. For the rest it is the task of the sword to see that the good men do not fall victims to the godless.

For centuries the states of the Protestant princes of Germany lived on the spirit of this teaching. Above all it was an educational state (as was the Catholic state after the Counter-Reformation); a Christian police state which was conscious, over and above its outward striving for power, of its duty of care for the spiritual well-being and for the administration of a strict and sturdy system of justice and material welfare of its subjects. So it educated the German people and in particular the peasant and middle classes to a strict and unpolitical sense of integrity, industry and respectability. The powerlessness of most petty German states outside their own boundaries, their position within the Empire as vassals of the Emperor, and the balance of power among the states themselves, were all factors which served to damp their ambition in foreign affairs, and to lengthen the life of their patriarchal form of government.

Today all this is a matter of the distant past. And Luther's individual pronouncements about just causes of war, the duties and rights of 'the man of war', about estates and kingship, about economic problems such as the levying of taxes, commercial competition, monopolies, and the use of law-suits for commercial gain, have faded into oblivion. For all these attempts to solve practical moral problems of his time from his not always adequate knowledge of the world were valid only for his own day. But was the attitude which governed all these pronouncements as temporary as they were themselves: the attitude of the prophet strong in the faith, who makes all earthly actions, including political actions, immediately answerable to the Eternal God? Of course, it is not always easy to see where the boundaries begin which such responsibility imposes on the individual's caprice. There are no ready-made recipes, no casuistic school-rules for our moral actions, either in the life of the individual or for the larger communities, the states and the nations. Every moral decision is a new risk, because no one can tell in advance where in any given case the boundary lies between a justified and indeed necessary desire for self-assertion and on the other hand mere presumption and arrogance; between moral right and immoral use of force, between the necessity of self-preservation and the necessity of sublimating the individual in a higher community. Even the rules and norms of positive law do not always tell us what is lawful and unlawful; for how many conflicts in the daily life of the individual and of the State are in no way legal conflicts, because they stand outside all legal norms! What positive law is immune from attack in the name of a higher, divine or natural law, and how many legal traditions are there which do not in time become obsolete? Must this necessarily lead to a moral relativism where the only law is the law of force? Even Luther was not so bound up in medieval concepts of law that he would have wished to bind the active development of historical life to fixed legal tenets which were valid for all time. Even he knew that positive laws and traditions become obsolete and that they must then in some circumstances be destroyed by force. For this purpose God raises up those 'healthy heroes', those great and exceptional men who pour scorn on all school-rules and popular wisdom; he strengthens them with his spirit and lets them boldly create new forms of order. But does this mean that they are exempted from all moral and religious responsibility? On the contrary! Their responsibility and with it the danger of their mission is redoubled: all too easily can they fall victims to the temptations of pride and irresponsibility, and are then cast down from their seat when God withdraws his hand from them: 'because then no counsel or advice is of any more avail'.

History itself teaches—even if this only becomes apparent afterwards—where the bounds of moral and political reason have been overstepped, and where presumptuousness begins. For the statesman who acts irresponsibly will, in Luther's opinion, one day infallibly be brought to account; indeed, both the records of history and our daily experience show that there is a living consciousness of true responsibility which does not allow itself to be shaken by any pressure of our concrete needs in life nor by any degree of force, nor by any uncertainty about the validity of positive laws. It soon becomes clear even in one's everyday life whether one is dealing with men who are acting out of a sense of such an ultimate responsibility. It is also true in the life of nations, in the world of international politics, that the statesman's own consciousness of bearing an inescapable moral and religious responsibility sets quite definite limits on his actions, as one can see quite clearly from the example of Bismarck. Although he had progressed far from the realms of the old German patriarchal state, into the higher spheres of modern national power politics, he was still, as a Lutheran Christian, perfectly cônscious of his responsibility before God, and saw his Christianity as the source of his power as well as his moral norm. Everything which contributed to his greatness as a statesman was essentially conditioned by this consciousness of his moral political responsibility; or, to put it the other way round, the limit of his historical and political achievement is to be found wherever his inborn warlike passions (above all in his domestic policy) tempted him to overstep the boundaries of these norms.

In a more general sense this example shows the limits of the historical influence of Luther. Bismarck was the last great champion of the idea of the old German monarchy: that princedom of 'God's grace', whose representatives the Reformer himself had been able to address as 'Christian authorities'. His preaching to men's hearts, indeed the whole structure of the

Lutheran Church, was ultimately based on this possibility. Yet its days were numbered ever since, in the train of the great French Revolution, the modern state broke away from the person of its ruler. Since then the latter has become more and more subject to the will of his people, to the nameless mass, and the old monarchy has now finally disappeared. It is, however, a much more difficult task to convince the modern nation as a whole that it is also called to bear this ultimate moral and political responsibility, both for the forms of its political life within the community and also for the practical effect of its desire for power and status in foreign affairs: a truly terrifying and serious responsibility, which even extends to the choice of which deeds and which men one should applaud! In the last century, Lutheranism, deceived by the continuance of the monarchist state, has paid far too little attention to the tasks of educating the people into a sense of Christian responsibility in public life, which became so urgent in that period of radical political change. For the Lutheran way of thinking, which preaches neither a divine natural law nor a political priesthood, this great and difficult task could only have been solved by an extensive organisation of the laity. This presented practical difficulties and raised fundamental objections which are closely connected (particularly in the eastern parts of Germany) with the whole structure of the Lutheran 'Pastor-Church'. It is only with the reorganisation of the German Evangelical Church, which has taken place since the collapse of the Third Reich, that it has been possible for Protestantism to make a serious contribution to the solution of these problems. Only now has the Lutheran Church become aware of its great omission, after not only the monarchy but the German State as such, and with it everything which enhanced its standing in the eyes of the public, has fallen in ruins.

Today people are very conscious of the Church's share of responsibility for the political and moral chaos which a godless German government unleashed on Germany and the world.

Today they are more conscious than ever before—possibly even for the first time—of their duty to assist in the infusion of the Christian spirit into public life, in the reconstruction of a form of law and order where moral norms are taken seriously into account. And in this, the most difficult of all tasks which confront the Christian, namely in his relationships in the world, they can and will take Luther's attitude as a model for their own. In his persisting hope in God's help in this task, he shows himself far superior to any of his followers. At times the task seemed completely hopeless to him. 'We serve here in an inn where the devil is master and the world keeps house, and where the servants are every conceivable sort of vice, and all of them are enemies of the Gospel.' But does he ever think of running away from this terrible house and retiring to the sure stronghold of his own devout community? Rather, he behaves himself like a true warrior, steadfast in the fight in spite of the certainty that he will never be able to drive the Devil out of the house. It is typical of the man who left the quiet of his monastery cell, which seemed to him the only place for which he was really suited, to brave the struggle with the powers of this world. However difficult it was for his trembling conscience, he nevertheless faithfully fulfilled the command of his master: 'Go. I send you as sheep in the midst of wolves!' For this reason his story does not belong to the theologians alone: because he placed himself in the midst of the moral tribulations and problems of this earthly existence and took up the struggle with them in the grand manner.

This is not to say that he came out of this struggle unscathed. It would be very un-Lutheran if we were to fête him as a pure 'man of God', as a sort of Protestant saint. Even he did not escape the hopeless entanglement of all human life in guilt and fate, in error, blindness and passion. Above all, his zeal in battle could reach such a pitch of intensity that it became quite simply impossible to distinguish clearly between spiritual and earthly motives, between a genuine care for that which is sacred and human arrogance, and indeed, at times, even hatred. There is a degree of anger which blinds the eyes and hardens the heart; even Luther was not without his share in the furious, self-righteous and unloving bickerings of his own followers over the right formulation of doctrine. It is, of course, a favourable aspect of Lutheranism that its adherents should take spiritual decisions seriously, and it has had many diverse effects on German life; but it can harden into a form of doctrinaire and pedantic arrogance, which then makes any true community in the spirit and in love impossible. Now Luther himself was neither doctrinaire nor pedantic, but a man with a very lively mind, and at the same time with a hot-blooded temperament. His prophecy is still far removed from the pure spirituality of the Pauline epistles, which are so free from everything earthly.

Despite this, at heart his struggles were inspired by his zeal for the holiness of his Lord, and for the true understanding of the divine revelation. Without his passionate temperament he would certainly not have been in a position to keep his life's work pure from all the thousands of temptations and dangers which assailed it. Without his vision of faith he would never have had strength to achieve this, and it is this central element in his life of struggle which rewards every new examination of it. The depth of meaning in his writings is unfathomable and inexhaustible. He will always continue to fertilise Christian theology from one generation to another. For not only his theological thinking, but everything, the power of his character and the creative achievement of his thought, has its root in the same mysterious depths: in the encounter of the believer with God. Because he is sure that God calls him, he knows no fear in his battle for his life's work:

> 'Here I stand. I can no other.
> God help me! Amen.'

CHRONOLOGY

1483	10th November: Birth of Martin Luther at Eisleben. 11th November: Martin Luther baptised.
1484	1st January: Birth of Ulrich Zwingli at Wildhaus in the canton of Toggenburg. Early summer: Hans Luther moves to Mansfeld.
1497	16th February: Birth of Philip Melanchthon at Bretten. Easter (at the latest): Luther sent to school in Magdeburg.
1498	Martin Luther changes to the St. George school in Eisenach.
1501	About the beginning of May: Matriculation and commencement of studies at Erfurt (George scholarship).
1502	29th September: Bachelor of Arts.
1503	16th April: Luther wounds himself with his sword on the way to Mansfeld.
1505	About 7th January: Master of Arts. 24th April: Begins to lecture as Master of Arts. 20th May: Begins to study law. June: Journey to Mansfeld. 2nd July: Luther is overtaken by a storm near the village of Stotternheim and vows to become a monk. 17th July: Enters the Augustinian cloister at Erfurt.
1507	3rd April: Luther ordained priest. 2nd May: First mass.
1508	Beginning of the winter term: Luther moved to the 'Black Cloister' in Wittenberg.
1509	9th March: *Baccalaureus ad biblia* (Bachelor of Theology). 10th July: Birth of John Calvin at Noyon. October: Luther moved back to Erfurt.

1510   Before the middle of November: Leaves for Rome; arrives there about the end of December.

1511   End of January or the beginning of February: Leaves Rome.
Beginning of April: In Erfurt again.
Between August 1511 and May 1512: Moved for the second time to Wittenberg.

1512   4th October: *Licencia magistrandi in theologia.*
19th October: Doctor of Theology.
25th October (?): Beginning of his lectures on Genesis.

1513   16th August: Beginning of his first course of lectures on the Psalms.

1515   April, after Easter: Beginning of the lectures on the Epistle to the Romans.

1516   7th September: End of the lectures on Romans.
27th October: Beginning of the lectures on the Epistle to the Galatians.

1517   31st October: Posts his ninety-five theses against indulgences.

1518   22nd February: 'Sermon on Indulgence and Grace'.
26th April: Disputation in the Augustinian convent at Heidelberg.
June: Printing of the 'Commentary on the Theses against Indulgences'.
    Preliminaries of the canonical trial of Luther in Rome
7th August: Luther receives summons to Rome.
23rd August: Papal brief to Cardinal Cajetan at Augsburg with the order to summon Luther before him.
25th August: Melanchthon moves to Wittenberg.
31st August: Polemical treaties against Prierias, the papal palace theologian.
26th September-31st October: Journey to Augsburg.
12th-14th October: Hearing before Cajetan.
16th October: Luther appeals from Cajetan to the Pope.
20th-21st October: Flight from Augsburg.
23rd October: Pickenheimer's guest in Nürnberg.
25th November: *Acta Augustana* published.

CHRONOLOGY 251

28th November: Appeals to a council.
8th December: Elector Frederick refuses to hand over Luther to Rome.

1519 4th–6th January: Conversation with Karl von Miltitz at Altenburg.
12th January: Death of Emperor Maximilian I.
28th June: Election of Charles V as Emperor in Frankfurt-on-Main.
4th–14th July: Disputation at Leipzig between Luther and Eck.
September: Printing of the Commentary on Galatians completed.

1520 January: Ulrich v. Hutten offers Luther his and Francis v. Sickingen's protection.
8th June: 'Sermon on good works'.
11th June: Sylvester v. Schaumburg offers Luther the protection of one hundred nobles.
15th June: Papal bull 'Exsurge Domine' gives Luther sixty days in which to submit, under threat of excommunication.
August: 'Address to the Christian nobles of the German nation'.
6th October: 'Of the Babylonian Captivity of the Church'.
12th November: Burning of Luther's writings in Köln.
November: *Adversus execrabilem Antichristi bullam* and 'Of the Freedom of the Christian Man'.
10th December: Burning of the papal bull and of the decretals in front of the Elster Gate in Wittenberg.

1521 3rd January: Leo X bull of excommunication: *Decet Romanum Pontificem*.
13th February: Aleander's speech before the Imperial Diet in Worms; exhorts the Emperor to carry out the papal condemnation of Luther.
6th March: Imperial invitation to Luther to go to Worms, together with safe-conduct.
10th March: Charles V's mandate against Luther's writings.
2nd April: Luther leaves for Worms.
16th–26th April: Luther in Worms.

17th-18th April: Appearance before the Imperial Diet.
4th May-1st March 1522: Luther at the Wartburg as 'Junker George'.
8th May: Edict of Worms; Imperial ban against Luther.
29th May: Alliance of Charles V and Leo X against France.
29th September: Evangelical communion service in Wittenberg by Melanchthon and his pupils.
12th November: Thirteen monks leave the cloister in Wittenberg.
3rd-4th December: Riots in the Churches in Wittenberg.
25th December: Andreas v. Karlstadt offers communion in both elements and in the German language.
27th December: The prophets from Zwickau in Wittenberg.
December: Beginning of the translation of the New Testament (1st edition Sept. 1522); revision of the first book of sermons; publication of Melanchthon's text-book on dogma (*loci communes*).

1522 6th January: Dissolution of the congregation of the German Augustine Eremites.
26th February: Marriage of Justus Jonas, provost of the Castle Church in Wittenberg.
1st-6th March: Luther's return from the Wartburg to Wittenberg; 'Faithful warning to all Christians to guard against riots and disturbances'.
9th March: Beginning of Luther's Lent sermons in Wittenberg.
April: Beginning of the Reformation in Zürich with Zwingli's tract against the laws of fasting.
September-May 1523: Sickingen's feud against Trier.

1523 6th March: Mandate of the Imperial Diet at Nürnberg: postponement of the ultimate decision to a new council; earnest exhortation to all Christians to beware of all uproar and rebellion.
March: 'Of the Secular Authorities, and how far one owes them Obedience'.
Whitsun: 'Of the Ordering of Divine Service in the Parishes'.

CHRONOLOGY

       1st July: Burning of the first martyrs of the Reformation in Brussels.
       23rd August: Death of Hutten.

1523–4 Publication of the first parts of Luther's translation of the Old Testament.

1524 January–February: 'To the Councillors of all the Towns in Germany, that they should Establish Christian Schools'.
       23rd June: Beginning of the Peasants' Revolt in the county of Stühlingen (in the south of the Black Forest).
       6th July: Alliance of Regensburg of the Catholic estates for the execution of the Edict of Worms.
       September: Polemical writings of Erasmus and Thomas Müntzer against Luther.

1525 January: 'Against the Heavenly Prophets'. First expulsions of the Baptists from Nürnberg and Zürich.
       24th February: Charles V's victory over Francis I at Pavia; capture of Francis.
       March: The 'Twelve Articles of the Rebellious Peasants'.
       19th April: 'Exhortation to Peace in Answer to the Twelve Articles of the Peasants'.
       5th May: Death of Elector Frederick the Wise of Saxony; accession of John the Steadfast (1525–32).
       5th May: 'Against the Plundering and Murdering Peasants'.
       15th May: Battle of Frankenhausen, capture of Müntzer.
       May–June: Suppression of all the peasant risings.
       13th June: Luther's marriage with Katherine von Bora.
       July: 'A Tract on the Severe Book against Peasants'.
       19th July: Alliance of Dessau of Catholic princes from Central and North Germany against the Evangelical teaching.
       Before Christmas: 'German Mass and Ordering of Divine Service'.
       End of December: 'Of the Unfree Will' (against Erasmus).

1526 14th January: Peace of Madrid between Charles V and Francis I.
       23rd February: League of Gotha between Saxony and Hesse for the protection of Evangelical doctrine.

22nd May: Holy League of Cognac against Charles V with participation of the Pope.

25th June–27th August: Imperial Diet at Speyer; prorogation of the Edict of Worms.

1527 January: 'Whether Soldiers can be in a State of Grace'.

April: 'That these words: this is my body: still stand firm, against the enthusiasts'.

6th May: Sack of Rome by the imperial troops.

1527–9 Second war between Charles V and Francis I.

1528 4th January: Imperial mandate with threat of death penalty against the Anabaptists.

22nd March: 'Instruction of Visitors to the Pastors in the Electorate of Saxony' with a foreword by Luther.

28th March: Luther's great 'Statement of Faith about the Last Supper of Christ'.

June: Offensive and defensive alliance between Zürich and Berne for the protection of the Gospel.

1529 26th February–12th April: Imperial Diet at Speyer.

19th April: Protest of the Evangelical estates in Speyer.

22nd April: 'Understanding' between Electorate of Saxony, Hesse and the Upper German States.

5th August: Permanent peace of Cambrai between Charles V and Francis I.

1st–4th October: Religious discussions at Marburg.

16th October: Conventions of Schwabach between Brandenburg-Ansbach and the Electorate of Saxony.

30th November: Lutheran convention in Schmalkalden. Saxony's break with the Upper German States.

German Catechism (so-called great Catechism); 'Army Sermon against the Turks'.

1530 24th February: Imperial coronation of Charles V in Bologna by Pope Clement VII.

16th April–13th October: Luther in the fortress at Coburg.

15th June: Arrival of Charles V in Augsburg.

20th June: Formal opening of the Imperial Diet at Augsburg.

25th June: Presentation of the Augsburg Confession.

CHRONOLOGY

19th November: Dismissal of the Imperial Diet at Augsburg.
31st December - 27th February, 1531: Formation of the Schmalkaldic League.

1531 April: Luther's 'Warning to his Dear Germans'.
11th October: Death of Zwingli in the Battle of Kappel.

1534 Completion of Luther's translation of the Bible; first complete edition of the German Bible.

1535 November: Visit of the Papal Nuntio Vergerio to Wittenberg.

1536 John Calvin's *Institution de la réligion chrétienne* appears in its first edition.
May: Pact at Wittenberg achieved by Melanchthon and Butzer with Luther's agreement for the restoration of relations between Saxony and the Upper German states.

1537 February: Luther's 'Schmalkaldic Articles' are laid before the Schmalkaldic League.
18th December: Luther's first disputation against the Antinomians.

1539 March to April: 'Of the *Conciliis* and the Churches'.
30th September: First volume of the Wittenberg edition of Luther's complete works with foreword by the author to the German writings.
10th December: Advice of Luther and Melanchthon given in confessional to Philip of Hesse about his marriage.

1540 12th June-28th July: Religious discussions at Hagenau (without the participation of Luther).

1541 14th-17th January: Religious discussion at Worms between Melanchthon and Eck.
31st March: 'Against Tom Fool' (pamphlet against Duke Henry the younger of Brunswick).
22nd April-22nd May: Religious discussions at Regensburg.

1543 4th January: 'Of the Jews and their Lies'.
July: Beginning of the printing of the great lecture on Genesis (held from 1535 to 1545).

1544 'Short Testament of Faith about the Holy Sacrament'.

1545	5th March: Luther's foreword to the *Opera latina* of the Wittenberg edition of his collected works (beginning of his autobiography).
25th March: 'Against the Papacy at Rome, Instituted by the Devil'.
End of July: Luther threatens to leave Wittenberg for ever (just as he had done at the beginning of 1544).
13th December: Opening of the Council of Trent.
1546	January–March: Two religious discussions at Regensburg.
18th February: Martin Luther's death at Eisleben, where he had travelled to mediate in a dispute of the Count of Mansfeld.
22nd February: Burial of Martin Luther in Wittenberg.